I0084721

Murderous Consent

Series Board

James Bernauer

Drucilla Cornell

Thomas R. Flynn

Kevin Hart

Richard Kearney

Jean-Luc Marion

Adriaan Peperzak

Thomas Sheehan

Hent de Vries

Merold Westphal

Michael Zimmerman

John D. Caputo, *series editor*

PERSPECTIVES IN
CONTINENTAL
PHILOSOPHY

MARC CRÉPON

Murderous Consent
On the Accommodation
of Violent Death

Translated by Michael Loriaux and Jacob Levi
Foreword by James Martel

Fordham University Press
New York ∎ 2019

Copyright © 2019 Fordham University Press

All rights reserved. No part of this publication may be reproduced, stored in a retrieval system, or transmitted in any form or by any means—electronic, mechanical, photocopy, recording, or any other—except for brief quotations in printed reviews, without the prior permission of the publisher.

This book was first published in French as *Le consentement meurtrier*, by Marc Crépon © Les Éditions du Cerf, 2012.

Fordham University Press has no responsibility for the persistence or accuracy of URLs for external or third-party Internet websites referred to in this publication and does not guarantee that any content on such websites is, or will remain, accurate or appropriate.

Fordham University Press also publishes its books in a variety of electronic formats. Some content that appears in print may not be available in electronic books.

Visit us online at www.fordhampress.com.

Library of Congress Control Number: 2019935377

Printed in the United States of America

21 20 19   5 4 3 2 1

First edition

Contents

Foreword

James Martel

There are many forms of opposing violence but few take the injunction against murder as seriously and thoroughly as Marc Crépon. In this book, which has been newly translated into English by Michael Loriaux and Jacob Levi, Crépon offers us a vision of what it looks like to forbid murder absolutely. To do so, Crépon refuses the various categories of identity that help us to rationalize and justify killing. These distinctions include those between the innocent and the guilty, legitimate and illegitimate targets, just and unjust wars, and the entire panoply of discourses that in the end only allow nations, communities, and individuals to be the arbiters (in their own minds anyway) of whom they may kill and whom they may not.

In refusing such distinctions, Crépon is undermining the idea of consent as an implicit marker of who may or may not be killed. Scholars don't usually think of consent and murder in the same breath, but Crépon is very persuasive that the one leads to the other. The notion of consent implies a world of perfect information where the consequences and purposes of a decision are all guaranteed, allowing fully informed persons to align themselves with some group or other. It is therefore the basis on which we tend to consider people's affiliations as chosen rather than required or enforced. Crépon is fundamentally uninterested in the question of whether people really and genuinely choose to be in this or that community precisely because, as he sees it, this question calls forth a deeper question: "May I kill this person? Is this person—by his or her own choice—a member of a group that is an enemy to me?"

We can recognize this logic as being applied all the time when determining who is a legitimate target of war and state violence. Discussions about "collateral damage," the killing of civilians versus armed combatants, all hinge on the idea of consent. It's OK to murder soldiers, this logic goes, because they have consented to fight for the state. But this argument can be flipped around: it's OK to murder civilians, some groups avow, because as citizens of this or that nation or polity, they have consented to be in a group that is hostile to us and hence are our legitimate target. Either way, the notion of consent, itself a complete fabrication (based on hypotheticals dreamed up by social contract theorists), serves its murderous purpose.

What Crépon is doing in this book, then, is to remove the shield of consent as a way to justify murder. Furthermore, because consent is one of the most foundational tenets of liberal rationalism, by attacking it— indeed, by rendering it *murderous*—Crépon is subverting the entire political apparatus of the liberal (or neoliberal) state, which is built precisely on the simultaneous denial and use of murder as its ultimate political tool.

This kind of argument is controversial. Crépon is, of necessity, going to ruffle many feathers (to put it mildly), especially those of the Fanonian postcolonial studies world or the world of the Antifa, who see violence as both necessary and valid as such. He may also perturb those groups who don't openly espouse violence but de facto condone it through careful ratiocinations (a lot of liberals fit into this group, although they probably wouldn't recognize this, much less appreciate having it pointed out to them). There doesn't even seem to be an appreciation by Crépon for the right of self-defense as a justification for killing; murder is murder, in his view.

Accordingly, Crépon takes on some positions that are distinctly out of joint with many current ways of thinking on the left and the liberal middle alike. He generally, if painfully, supports Camus's position on the Algerian revolution, for example, condemning both sides for their violence. This is a move that might smack of Trump's "there are good people on both sides" (meaning that white supremacists are good) were it not for Crépon's deep commitment to what he calls ethicosmopolitics, a sense of allegiance not to this or that group (via consent) but rather to humanity as a whole (in which case the very idea of consent is meaningless; we cannot not be human beings).

Without the right to murder, and without a core theory of consent to underpin that right, the very building blocks of nation-states, affinity groups, and the like require an entirely different basis to come together (if they require one at all). If, for some, to think this way skates dangerously close to liberal individualism ("there is no black, there is no white, we are all consumers," etc.), I don't think that this is at all what Crépon has in mind, nor do I think that his ideas readily lend themselves to this kind of logic. After all, liberalism, as already mentioned, is highly dependent on a theory of consent to exist at all, and no sense of identity can be innocent of consent (nor its dark links to murder) in liberal—or even illiberal—capitalism.

Another fairly radical idea that Crépon holds—which comes out toward the end of the book—is to think about nuclear weapons and drones in a surprisingly optimistic way (not that he downplays the horror of these things; quite the contrary, it is the source of his optimism). Here, we have come to the end of consent: these weapons are so detached from their operators, not to mention the people to whom they deal death, that they barely have any element of the human in them at all. Even so, for Crépon, the very fact that nuclear weapons in particular suggest the possibility of annihilating all human life on the planet also suggests the fact of our shared life together in this world, making it harder to think in terms of the us/them gradations that are the stuff of murder in Crépon's view. Furthermore, insofar as these weapons can kill without warning literally anywhere on earth, he offers that a new sense of place—the planet itself as place—reemerges via this common and ultimate threat (although I think that, in practice, this realization dawns far more readily on those who, for example, live under the constant threat and buzzing noise of unseen drones than on those who watch such murderous acts on television).

Related to this point, one of the ideas that I think is most striking and innovative in this book—more of a tendency than an idea, actually—is the way that Crépon treats human frailty, error, and imperfection without judgment or rejection; he always seeks to recuperate the positive and the beneficial even out of our darkest moments (including Hiroshima and Auschwitz). Recognizing that our desire and willingness to kill usually have some positive motive behind them—a desire for justice, a desire to promote one's community, a general "complicity among men" (citing Camus)—Crépon thinks about how this very same set of values might be turned around to serve the cosmopolitan rather than the particular. Crépon seeks to turn this original complicity into something else, a complicity among and between one another as members of a species, or into what he calls a "fidelity to the human condition."

What is refreshing about this approach is that Crépon, in demanding so much of us, does not demand our perfectibility. He works with what and where we are, with what our motivations are, our limited knowledge (vs. "consent"), and our histories of violence and pain and oppression. In fact, considering the way he often sounds like a universalist, it is striking how dedicated Crépon can be to the local and the particular so long as that particularity is oriented toward the human rather than gradations of our species. Indeed, I would say that for Crépon the human appears to us only via its particularities; grand declarations of human nature in the abstract are what get us into trouble (that is, they allow us to murder) in the first place. He thus fundamentally accepts human beings (in a way that accords with Camus, Freud, Levinas, and Butler, four of his main interlocutors) as they are.

Crépon even accepts the ongoing fact of human rebelliousness and the desire for revenge, so often the source of violence as one group seeks to upend the domination of another, causing endless repetitive cycles of violence and counterviolence. He wishes only to have rebellion be, not against this or that faction, but against murder, which comes at the cost of the human itself. In this way Crépon again seeks to turn what is often the source of violence and murder into its opposite.

One of the most critical discussions in the book comes when Crépon (citing Levinas) seeks "what is human in human beings." This search animates several chapters, engaging with Freud, Levinas, and Butler respectively. This desire comes from the idea that when we kill (or when we consent to have others kill for us), we are acting out of our own nonhuman attributes rather than as fellow human beings (although this gets complicated because, of course, the division of subjects between human and nonhuman itself may smack of the very kinds of gradation that Crépon ardently opposes).

To be human is, per Butler, to be vulnerable. Crépon suggests that even as such vulnerability is endlessly promoted as the reason to kill others, it is also precisely this that we all have in common; this common vulnerability, you could say, is where the particular and the universal meet in Crépon's system of thought (each of us experiences our vulnerability as absolutely local and particular, but it is the one thing that we share with absolutely every other human on the planet).

Insofar as we are all vulnerable and all too human, we already have everything that we need, Crépon states plainly and boldly, to cease to murder one another. Nothing needs to change or be introduced; we do not need to alter "human nature" or reeducate ourselves. When we murder the other, we are doing violence to our own humanity, and for this reason, so long as we actually do remain human—and we can never cease to be human in his view—we can never fully extinguish that side of us that opposes murder and that wishes only to live in peace with other human beings.

That is the good news that Crépon brings to us. That he does so in the context of a book that addresses the horrors of Auschwitz, Hiroshima (with a superb reading of Kenzaburō Ōe's writing on the subject), and countless other atrocities demonstrates the peculiar character of this book. Crépon "goes there"; he looks death and murder right in the eye but he doesn't blink. His opposition to murder comes, not from an effort to deny it, but to go right through to the other side (perhaps engaging in what Žižek calls "traversing the fantasy").

Even if one were to reject some of Crépon's basic tenets (including the absolute injunction against murder itself), this book helps us to see what it takes to think about a politics that seeks only life and not death. Perhaps the cost of such a position will be too high for those who see all the problems that come from subscribing to such a view (starting with the question of moral equivalencies, which is exactly the bugaboo that Crépon seeks to take down). But if nothing else, Crépon shows that it is possible to reject murder in all its forms, to refuse to be a passive enabler of murder, to refuse to kill or even to be killed—at least in the abstract—because, as Crépon ably shows, human beings are not fated to be killers. When we kill, whatever else we say about it, we are *choosing* to do it, and for that reason, we must bear the responsibility for our actions, including the cost of possibly losing a part of what it means to be human (to abandon our faith in the human condition) in the process.

Murderous Consent

Introduction

I

No critique of violence, no denunciation of cruelty, *to the extent that both the one and the other are partial* [*partiel*] *and partisan* [*partial*], can elude the risk of consenting, actively or passively, implicitly or explicitly, to the very violence it critiques and the cruelty it denounces. It suffices that the critique apply only to violence and the denunciation only to cruelty that take place *elsewhere* and *otherwise*. This is the paradox of every protest and every expression of indignation, whether moral or political. No matter how legitimate our protestations may be, the silence, the incomprehension, the small and not-so-small concessions regarding the various forms of violent death that they imply or tolerate, which weave the fabric of our history, compromise death's meaning and their import. As soon as such protestations accept or even draw a line of (political, ideological, economic, military, or industrial) separation between people whose wounds are judged unacceptable and people whose sufferings might be seen as tenable, they expose their lack of coherence with the principles they espouse. As soon as such protestations find "good" reasons *here* for the destructions that they condemn *elsewhere*, they lose their essential credibility, unless we concede that violence is natural and has primacy over considerations of ethics. We cannot, in other words, claim for some what we refuse to others. Our awareness of violence and its effects cannot depend on the affiliation of those who suffer, no matter how that affiliation is defined, whether geographically, "ethnically," "factionally," "culturally," politically, or religiously.

II

In the following pages I call "murderous consent" any accommodation with violent death, any habituation to murder, any compromise, in reality untenable, with principles (enumerated below) that should forbid even the slightest exception, *regardless of who the victims are*. I will not shy away from the question of whether the concept remains valid or not when applied to the executioner's own punishment. The forms assumed by murderous consent are multiple and diverse. But even if it is true that we cannot place all these forms on the same plane and that they elicit endless distinctions—such as those that differentiate war from war crimes from crimes against humanity from the multiple "states of violence" that often substitute for war, or those that make a distinction between acquiescing in terror and encouraging cruelty, not to mention active participation in mass murder, pogroms, or genocide, and, to conclude, remaining silent, indifferent, or unaware—it is nevertheless worthwhile to bring these forms together into a general concept.[1] They demand it, in fact, because there is nothing more questionable than distinctions like these, especially when they idealize and exonerate from blame some or other conflict, some or other military intervention, some or other "reprisal" or "retaliation," or war in general. And even if such distinctions are necessary, they nevertheless lend themselves to all sorts of circumventions and instrumentalizations (whether by the media or by politicians). Acts of violence and terror remind us that one of the most fertile sources of conflict is found in the way we interpret and categorize civil and military actions. And yet, as we know, no "war" has failed to produce exactions and violations of the law. No military will deny it, and yet no military will hesitate to defend itself from such accusations. Inversely, no military can legitimately claim that it abstains (or has abstained) from murder, and no political power that is engaged in conflict can remain (or has remained) above publicly organizing propaganda for and acquiescence in the deaths of others.

III

Such ambivalence is also characteristic of forms of murderous consent that are, in appearance, more passive. How do we judge the compromise between violence and silence, or indifference? Is closing our eyes and plugging our ears not also a way of "participating" in murder? Could we (or someone else) not say that, in peace as in war, there is no difference between active engagement and tacit acquiescence—in full knowledge of the facts—in the torture, abduction, and execution of anonymous members of some "community" or other, whether for reasons of prudence or cowardice or because of our "unconditional" attachment to some principle ("identity," "security," etc.)? And why, in certain circumstances, do we hesitate to say it? What is the meaning of this inconsistency in our ability to judge a crime? Such questions haunt, incessantly though diversely, our memory of the past and our judgments of history, which participate in the conflicting perceptions that we have of the present and in our various apprehensions regarding the future. With each new explosion of violence, our memories hurt us, divide us, and fuel interminable polemics and even future wars, proving that murderous consent is not simply about questioning our *partisan* attitude regarding the death of others on a world scale but also about unsettling and even disrupting the geography, the history, the politics, and the economics that nourish and orchestrate killing—beginning with the distinction between "near" and "far" and between "familiar" and "foreign," as instrumentalized by one or several of these disciplines.

IV

But this is not all that is at stake. Not only does murderous consent "haunt" us, but it also drives a wedge between politics and the *necessary* injunction addressed to politics by ethics. The shadow of murderous consent darkens the unavoidable invocation of moral principles in human affairs—the very principles that commit us to providing populations with security and to respecting their freedom—and indelibly marks their limits. Why should some "victims," past or present, merit more consideration, the particular *attention* that they are given, to the exclusion of or in ignorance of others? Why must we take such principles into account *here, in one place, and not elsewhere*? How are we to understand the complexity of the partitions that organize our mercurial perception of suffering and our erratic sensitivity to the death of others? Is such inconsistency *inevitable*? And if so, what conclusions do we draw, and how do we answer for it? As we take up these questions, we become aware of a twofold temptation. The first is unconditional pacifism, which ignores the reasons that might make war necessary. The second is the rejection of any moral and political engagement against violence because we feel discouraged and weary in the face of all the world's atrocities. Murderous consent's unassailability, in all its various manifestations, is strengthened by resignation and a fatalistic "acquiescence," which only encourage murder and even participation in murder. Doing nothing, saying nothing, or refusing all feelings, because nothing will ever change (this is the hardest thing to admit), is always to consent to murder a little bit. "There's nothing we can do"; "that's just the way the world is"; "what's the point!"—so many avowals that, when taken together, form a kind of credo of violence. In the following chapters, I confer the name "nihilism" on all such utterances, though I endow the word with a meaning that deliberately challenges its Nietzschean signification.

V

The questions asked above are the focus of this book. I seek, in a less introductory and provisional way, to formulate a hypothesis regarding what ethical obligation means if its conditions are placed in doubt by the problematic of murderous consent. The answer is not obvious. At a minimum we have to probe the relationship between ethics, law, and politics, at least to the extent that the latter is the object of a common construction. What is our obligation? First, and above all (this is what I try to show), it is one of the attention, care, and assistance that the vulnerability and mortality of the other enjoin *everywhere*. If it is true that our existence is a fabric of relations that evolves over time—in other words, that every *life singularly* is a *living-with* unfolding in time [*en devenir*]—then the meaning of the "with" that bears life, from life to death, can be revealed in a *prinzipiell* way in this supplication. This is so for at least two reasons. First, there is no knowledge or awareness that we hold more clearly in common, and that more clearly transcends every frontier that separates us (geographical, cultural, linguistic, and political), than our knowledge of our shared mortality. One thing that we know about everyone, whatever her affiliation or attachment, whatever her convictions or beliefs, is that she knows that she *herself* is mortal, that she knows that *we* are mortal, and we know this about her as much as we know it about ourselves. And we can also assume that she fears death, her own and that of her loved ones, with an intensity that varies according to her exposure to it. Nothing about our existence is more mysterious than the origin of this knowledge. No one knows the exact date or circumstances of its origin. But one thing is certain: from the day we know it *about the other*, we also know it *about ourselves* and, in time, about *everyone*. From that day forward, we can no longer deny or refuse to acknowledge the supplication of the other without jeopardizing the possibility of a moral *and* political relationship with him or her. If we put at risk our "encounter" with someone, whatever the nature of that encounter (real, imaginary, fictitious, conceptual), by deciding in advance that we are indifferent toward her death and not concerned by it, that she can therefore die if it "humors" someone else, then have we not already consented to murder?

VI

This, then, will be my point of departure: any relationship, moral *or* political, assumes, from the beginning, that we are prepared to heed the appeal of the other for attention, care, and help, as enjoined by his or her vulnerability and mortality, *without exception*. Inversely, any denial of that call, any refusal to hear it, affects, rejects, or extinguishes this relationship. We experience such denial too often. It is an "ordinary" experience. There are those who presume, for ideological, religious, or other reasons, that they have nothing (and never had anything) in common with men and women of a given "origin" or a given "community," who therefore are perceived as "different" and stigmatized. They presume that no relationship with the other of that origin or community is (or ever was) possible.[2] Whoever they might be, the wounds and the deaths of such men and women do not count for much. Nothing can limit the extent of murderous consent when it is empowered by this ordinary experience. Violence breaks out among neighbors, for example, former "brothers" or friends, between whom attention, care, and help were a matter of course, and who, through the years, had constructed a durable relationship, a neighborhood, a coexistence, a life of mingling and sharing. When violence erupts (the conditions for which may have been developing for a long time), the same process of destruction of old ties is always set in motion: no longer is it a question of the vulnerability and mortality of either the one or the other, though they were once the object of shared concern. On the contrary, each now sees only the wounds of *his* wounded and the suffering caused by *his* "own deaths." The possessive pronoun becomes exclusive. Our solicitude, now compartmentalized (and often intensified), for the vulnerability and the mortality of *our own* becomes the incubator of new divisions that surface and calcify. Such divisions take root in the litany of victims who fall on each side of some line of combat; their numbers are not added together.

VII

This is why both vulnerability and mortality define the threshold of an initial responsibility. To hear their call is to respond with the words and acts that they mandate [*donner droit*]. Cries of alarm and revolt, signs of protest, commitments to help, interventions, emergency aid, all these gestures have in common the expression of an enduring opposition to the proliferation—a sign of the times—of murderous consent. Murderous consent is cultivated, inversely, by the strategic calculations of unprincipled geopolitical visions, by the global arms economy, and, more generally, by all the sovereign logics that attach to the blind defense of particular interests. In the end, all such cries lead us back to the most important question, which delineates the horizon of my reflections, which is that of the articulation between ethics and politics. If it is true that the responsibility that I have just described constitutes the essence of the "with," understood as the basis of the relational character of existence, how far does this responsibility extend and what limits are imposed on it? I do not reject the idea that this responsibility produces its own distinctions and that, in practice, because it is dependent on the nearness of some and the remoteness of others, we do not feel or assume this responsibility in the same way with regard to everyone or with the same degree of involvement. Nevertheless, this does not mean that we can decide or decree in advance how such limits are to be defined. Assuming that we experience these limits, they are necessarily—and this is my second hypothesis—de facto and not de jure, despite all the arguments to the contrary that are advanced by political, ideological, and religious forces. This is why the work of international legal forums remains an indispensable line of resistance against murderous consent.

VIII

For this reason, I will differentiate between degrees of violence. Insofar as we cannot avoid the eclipse or the suspension of the principle that attaches us to the vulnerability and mortality of the other (this is the meaning of the "with"), we must begin by recognizing that no one *in good conscience* can consider his or her life, as being-in-the-world, immune from murderous consent. Whether we like it or not, whether we are ready to admit it or not, the responsible "with" that weaves the fabric of our lives is sullied with violations of constitutive obligations that derive from this same principle. It is sullied with *gaps* [*failles*] and *failures* [*faillites*] in what should give meaning to our belonging to the world. We can invoke the finitude of our faculties as justification all we like. But our derelictions will not be erased. It will always be futile and somewhat facile to use finitude as an excuse or as an explanation of why things cannot be otherwise. It is better to admit that such derelictions constitute an unavoidable feature of our way of living in and sharing the world, and to interrogate them as such. We bear without difficulty, and without much thought, our "being-in-the-world" while having only a more or less hazy awareness of the scandal that is the persistence of famine in so many countries, the inequitable access to health care between North and South, the endemic misery of slums and refugee camps, the global arms trade, and, lest they be omitted, the interests (economic, political, military, and industrial) that perpetuate forgotten wars and "conflicts" almost everywhere. It is too late today to push for political decisions that would try to curb all the resulting deaths, to demand that such concerns be more central to our political preoccupations, or to believe that the will to make them more central will engender proposals that might actually appear on a campaign platform or exert influence over our political choices. The murderous consent that follows, whether tacit, implicit, negligent, or oblivious, already signifies a kind of fatalism regarding the violence that lingers at the heart of our sense of belonging, or in what Malraux calls the "human condition." Nevertheless, we should be careful not to exaggerate the existential weightiness of our human condition by adding to it some irredeemable culpability or the onus of some fatality. It is enough to acknowledge that the irreducible nature of murderous consent suspends, as if it needed to be suspended, the unconditional esteem in which we might want to hold "human nature" and its "progress," especially since we cannot be entirely confident about the state of the world and its evolution—unless we are pushed to seek a way out in rebellion, goodness, critique, or shame, as we shall see below.[3]

IX

But this form of "acknowledgment"—tied to the finitude of our belonging to the world—marks only a first step in our relation to the violence that affects our existence. The second, of much greater gravity, consists in the *alleged, desired, and avowed* passage from simple contingency [*état de fait*] to the rule of law. In this case, murderous consent assumes a different character altogether. It is no longer about our incapacity to assume responsibility for the attentiveness, care, and aid that the vulnerability and mortality of the other demand of us, but about our active participation and deliberate acquiescence in what I will call, following Frédéric Worms, the "violation" of the moral and political relations that this responsibility establishes.[4] There are times (history repeatedly, on every continent, provides us with new examples) when men and women, no longer content simply to neglect such responsibility, either assume or are granted the right not so much to suspend it as to flout it. They empty it of meaning, contradict it in act and in speech, and destroy it with all the force granted them by their political, military, or religious authorities, who have given themselves the power of granting it. The most terrible moment of pogroms, genocides, civilian massacres, and crimes against humanity is the moment at which nothing more restrains yesterday's "peaceful" neighbors—the same ones with whom life's joys (weddings, births) and the pains and sufferings of misfortune, loss, and death could still be shared—from turning themselves into executioners. Such a metamorphosis presupposes that the comportment—the mourning, the grief, the sorrow, the signs of compassion, the words and gestures of solace—that we ordinarily adopt when confronted by the death of those with whom we are in some "relation" is overturned. This is the most extreme "violation": the convulsion that shatters the first and most universal of bonds that attach us to others. Subsequently, there is no wound, no humiliation, no outrage that the enemies that emerge from this convulsion are not prepared to inflict on one another. There is no perspective on the other's suffering that restrains them. Instead of dread, fear, and shared suffering, the death of the person who now appears as "adversary"—that is to say, the person whose life itself is suffered as "adverse"—if not simply taken for granted, becomes an object of desire, encouragement, and applause.

X

But the question of murderous consent takes us farther. No one can ignore the fact that, across the world, there is no act of violence that humans are not prepared to commit (if they have not already committed it), no life that they are not ready to sacrifice, in the name of whatever they consider to be "justice" or whatever, in their eyes, "being free," their ambition, or their vision of the world demands of them. Not only does the recurrence of violence—and our powerlessness to break free of the downward spiral of savagery and its snares—make us vulnerable to the risk of nihilism (as we saw), but it also threatens us with doubt and denial regarding our ideas of "justice" and "freedom." It threatens our confidence in what is presented to us as the "truth," which we want to believe. How can we support those who demand justice for themselves if it means persecuting others? How can we follow those who demand freedom if that demand is accompanied by terror? What credence can we give to discourses and images that claim to describe the world if we find ourselves wondering if they are fabrications, manipulations, or instrumentalizations that encourage a partial and partisan vision of violence, injustice, and oppression? We cannot avoid such questions. But we also have to be wary of drawing premature conclusions if the only consequence is to give the last word to murderous consent. If that were the case, it would mean that most of the relations that bind us to others cannot be simultaneously moral *and* political—or, moreover, that we can never elude the grand designs and gambits of history, even when we claim to act according to ethical principles.

XI

Everything therefore depends on how we conjoin and coordinate politics and morality. Under what conditions can the political relations that bind us *to one another* be moral *as well*? How do we (re)endow ideas of justice, freedom, and truth with some chance or possibility of sounding sensible and not "going bad" and turning into their antithesis? It is our belonging to the world that is at stake, because there is one thing about which there can be no doubt: as soon as a different logic *prevails*, that of an unconditional attachment to a circumscribed community (however defined, whether political, "ethnic," "religious," "cultural," "civilizational"), there will follow just this kind of reversal. Nationalism, racism, and xenophobia, in all their forms, from the most subtle to the most virulent, remind us that whenever we evoke security and identity—what I have called elsewhere "securidentity" [*sécuridentité*]—there is no vindictive discourse, no recourse to exclusion or discrimination, that we are not prepared to embrace.[5] However much we might wish for lines that cannot be transgressed (such as the one between stigmatization and murder), such violence breaches the lines more readily than we can imagine. However much we want to believe that there are institutions that guarantee us against it, such violence—whether spurred by some malicious utterance, some governmental decree, or some law that turns out to be one too many—nevertheless breaks free from them with greater ease than we can think possible. This is why the problematic of murderous consent allows only one point of view from which the articulation of morality and politics becomes possible and tenable: the point of view of the world as a whole. Assuming, from this perspective, that we agree that the necessary organizing thread is our responsibility for care, aid, and attention as enjoined by the vulnerability and the mortality of the other, then this responsibility should give rise to what I will call henceforward, using a word that evokes a now-unfashionable tradition, an "ethi*cosmo*politics" of relations. This will be the focus of this book. Naturally, I will seek to assess the significance of murderous consent as an irreducible and structural dimension of the human condition, understood as being-in-the-world. But beyond that, and perhaps more importantly, I will seek to explore the ways that enable us to take up the burden of murderous consent and construct an ethi*cosmo*politics, and do so deliberately (that is to say, knowingly and without excuses), fully cognizant of our negligence, our omissions, our indifference, our distractions, and the persistent potential of a reversal in our relation to the death of the other.

XII

We begin to see that vulnerability, mortality, attention, care, and aid form the backbone of such an ethi*cosmo*politics. Each term therefore calls for an explanation, both of what distinguishes it from and of what attaches it to the other terms, within the framework of murderous consent. Judith Butler, Joan Tronto, and Sandra Laugier have shown how crucial vulnerability is to the articulation of what is called the ethics and politics of *care*.[6] The literature on care understands "vulnerable being" in a much broader sense than the one I will employ here. Vulnerability, in this literature, refers to the forms of insecurity and precarity that affect the most destitute, as well as to the inequitable distribution of the risks of epidemics, health and climate crises, and the accidents and erosion of life that are illness and old age. More generally, the term refers to that which, in the everyday life of any individual, requires care, attention, and/or assistance and thus renders the individual, in the most "ordinary" way, dependent on the "care" provided by others.[7] Vulnerability is a structural given of existence. It interjects obstacles and vexations into life and imperils life through the wounds, trials, and upheavals that life confronts in the most ordinary undertakings: finding housing, clothing, nourishment, schooling, and work.

But *care* also has a *cosmopolitical* dimension that I wish to highlight. This dimension is apparent in the definition proposed by Berenice Fischer and Joan Tronto: "the task of care is to maintain, continue, and repair the world so that we can live in it as well as possible."[8] If we take seriously the idea of "world," as evoked by this definition, then we are being pointed toward an extension and expansion of our responsibility beyond the political, national, or cultural [*communautaires*] frontiers in which we are tempted to confine it. Doing so turns the attention, care, and aid that are enjoined by the vulnerability of the other into "concern" [*souci*] for the world. Because it is about "liv[ing] in [the world] as well as possible," Fischer's and Tronto's injunction cannot be given a meaning that is exclusively or even primarily "local." If, as a matter of principle, nothing is more foreign to *care* than some argument for the individualistic or egoist retrenchment within a private sphere that excludes certain kinds of people whom we designate in advance, then *care* is of necessity cosmopolitan.[9]

XIII

Therefore, neither ethics nor a politics that calls itself ethical can evade the question of what *seems* to be damaged in the "world"—broken, "out of joint," unhinged, perhaps even irreparable—and which we must try, despite everything, to "put back together."[10] If the world is really the yardstick by which we evaluate the justice and efficacy of *care*, then we cannot call the world repaired as long as men and women in it are exposed to death by war, poverty, famine, or some form or other of terror. In the pages that follow I use the phrase "incompleteness of the world" to represent the fractures, breakdowns, and flaws that enjoin our responsibility. Every life, I noted above, is a living-with—and nothing is more fragile, more reversible, more destructible than the fabric or network of ties that composes this "with" as it expands outward toward the world as a whole. It is in the relations that attach us to others that we, over time and in all facets of life, are most vulnerable. As Frédéric Worms has observed, the most extreme form of vulnerability is the potential "violation" of such relations, that is, "the act of shattering a human relationship from within this very relationship."[11]

The problematic of murderous consent intersects with this last observation in a number of ways. It does so by urging us to conceptualize relations that are simultaneously moral *and* political and analyze these relations at an ethi*cosmo*political level. It shifts the emphasis away from such "violations" and focuses on the particular form of radical vulnerability that is our exposure to lethal violence. The constitutive relationship, whose suspension or rupture murderous consent interrogates, is the responsibility that binds us to the life of the other. It is this responsibility that locates the primary form of vulnerability that can affect this relationship. The most radical and daunting form of this vulnerability is the other's mortality. The relationship of responsibility therefore hews to an ethics of *care* to the extent that it requires us to take into account the multiple ways that a person's existence can be crippled by the prospect and experience of death. This is why, as our relationship to the other confronts us with our responsibility for attention, care, and aid (which are constitutive of this ethics), the problematic of murderous consent directs our attention first and foremost to the possibility of a *radical extinction* of attention, care, and aid, of their *eclipse* or their *suspension*—of their neglect, on the one hand, or their transformation into a savage drive, on the other, that is, the irruption of evil and cruelty.

XIV

In our efforts to follow the traces of murderous consent that haunt our rec-
ollections of war, oppression, and terror in the twentieth century, we do
not encounter the memory of its victims alone. The reflections and thoughts
of others accompany us, as do the testimonies and the accounts that are
that memory's custodians and mediators. As we become aware of the faults
and chasms, past, present, and ongoing, that the eclipse of responsibility
has revealed (and continues to reveal) in our belonging to the world, we
become mindful of texts, phrases, propositions, and expressions that take
possession of the mind and cause long nights of sleeplessness. In the following chapters I borrow phrases, propositions, and expressions from Camus, Freud, Grossman, Levinas, Kraus, Anders, and others. Their recitation
and meditation, reprised again and again, impart a certain rhythm to the
composition of this book. Indeed, it is around such phrases that the book
is articulated. What phrases? one might ask. For example, the following:
"The whole world stood open to us." "There is no eradication of evil."
"Everything inhuman is senseless and useless." "Isn't the messenger guilty,
too?" "We were ashamed to be human." "We are really neighbors—at the
very least as mortals."[12] These words serve not only as beacons to guide our
efforts to comprehend murderous consent in its existential dimension but
also as buoys to which to moor our thought as we search for a way out.

XV

There are several reasons to adopt such an approach. First of all, philosophical writing always assumes, whether we admit it or not, that our words are
forever grafted on to those of others. Even if this grafting is not obvious,
our writing is nevertheless colonized by citations. Our writing, in one way
or another, recollects other texts, propositions that have been analyzed and
internalized and that contribute to our composition. In this book I plead
repeatedly in favor of this way of writing. The development of thought in
its singularity implies neither rejecting such a practice nor pretending to
ignore it. It always refers, at least implicitly, to a tradition made up of texts
and propositions. No doubt there are occasions when thought seeks to displace its heritage. But even when the gesture is critical or "deconstructive," it still secures the transmission of that legacy. That transmission is
more necessary today than ever because, as a product of rumination and
close reading, it is threatened from without by new configurations of knowledge production, and from within by the administrations that are expected to manage this inheritance and safeguard it. If we want to preserve

the memory of such texts, not, as some might say, as an inheritance, but because they take part in the life of thought, then we must continually re-call and reintroduce them in a way that is each and every time *singular*. This is the first principle of the method I adopt here: we write always, and as a matter of course, to transmit something more than our "own thought." This is the most effective way to combat the mistaken impression that some "cultural tragedy" has rendered us powerless to oppose the manipulations of violence.

XVI

It is not only philosophy that is solicited in the chapters that follow but, in equal measure, novels, plays, and poetry. This does not mean that philosophy will provide interpretations of these literary texts. Rather, literary texts will be asked to back up my conceptual analysis and even substitute for it when the latter's limits are being tested. No problematic demands literary treatment more than murderous consent. Nothing can substitute for the singularity provided by testimonials and narratives as we try to imagine, at the limits of language, the cruelty of the regimes of terror, the mass murders, and the violence that has been woven into the fabric of twentieth-century life. Varlam Shalamov's *Kolyma Tales*, Yevgenia Ginzburg's *Journey into the Whirlwind* and *Le ciel de la Kolyma*, Yury Dombrovsky's novel *The Faculty of Useless Knowledge*, not to forget Vasily Grossman's *Life and Fate* and *Everything Flows*, Paul Celan's poems, Primo Levi's *If This Is a Man*, or Robert Antelme's *The Human Race*, and so many others, for example, the books of Kenzaburō Ōe or, closer to us still, Boris Boubacar Diop's *Murambi, the Book of Bones*, which explores the Rwandan genocide, all arrest our thought and subject it to a hearing that exposes the inadequacy of our generalizations. They subject it to the intensity of an "experience" that, if it does not force our silence, at least invites the reserve and restraint that the singularity of every experience of suffering demands of abstract thinking. Not all these works are cited in this book, but they have all participated in its composition.

XVII

Literature (novels, tales, and testimonials) takes us down paths that thought might otherwise hesitate to follow. Given the power of murderous consent, we might well smile dismissively when revolt, benevolence, or the critique of shame are defined as *ways out* [*dégagements*]. But when revolt is understood in the light of the paradoxes and the aporias confronted by Camus's characters, according to one of the organizing threads of his thought, or when, in *Life and Fate*, benevolence emerges as the heart of the message of hope that Ikonnikov conveys to us from the abyss of horror, or when critique (ironical and polemical) is the only weapon that Karl Kraus can muster against the aggressive censorship, lies, falsifications, and deceptions of his time, or when Kenzaburō Ōe and Günther Anders describe shame as the only legitimate response to the brutal cataclysm that befell Hiroshima and Nagasaki and as the only defensible attitude that we can adopt with regard to the cross-generational hardships experienced by the *hibakusha*, the idea of a way out takes on a dimension that we cannot treat casually. Revolt, benevolence, critique, and shame buttress one another with the force of evidence, imposed on us by that which in the words and writings of literature is irreducible and irreplaceable. They proclaim resistance, restoration, and even redemption by the attention, care, and aid that the vulnerability and the mortality of the other demand of us, both in the face of and in opposition to all of history's violence. We need more than a concept to make possible such a proclamation. Revolt, benevolence, shame, and even critique must make themselves heard in singular speech, in its distinctive idiomatic turns, its deployment of thought, style, and rhythm. They must make themselves discernible in the expressions of a face, in gestures, in what Iris Murdoch calls the "textures of being" of a man or a woman, a "personage," as depicted by a novel, story, portrayal, or stage dramatization.[13]

It is true that literature often loses itself in the blind approval of terror and cruelty and thus bears no small degree of responsibility in the production and perpetuation of murderous consent. But it has also helped, in an incomparable way, to keep alive the possibility of escaping from the perversion of violence. It has shown that we can struggle *against it*, even if not on its own terrain and with its own weapons. It has shown that concessions are not inevitable. There are alternatives. If literature inherits a promise from the language that it weaves together or translates, this must be it. The promise is twofold. First, literature exemplifies and evokes repeatedly that which, in confrontation with the powers and ideologies of destruction and all their justifications of murder, makes up the *idiomatic* singularity of each and every existence. Second, as shown by the poems of Paul Celan or Osip Mandelstam or by the novels of Vasily Grossman, it brings to life, through language, the hope of a bond that will stand up to destruction. By the simple fact of offering itself up as something to be shared, literature proclaims (and this is why I appeal to literature in the chapters that follow) that it cannot and will not let violence have the last word.

XVIII

Finally, this book seeks to respond to one last need. When, twenty years ago, I undertook to "deconstruct" the "characterizations of peoples" and their corresponding "imaginary geographies," when I undertook subsequently to question all the ways that belonging (national, linguistic, European, civilizational) is invoked so as to foster and reproduce itself, I did so with the conviction that peoples and geographies, because they are reductionist and exclusive, are the sources of violence. Thus, the question of murderous consent was always in the background of my writing; it defined the horizon of my research. But nurtured by its frequent manifestation as "news," murderous consent persistently elicited new research and new writing. I could not begin to cite all the place-names (cities, regions, countries) that bring to mind instances of murderous consent (they are too numerous) without worrying that I had omitted some. But having studied several instances (potentially though not necessarily murderous) in which the use of the first-person plural ("*we* who share the same culture," "*we* who speak the same language," "*we* who practice the same religion," "*we* who belong to the same civilization") was enabling murderous consent, it became impossible to approach the horizon they define without analyzing them from a global perspective. Thus was born the project of an ethi*cosmo*politics, the purpose of which is to find answers to the questions: what is meant by the expression "*we* mortals" and what relationship and what responsibilities does this expression imply?

XIX

Thought must therefore confront this complicated and problematic use of the first-person plural. The *we* is no doubt gesturing toward the confinement of moral *and* political relations within reductionist and exclusionary bounds. But the mortality with which it is associated also interrogates, in an even more enigmatic fashion, humanity's relations, if not with animals in the abstract, then with some animals specifically.

They are "vulnerable" and "mortal," too, perhaps now more than ever, given the conditions in which some are raised and given the many experiments to which they are subjected.[14] Should we use the term "murder" to describe the most violent and most cruel aspects of these relations and characterize the way our societies adjust to these relations as murderous consent? We should not rush to judgment. But ultimately we will not be able to elude the question of whether, beyond humanity, it is not the entire "community of the living" with which humanity shares the earth that is concerned by the problematic of murderous consent.

1

Justice

Who among us can say that we have never *consented* to violence or desired someone's death or allowed it to happen? Who among us can claim that the desire for or indifference toward murder is, has been, and always will be foreign to us? Consent to violence and murder can occur unbeknownst to the person who claims to resist it. The haunting litany of names that expose consent, and the forms that it assumes, are boundless. These include resignation, passivity, the absence of revulsion at the spectacle of savage injustice in all its forms, acquiescence in the murder of others, and even a taste for assassinations, the temptation of terror, and the fascination of war and all the cruelty that accompanies it. We know how complex and diffuse is the sentiment of consent, whose infinitely variable forms give shape to the course of history and engender a geography of mourning—a history and a geography that chart the difference between the deaths that affect us and the disappearance of those who do not.[1] The problem of consent is the line of separation that it draws. On one side are those who will never be touched, shaken, or worried by it, who will always judge the scruples it engenders unreasonable, excessive, "idealistic," and who will even find (politically, economically, and indeed philosophically) good reasons to avoid resisting consent so that it does not trouble their comfortable lives. On the other side are those who experience consent as an injustice that is tolerated—if not encouraged—and that dwells at the heart of their lives. Whether it concerns populations exposed to famine (even though the richest countries grapple with the overproduction of foodstuffs), the growing numbers of people deprived of health care (despite the fact that the pharmaceutical industry enjoys sizable profits), all the wars that have been forgotten (which have filled the coffers of weapons manufacturers from the very countries that proudly appeal for peace), the civilian massacres, or the refugee camps where death en masse is met with nearly total indifference, those who are on this latter side of the line know that *in saying and doing nothing, they are consenting to murder.*

If we are struck by the injustice revealed through this analysis, how can we resist the temptation to violence that it conveys? How do we escape the legitimate desire to eradicate, through violence, the causes and reasons, real or supposed, of violence and injustice? How can victims, biased by their own plight, abstain from punishing those responsible for their suffering? The refusal of violence and the consent to violence are inextricably linked, and no ethicopolitical question has proven more difficult to resolve. If I say and do nothing, I consent. But is it possible to speak and act against injustice and the many forms that violence takes *without* violence? In other words, is it possible to make the impossible possible—daring to believe that such a possibility could arise—without consenting to violence? If we give in to the temptation or the convenience of consent, is this possibility not ipso facto invalidated?

"A Lunatic's Pastime"

This is the paradox that haunts the thought of Albert Camus. It is the central theme of *The Rebel*, most notably the last chapter, "Thought at the Meridian"; it informs his positions in *Nuptials, Summer, The Stranger*, his *Actuelles*, dedicated to the war in Algeria, and many of the articles published in the newspaper *Combat*. It is also the focus of several of his plays, which is where we might begin our analysis—with *Caligula* and *The Just Assassins*. We remember the murderous folly of the Roman emperor whose destructive impulses Camus represented onstage for the first time in 1945 (the date is significant). What is surprising about Caligula's madness is that it is not bereft of logic or reason. While Caligula's crimes may seem arbitrary and blind in the spectator's eyes, they pursue a goal, as the emperor reminds Scipio toward the end of the first act.

> Caligula: I repeat—that is my point. I'm exploiting the impossible. Or, more accurately, it's a question of making the impossible possible.
>
> Scipio: But that game may lead to—to anything! It's a lunatic's pastime.

Caligula: No, Scipio. An emperor's vocation. [*He lets himself sink back wearily among the cushions.*] Ah, my dears, at least I've come to see the uses of supremacy. It gives impossibilities a run. From this day on, so long as life is mine, my freedom has no frontier.[2]

There is much to say about the fatigue that weighs on the shoulders of the person who, in the name of a certain idea of justice, wants to make the impossible possible. We could write a history of the twentieth century simply by recalling the names of those who have been exhausted, driven mad and blind, sometimes for the better but more often for the worse, by the idea of justice and then were propelled down the path toward murder. But what is the impossibility that Caligula wants to make possible? Two scenes later, he reveals it to Caesonia, who considers the inexplicable reasons for his torment:

Caligula: Men weep because . . . [3] the world's all wrong.

. . .

Caligula: . . . I shall make this age of ours a kingly gift—the gift of equality. And when all is leveled out, when the impossible has come to earth and the moon is in my hands—then, perhaps, I shall be transfigured and the world renewed; then men will die no more and at last be happy.[4]

Caligula's murderous folly finds justification in a dream of justice and equality that touches on the question of human mortality. Tragically, his folly is grounded in his unbearable awareness (lived as suffering) that such justice and equality are abidingly deficient and in his mad desire to remedy it, no matter the cost. "To make possible the impossible" is a motivating theme that all rebellions share. There is probably no perspective on the world (since I am talking about the world) that is not troubled or undermined by the need to renounce this ambition. This same phrase, however, will undergo a strange revision. Half a century later, in new thought on possibility, Derrida employs this same expression to define the aporetic character of *responsibility*[5]—for example, the responsibility that requires an impossible transaction between the demands of justice and the rule of law or between the principle of unconditional hospitality and the regulations, decrees, constraints, and controls that govern the conditions of hospitality, as offered (or refused) by sovereign states. For Derrida, there is no ethics (and no politics derived from ethics) that is not burdened by the task of "making possible the impossible." According to Camus's depiction of the bloodthirsty emperor, however, this same task justifies all forms of cruelty and, as one of the conspirators (Cherea) complains, drives Caligula to "count mankind, and the world we know, for nothing."[6] For Derrida, this task is inseparable from the deconstruction of sovereignty whose sole perspective is to search for the *impossible beyond* cruelty.[7] At the end of the play, however, as Caligula stands in front of the mirror, he has no choice but to acknowledge that his destructive logic has led him into an impasse. All that is left of his dream of justice is the mirror image that is violence. Ultimately, having pursued his dream to the ends of the Earth, he finds only a distorted image of his own freedom—neither the world nor justice:

> Caligula: . . . There's nothing in this world, or in the other, made to my stature. And yet I know, and you, too, know [*still weeping, he stretches out his arms toward the mirror*] that all I need is for the impossible to be. The impossible! I've searched for it at the confines of the world, in the secret places of my heart. I've stretched out my hands [*his voice rises to a scream*]; see, I stretch out my hands, but it's always you I find, you only, confronting me, and I've come to hate you. I have chosen a wrong path, a path that leads to nothing. My freedom isn't the right one.[8]

Camus always defended himself, rightly, against the claim that he had written a philosophical play. By invoking what he called a "tragedy of the intelligence," he was not seeking to illustrate, demonstrate, or verify some particular "thesis."[9] Nor will this be the case later in *The Just Assassins* and *The Stranger*, in which murder occupies a central position, or, in a completely different context (all this requires much nuance), in his subsequent *Reflections on the Guillotine* (1957). I began with the play because it exemplifies from the outset one of the diverse and complex forms of what I will attempt to analyze in this book using the term "murderous consent," which I will examine through readings of Sigmund Freud, Emmanuel Levinas, Vasily Grossman, Karl Kraus, Judith Butler, and Günther Anders. But few bodies of work are more haunted by the possibility of murder than Camus's. Recall Mersault's marvel, vertigo, and dizziness that constitute the tipping point of *The Stranger* (1942):

> That's when everything began to reel. The sea carried up a thick, fiery breath. It seemed to me as if the sky split open from one end to the other to rain down fire. My whole being tensed and I squeezed my hand around the revolver. The trigger gave; I felt the smooth underside of the butt; and there, in that noise, sharp and deafening at the same time, is where it all started. I shook off the sweat and sun. I knew that I had shattered the harmony of the day, the exceptional silence of a beach where I'd been happy. Then I fired four more times

at the motionless body where the bullets lodged without leaving a trace. And it was like knocking four quick times on the door of unhappiness.[10]

In his 1957 preface to the American edition of three of his plays, Camus writes that Caligula, "obsessed with the impossible and poisoned with scorn and horror, . . . tries, through murder and the systematic perversion of all values, to practice a liberty that he will eventually discover not to be the right one."[11] In so doing, Caligula becomes the herald of an ambivalence that still preoccupies us. But we should not forget that the heroes of *The Just Assassins* (1950), Kaliayev and Dora, are no less ambivalent. Recall the following exchange, which betrays Camus's own attachment to these characters, concerning the planned assassination of the grand duke in czarist Russia. Several lives hang in the balance, those of the grand duke, the grand duchess, their nephew and niece (whose "innocent" presence will ward off the assassination), and, in particular, the "terrorists." All these lives are tied to one another by the responsibility to dispense death in the name of an ideal of justice. In the scene in question, Dora reminds Kaliayev how difficult it is to endure the gaze of the person one intends to kill. This is why it is "preferable" that murder take place in the absence of any "human" interaction that might restrain the hand of the avenger. Death, she tells him, is most easily administered when the face-to-face encounter is interrupted. Execution requires that we not (or cease to) see what the other's face might be expressing. In terms that are not those of Camus but that compose one of the main themes of this book, I would write of the other's *vulnerability* and *mortality*. Execution requires that we be deaf to the appeal for attention, care, and assistance that is expressed by the condemned. It demands that we ignore, forget, or erase the potential victim's irreplaceable singularity (his or her gaze, voice, emotions, and thoughts) in the name of some abstract idea that justifies murder. All that counts are the strategies, discourses, ruses, and grandiose phrases that make murder sound necessary. Today, as in the past, condemning the other to death is always grounded, in word and image, in a logic of necessity:

> Kaliayev: It's not he I'm killing. I'm killing despotism.
>
> Dora: That's quite true. And despotism must be killed. . . . But, then, I don't know the Grand Duke; it wouldn't be anything so easy if while I was screwing in the tube he were sitting in front of me, looking at me. But you'll see him quite near, from only a yard or two away.[12]

Kaliayev, looking into the eyes of the children (the nephew and niece of the grand duke), cannot throw the bomb. He meets with condemnation by another "terrorist-avenger," Stepan, who denounces his hesitation in words that provide one of the most complete formulations of murderous consent (wherever it is engendered, and no matter how it is justified): "Not until the day comes when we stop sentimentalizing about children [that is, to look away from their gaze and what we see in it: innocence, vulnerability, fragility, the promise of a future, etc.] will the revolution triumph, and we be masters of the world."[13]

This is not the place to recall all the landscapes throughout the world in which we see this "neglect of children," whether war in the former Yugoslavia, Rwandan genocide, war in Angola, Liberia, or Sierra Leone, or the "attacks" that take place all around the world in (more or less blind) retaliation.[14] They all contribute to the infinite spiral of violence that feeds murderous consent. I will return to this issue subsequently, when I interrogate the use, manipulation, and "dissimulation" of the images of dead and murdered children by the technologies of "consent."[15]

I cannot provide a reading of the entire play here—doing so would, at the very least, call for comparisons with Sartre's plays *Dirty Hands* (1948) and *The Condemned of Altona* (1959). But I can evoke the response to murderous consent that emerges from one of the play's most dramatic and emblematic confrontations, revealing the importance of the question of whether murder can be justified in the name of rebellion and justice in Camus's thought. When the attack fails, multiple logics clash: the logic that gives the revolutionary cause the absolute right to determine life or death for those whose sacrifice it considers necessary and the logic that rejects that price. After Kaliayev's unsuccessful attack in act 2:

> Stepan [*vehemently*]: There are no limits! The truth is that you don't believe in the revolution, any of you. [*All, except* Kaliayev, *rise to their feet.*] No, you don't believe in it. . . . if you draw the line at killing these two children, well, it simply means you are not sure you have that right. So, I repeat, you do *not* believe in the revolution. [*There is a short silence.* Kaliayev, *too, rises to his feet.*]
>
> Kaliayev: Stepan, I am ashamed of myself—yet I cannot let you continue. I am ready to shed blood, so as to overturn the present despotism. But, behind your words, I see the threat of another despotism which, if ever it comes into power, will make of me a murderer— and what I want to be is a doer of justice, not a man of blood.
>
> Stepan: Provided justice is done—even if it's done by assassins— what does it matter which you are? You and I are negligible quantities.[16]

Showing the complexity of what I am analyzing here as murderous consent would require multiplying my references and comparing Camus's texts with those of his contemporaries.[17] It would require placing books published during or just after the Second World War in conversation with one another and resurrecting the memories that were hollowed out by so many crimes, murders, and violent deaths. We would see that everything cannot be so easily placed in some category or other. As I have emphasized from the beginning, one of the most difficult issues concerning murderous consent is the necessary distinction between the various forms of consent. They can be neither easily merged nor easily separated such that no blurring of the boundaries separating them would render them undecidable. The murder of the Arab on the beach (*The Stranger*), Caligula's crimes, and the murderous acts of the Russian nihilists (*The Just Assassins*) are *incommensurable*. This is also, more generally, the case of the death penalty, of the "license to kill" that is war, of war crimes that transgress or pervert the rules and limits set by international law, and of crimes against humanity—to say nothing of the "culpable" silence that greets such crimes, the passive or active support for them, or their justification or encouragement. Nothing is more worrisome than our willingness to disregard this incommensurability. We do so whenever we submit our relation to the mortality of the other to *one and the same* standard. Nor should we ignore the fact that these books confront this relation in modalities other than that of providing help, support, and care or of *being opposed to, refusing,* or *being against* the death of others. Any possibilities (*living-with* [*vivre-avec*], "solidarity," or "support") that exhibit such opposition, refusal, or being-against are suspended, eclipsed, and even erased by the notion that I am trying to understand here as "murderous consent."[18] Such is the distinctive trait of consent's violence. It destroys an essential modality of our relation to the mortality of others. The challenge is to understand the importance of this modality and how it is destroyed.

"The Small Part of Existence That Can Be Realized on This Earth"

If our age admits, with equanimity, that murder has its justifications, it is because of this indifference to life which is the mark of nihilism.[19]

What is the origin of this notion that I am calling, with some reservation and at the risk of blurring the lines, "murderous consent"? Why does it seem that this expression resonates with our everyday experience (and not the least obscure part of that experience)? What "historical condition" does it reference? What ordeal does it evoke? The response I will try to sketch out in the following pages concerns both our manner of living in our modern-day era (haunted, as it is, by the memory of war) and our contemporary experience of the world (whose unity is jeopardized). I seek to show, in other words, that "murderous consent" both designates a distinctive characteristic of our era and describes (unquestionably, but difficult to admit) a dimension of our being-in-the-world. With murder as my central theme, I will begin with the first half of this proposition (our own times, along with the memory we retain of the wars and atrocities of the last century, among others) so that I may arrive at the second (our belonging to the world, both present and future).

To begin with our era, in which murderous consent is a distinctive trait, I return to Camus, specifically to *The Rebel*, published in 1951.[20] It is a masterpiece, which incited lively debate, and is notable for its incomparable lucidity. Its last chapter, "Thought at the Meridian," remains to this day the exception to the blind, confused, and shameful compromises that so many literary figures brokered with (state, revolutionary, nationalist, etc.) violence. It is one of the greatest moral and political lessons that the twentieth century—so destructive and so lethal—has bequeathed to us. Just as Camus's books are concerned with the possibility of murder, they are also haunted by a specter that in and of itself defines his era: "nihilism" (the point of departure that we seek and that we rediscover again and again). "Murderous consent" is another name for "nihilism." Nihilism is less directly, as Nietzsche maintains, the "devaluation of values" than it is the *logical and rational* "justification" of crime. The distinction is important. The history of the "collapse of values" is one thing, but the history of "criminal justification" is another. We should refrain from equating them. Nor should we assume that the decline of certain values (indicative of a moral, political, or other "civilizational order") is responsible for the "proliferation of crimes."

At issue are both a disaffiliation and the risk of a false start. The false start consists in assuming from the outset that murderous consent is rooted in the "death of God"—that our era is "nihilist" because it has ceased to believe, and thus, by the same token, "everything is permitted," as the Grand Inquisitor says to Ivan in *The Brothers Karamazov*. We should therefore refrain from theological-moral reductionism concerning our ability to murder, as Freud urges in *The Future of an Illusion*. As for the disaffiliation, we should not fall back on historical, political, and moral avatars of the divine commandment "Thou shalt not kill," as if it were self-evident. Nor should we discourage questions regarding its origin. But this approach and this perspectival distance are necessary. If we reduce consent to the transgression of the prohibition of murder, we miss all the cases that do not fall under this prohibition (whether understood as human or divine). I refer to all those cases in which we "consent" *without killing*, that is, to the cases in which our relation to the mortality and vulnerability of the other has been suspended or eclipsed, but *no one*, in the rigorous sense of the law, can be held legally responsible for the other's death. All these cases produce the same outcome, a fault [*faille*] or rift in our being-in-the-world.

The Rebel proposes a different approach. Camus does not study murderous consent for its own sake. Murderous consent, for Camus, is the crux of a paradox. The hallmark of the twentieth century (the "century of totalitarianism") is its profusion of good excuses for murder, whether discovered or invented. Never has murder been invoked so frequently as in these times of terror and in the name of some legitimate revolt against misery and injustice. Never have so many millions of lives been destroyed, en masse, in the name of some supposedly more just or equal relationship between the living (more in line with some "principle" or other of justice, a dangerously credible notion even when aberrant). This alleged relationship is what makes historical judgment so difficult and ambiguous. However we approach this century, we cannot minimize the "thirst for justice" that animates and elevates its protagonists in combat with their opponents—including those whom we deservedly remember as the "incarnation" of absolute evil. How can we escape this confusion? How do we avoid rejecting what is incommensurable without renouncing the notion of justice? How do we preserve principled distinctions, without which there would be no "values" left for us to hold on to? If the temptation of nihilism emerges as the problem of our era, it is because it is haunted by questions such as these.

This is why reading *The Rebel* is so important. To this day, Camus's work remains the most developed effort to breach this impasse. Camus reminds us that there are always two paths that are available to us in our disagreements over what could be foreseen or denounced, wrongly or rightly, in a rational, obsessional, or exuberant way, as an injustice. His distinction is significant. The first path recuses those ideologies that provide a justification of violence. That justification is more often than not intrinsic to ideology itself. It engages ideologies in a contest that provides them with yet more reasons to justify murder. The revolt of one ideology against the "inhuman principles" of some other ideology demands a response, a reprisal, vengeance—such that the respective claims of each in favor of *another* justice constantly *turn against life itself*. The history of the twentieth century, as we know, is made up of such confrontations. These confrontations have also provided literary and intellectual history with one of the axes around which it is articulated. Murderous consent is very much the business of historians, philosophers, writers, and poets. There was a time, not so long ago, when simply mentioning certain names sparked controversy—some of the more obvious names (limiting ourselves to France) being Brasillach and Céline on the right, and Aragon, Éluard, and Sartre on the left. Closer to the present, we might recall Alain Badiou's writings on the Khmer Rouge, Maoist China, or Slobodan Milošević's Serbia.

From this perspective, it is not surprising that *The Rebel* provoked a violent polemic following its publication shortly after the Second World War. In June 1952 Francis Jeanson published an incendiary text in *Les temps modernes*. It was followed by Camus's and Sartre's responses (and a second response by Francis Jeanson) two issues later.[21] Camus's detractors could not tolerate the alternative path (foreign to all ideological commitment and, for this reason, to all ideological justifications of violence), which condemns murder, that his reflections uncovered. It was a difficult path to follow at a time when identifying consent to violence most often meant contesting others' crimes while justifying or idealizing one's own. This path is the focus of this book. First, and in a foundational way [*de façon principielle*], it is the path of rebellion against servitude, lies, and terror—a rebellion that does not let itself be recuperated by dogma or circumvented by a mythical past, any more than it permits itself speculation regarding some radiant future. Rebellion cannot calculate or plan in advance, nor can it swear allegiance to a program or organization or to its organizers and leaders. We follow the path of rebellion in a present that constantly reinvents itself, always in a singular and irruptive way. Its temporality does not unfold as a continuous thread, and it does not comply with some negative dialectic. Rebellion is an insurrection of sense, or meaning [*sens*: sense, meaning, orientation, direction], against the forces that confiscate its possibility (political and religious authorities, the dogmas they support, churches, political parties, etc.). Camus reminds us of this forcefully in the first pages of "Thought at the Meridian":

> But its reasons [the reasons for rebellion]—the mutual recognition of a common destiny and the communication of men between themselves—are always valid. Rebellion proclaimed them and undertook to serve them. In the same way it defined, in contradiction to nihilism, a rule of conduct that has no need to await the end of history to explain its actions and which is, nevertheless, not formal. Contrary to Jacobin morality, it made allowances for everything that escapes from rules and laws. It opened the way to a morality which, far from obeying abstract principles, discovers them only in the heat of battle and in the incessant movement of contradiction. Nothing justifies the assertion that these principles have existed externally; it

is of no use to declare that they will one day exist. But they do exist, in the very period in which we exist. With us, and throughout all history, they deny servitude, falsehood, and terror.[22]

Several remarks are in order here. First, note that rebellion is discussed in the *past tense.* Why? Precisely because the present (1951 for Camus but, perhaps, in other ways, our present as well) is dominated no longer by rebellion as defined here but by the various forms of nihilism that smother and pervert it—that is, the confrontations, combats, and commitments that merely have the appearance of rebellion and in which the meaning [*sens*] of rebellion has been compromised. As we have seen, and as Camus constantly reminds us, nihilism is characterized by the *proliferation of crimes* that have been committed in the name of history, equality, justice, revolution, and even truth. For someone who protests against the murderous excesses of the era, to speak of rebellion in the past tense is therefore to confess that his or her thought belongs to a time when the sense [*sens*] of rebellion as alive to (and enlivened by) the injustices of the present, vigilant against servitude and untruth, and alert to terror has been lost. The meaning of rebellion was lost in a wave of multiple murderous consents, whether in the name of Jacobin morality, rules, or laws or in the name of abstract principles or supposedly eternal truths. Rebellion is thus an "insurrection of sense" because it disappears, because it is compromised and goes astray as soon as this sense is commandeered by some truth imposed by dogma or rule, which is always potentially murderous. One could recite a litany of writers, intellectuals, and philosophers (they are not alone, though the public character of their words increases their responsibility) who lost their way—not to judge or condemn them but to highlight the force of the paradox (rebellion's inability to match and balance murderous violence) that Camus depicts.

The second important remark concerns the reasons for rebellion. The reasons are crucial and will help situate my central theme going forward. "The mutual recognition of a common destiny and the communication of men between themselves" are reasons, Camus writes, that are "still alive." Later he makes clear that injustice is critical for the rebel, not because it impedes or contradicts a certain supposedly immutable and principled idea of justice, but because "it kills the small part of existence that can be realized on this earth through the mutual complicity of men."[23] I will parse these words carefully because they display several threads that I wish to weave together. The following expression should retain our closest attention: "the small part of existence that can be realized on this earth through the mutual complicity of men."[24] I focus on this phrase because it is about the world, what happens to the world, and thus, necessarily, being-in-the-world, or what makes the world a world. It concerns the necessary conditions for the world we live in—the world we share—to really be a world. Our relation to the world is counterfeit—it lacks being—it obstructs the "worldization" [*mondialisation*, "globalization"] of the world [*monde*], because nihilism prevails without reserve. Our being-in-the-world is bereft of being because our relation to the mortality and the vulnerability of others is no longer sustained by a rebellion that could locate sense [*sens*, or meaning] in the rejection of that relation's eclipse, effacement, and perversion.

There is more. We need to examine, and at length, this "mutual complicity of men." It constitutes one of the distinctive aspects of Camus's work, as a close reading of *The Plague* and other texts demonstrates. The sharing, alliance, and covenant that this "mutual complicity" supposes are not simply one literary theme among others. For Camus, they define the task that, in the end, makes mutual complicity, as complicity, the fragile and precarious counterweight to nihilism. Nothing is ever simple, however, and if we need to examine Camus's reflections, it is in part because "complicity" can prove to be murderous itself if it is exclusivist and turns against those that it marginalizes. As we know—and as persecution and discrimination always teach us—we can be "complicit" [*complices*] in crime.

At stake, therefore, is the possibility of a world that is not torn apart by the antagonism of murderous consents. This expression should be written in the plural. Whatever the form assumed by consent, the central characteristic of murder is that it divides. It never creates unanimity, and its endorsement can never claim universality. On the contrary, it traces a thousand and one borders, despite the fact that our experience of murderous consent is increasingly *global*. Regardless of what Camus means by the "mutual complicity" of (all) people, one thing is certain: murder disrupts it. It creates bonds of (murderous) solidarity so as to break other bonds that are "universal" or, if I dare use the word, "cosmopolitan," and it forgets that these are the only bonds that can justify rebellion. This is what makes the proliferation of contradictory and antagonistic murderous consents the principal symptom of nihilism: it breeds ruptures, interruptions, and suspensions. The first bond it breaks has its source in language. It is the possibility of speaking with others, with or without an interpreter, the possibility of dialogue. For a man of the theater like Camus, this last term is essential. The speech of murderous consent is, by definition, "monological." It listens to no one; it bends for no argument; its logic is unshared, like that of Caligula or Stepan. It receives nothing from anyone and is imposed on others by violence.

The mutual complicity and communication discovered by rebellion can survive only in the free exchange of conversation. Every ambiguity, every misunderstanding, leads to death; clear language and simple words are the only salvation from this death. . . . Every rebel, solely by the movement that sets him in opposition to the oppressor, therefore pleads for life, undertakes to struggle against servitude, falsehood, and terror, and affirms, in a flash, that these three afflictions are the cause of silence between men, that they obscure them from one another and prevent them from rediscovering themselves in the only value that can save them from nihilism—the long complicity of men at grips with their destiny.[25]

Again, there are several elements here that help us advance. The contradiction between nihilism and rebellion intersects the contradiction between "murderous consent" and the "plea [*plaidoyer*] for life," which in turn encompasses the contradiction between monologue (the soliloquy of ideology and terror, of their lies and their censorship) and dialogue. In other words, all opposition to the justification of murder must associate and combine these three forces: the rebellion against injustice, the "plea for life" that resists the fascination of death, and dialogue as opposed to imprisonment in a speechless logic. Rebellion must plead *for life* or cease to be rebellion. Rebellion speaks, protests, and tries to convince. Even when it cries out, it uses words. This is what (as a matter of principle) opposes rebellion to the sanction of murder, if such a sanction assumes that we have renounced language and ceased to uphold life. Rebellion betrays itself if it makes the slightest concession to violence that imperils life—this is the red line that must not be crossed. It is in life, in the care and protection of life, of life worthy of its name, that rebellion finds its justification.

I cannot overstate the importance of this red line: it alone dissociates rebellion from power calculations—and even the will to power—which are often the concealed reason behind murder.[26] But above all, it warrants the extension of rebellion beyond the limits of some given community. If to rebel is to "plead for life," it is not enough to "plead" simply for the lives of brothers, fellow citizens, or the members of our own religious community, while ignoring others or holding them in contempt. The red line cannot separate those whom it privileges in dialogue from those whom it might exclude on the basis of some principle or other. The distinction between rebellion and nihilism is rigorous. It results in a different relation to the world, a *completely other being-in-the-world*. It is this relation that defines the horizon of my reflections in this book. When rebellion becomes murderous consent and turns against itself, it is only because it has been subjugated and perverted from within determined borders, be it the borders of a village or a city, a region or a country, or some circumscribed notion of the "international." This is how connections are broken and the dream or ideal of a "mutual complicity of men" fades away. This is why this "unity of the human condition" depends on this other way of thinking of the world, as Camus reminds us in this decisive passage from "Thought at the Meridian": "It is then possible to say that rebellion, when it develops into destruction, is illogical. Claiming the unity of the human condition, it is a force of life, not of death. Its most profound logic is not the logic of destruction: it is the logic of creation."[27]

Several threads come together here that help orient our thinking. Three points merit consideration. First, there is no relation to the "just" world that can or even should be lived, thought, and shared other than rebellion. In other words, the rebellion against servitude, lies, and terror is foundational [*principielle*], if only because they jeopardize the possibility of such a relation. Second, what places that relation in jeopardy is, always, a lack of recognition—and what is not being recognized is the object of an imperative, the "unity of the human condition." But because parts of the world are exposed to servitude, lies, and terror, the human condition is divided (and for this reason we must demand that it be unified), and therefore, the world is not (or is no longer) a world (and so must be re-created). Finally, this failure of recognition is always murderous—and it is always in language, or in a certain relationship to language, that death looms.

Yet nothing is easy, because rebellion is aporetic. On the one hand, it should, in principle, imply the renunciation of violence. If rebellion makes concessions to murder, it contradicts its own finality, which is both to protest against death and to introduce unity into the world. Because rebellion is committed to both, it also engages our attitude toward death (especially the death of others) and our being-in-the-world. If rebellion renounces one of these engagements, it loses the other. In other words, it loses its meaning [*sens*] as soon as it chooses to sacrifice some part of humanity to perverted ends. Inversely, rebellion combats forces that resist it, in the face of which it must not surrender lest it become mired in the vanity of mere incantation. Renouncing these engagements exposes rebellion to erosion by nihilism, as conveyed by popular sayings like "What's the point!" and "There's nothing we can do"—expressions that are themselves, in their own ways, versions of murderous consent. I will question such resignation below. I will seek to know how much these exclamations owe to the media, especially the televisual, numerical, and related technologies that determine our relation to the world. By the same token, I am anxious to know if there is such a thing as *habituation* to violence, misery, injustice—and to the death of others.[28]

"Undeniably Human"

I began by asking: "Who among us can say that we have never *consented* to violence or desired someone's death or allowed it to happen? Who among us can claim that the desire for or indifference toward murder are, have been, and always will be foreign to us?" Camus has enabled us to grasp the terms of this inquiry more clearly. We find ourselves caught between two forms of murderous consent. On the one hand, we are exposed to the paradox of rebellion, according to which the introduction of unity in the world (for example, a dream of justice that aspires to become reality) consistently turns the protest against death (which should inspire our dream) into murderous consent. On the other hand, our denial of the necessity of such unity is itself influenced by our acceptance of the death of others. We must account for all forms of negation: from the most criminal politics (which never troubles itself with some or other notion of unity of the human condition), which deliberately organizes the world's partitioning through discrimination and extermination, to all those forms of compromise [*compromission*] (both active and passive) that, though various, nurture and endorse negation by all possible means.

This is why "the small part of existence that can be realized on this earth through the mutual complicity of men" (to repeat Camus's exemplary words—and each word is important), this "small part of existence," this "realized on this earth," and finally this "mutual complicity of men," articulated together, define the pole around which we can structure our thought regarding murderous consent. This is what binds being-in-the-world not to being-toward-death (Heidegger's *Sein-zum-Tode*) but (in an ethical and political sense) to the mortality and vulnerability of *all* people. At stake is a feeling of belonging to the world (a *cosmopolitanism*) that is grounded in our relation to the death of others, and whose distinctive and constitutive trait is to oppose all forms of murderous consent that eclipse care, assistance, medical relief, attention, and all the comforting words and gestures that ought to establish this relation *everywhere* and *for everyone*. What is ultimately at stake is the very possibility of rebellion that does not pledge allegiance to allegedly absolute laws of history or to some planned vision of the future. At stake is rebellion that will not divert us from what we should consider the only legitimate adversary of insurrection, that is, all the forms of murderous consent orchestrated through servitude, lying, and terror.

If the question of being-in-the-world is decisive, it is only because, by revealing its foundation in our relation to the mortality and vulnerability of *all others*, it opens a dimension of living-with that rejects the separation of people into communities of brothers, friends, fellow citizens, coreligionists, or other predetermined forms of community. This is not to say that life, understood as living-with, denies or refuses such attachments, but rather that it can accept them only to the extent that the sense of belonging is not founded, desired, or promoted in a way that implies the denigration, rejection, humiliation, or destruction of others. In other words, there will always be ways of defining belonging that legitimize, call for, or encourage murder, and ways of defining belonging that see in justifications of this sort a red line (another one) that belonging must not cross.[29] It is the line that separates those who tolerate the death of others because of their passion for their native land or because of aggressive, jealous, and vengeful notions of what is specific to their identity, on the one hand, and, on the other, a community that is complicit [*communauté complice*] in extending its horizon to include the totality of the world.

Camus reminds his imaginary correspondent of this in *Letters to a German Friend*, written and published between 1943 and 1945, which we should read with reference to their historical setting. The letters are articulated around four antithetical concepts.[30] The first letter opposes two logics behind the "license to kill," the second discusses two conceptions of the nation, the third identifies two ideas or visions of Europe, and the fourth isolates two conceptualizations of the world. Beginning with the problem of the legitimacy of murder and culminating with the unity of the world, the letters chart a path that helps us grapple with the problem of murderous consent. I will therefore follow Camus's analysis step-by-step. The question of death (whether it is consented to, given, or wanted, be it one's own death or someone else's) emerges in the first sentence of the first letter in the form of total sacrifice, an idea that follows all forms of murderous consent like a shadow: "You say to me: 'The greatness of my country is beyond price. Anything is good that contributes to its greatness. And in a world where everything has lost its meaning, those who, like us young Germans, are lucky enough to find a meaning in the destiny of our nation must sacrifice everything else.'"[31] There are two points that we must keep in mind from the outset. The first is the poverty of the meaning accorded to the world (its lack, its absence) and the exorbitance (literally: out of the world's orbit) of meaning bestowed on the nation. Because being-in-the-world is no longer supposed to mean anything, and because, apparently, it no longer enjoins any responsibility, the destiny of the nation is credited with the totality of meaning. But if our "responsibility" for the world is eclipsed by the "future" of the nation, it is also because the sense of belonging that might ground this responsibility is no longer recognized as *valuable*. The second point we must retain from this letter is that this missing value—which, if it exists, would diminish the importance we accord to the "greatness of the nation" and which is veiled if not hidden, abused by propaganda, neglected by politicians and members of the military—is that of life itself. The warmongering writers, eulogists of heroic death, and others who pine nostalgically for a more authentic existence must be reminded of this: the effacement of the "value" of life, no matter what they say, has an impact on the apology of sacrifice. Camus reproaches the Germans for not knowing how great is the cost of suppressing [*ôter*] life (or allowing it to be suppressed). Yet it is at this price (and only at this price) that they can profess their desire to give and do *everything* for the "destiny" of their nation. Such is the logic of their murderous consent, against which the "license to kill" of those fighting in the Resistance rises in opposition. Here, I must quote Camus at some length:

> We had to overcome our weakness for mankind, the image we had formed of a peaceful destiny, that deep-rooted conviction of ours that no victory ever pays, whereas any mutilation of mankind is irrevocable. . . .
>
> Now, we have done that. We had to make a long detour, and we are far behind. It is a detour that regard for truth imposes on intelligence, that regard for friendship imposes on the heart. It is a detour that safeguarded justice and put truth on the side of those who questioned themselves. And, without a doubt, we paid very dearly for it. We paid for it with humiliations and silences, with bitter experiences, with prison sentences, with executions at dawn, with desertions and separations, with daily pangs of hunger, with emaciated children, and, above all, with humiliation of our human dignity. But that was natural. It took us all that time to find out if we had the right to kill men, if we were allowed to add to the frightful misery of this world.[32]

The difference concerns time. The murder that is authorized by total sacrifice, and to which Camus's German friend consents, allows for no vacillation. Its justification cannot be hampered by scruples and reservations, since human life *no longer has value* and does not give meaning to the world. Sacrificing everything sacrifices nothing that Camus's friend values, neither the lives of *others* (which mean nothing to him) nor the unity of the world (in which he does not believe). No friendship, complicity, or solidarity between people is imperiled through or by his sacrifice, because he does not recognize such goods as a constitutive dimension of his existence. This is nothing like the "license to kill" that the Resistance grants itself, though reluctantly. This license, Camus explains, requires that the moral and political relations that preserve the world from violence have *already* been (unilaterally) suspended. It requires *ex ante* the conviction that "collaboration" is unacceptable, even in the form of mere silence, with those who themselves have *already* made the irrevocable choice for violence. As the litany of pains endured (the imprisonments, separations, executions, famine) makes clear, the human bonds that Camus calls the "mutual complicity among men" had to have been broken. Even the possibility of "friendship" has to have been irremediably compromised in order that those who choose to resist can *consent* to kill. We must recall this difference when terror represents itself as resistance (or claims the right to resist). The meaning of the "behind," the "detour," and the "all that time," which Camus underscores, is decisive: nothing less, but nothing more, than some unpardonable violation of moral and political relations can, as a matter of principle, precede consent.

Consent, nevertheless, is not a solution. This is the second lesson that we must retain from Camus's first letter. Contrary to what the executioners and those who applaud their crimes might imagine, the fact of killing [*la mort donnée*] "resolves" no problems and "settles" no questions. On the contrary, Camus writes, it "*add[s]* to the frightful misery of this world." We recall that Caligula thought he could transform the world by terror. Convinced, like all despots, that murder is the price to pay to rid the world of its misery and improve it (as he understood or reconstituted it in his fantasies), his deadly reasoning embroiled him in a spiral of violence that could only end in his demise. Ultimately, in the absence of any exchange, confrontation, or dialogue with those he neither could nor wanted to listen to, he is left with nothing more than a looking glass to restore his own sight and to see that his freedom, as the acolyte of destruction, did not resolve any of the world's problems. It is nevertheless uncertain whether this criminal emperor ever became aware of the "misery" he exacerbated.

Thus, the confession found in Camus's letter gives it an unexpected tonality. What prevails, in a foundational way [*de façon principielle*], is the awareness that acquiescing to violence always increases the world's misery. What prevails is therefore the will not to be easily taken in by the nature and necessity of murder. What prevails is the courage not to harbor illusions about the possibility of building or consolidating a world on such a lethal basis. The difference is in our awareness of loss. To argue, with Camus, that murder *adds* to misery, is to realize that, whatever the reasoning, as soon as the sword is drawn, as soon as we allow our weapons to do the talking, as soon as the recourse to force becomes necessary, *something is lost*. What is lost is our undeniable faith in the unity of the world, as promised by the dream of a "mutual complicity" between people. Inversely, when we make light of this loss, when we buy into the fables that rationalize it, when we find greatness in executions or subscribe to some or other mystique of violence, there are no longer any restrictions that we can impose on servitude or on lying, as we will see in my discussion of Karl Kraus and Judith Butler, or on terror, as we will learn from my reading of Vasily Grossman. Camus reminds us that it is the very possibility of preserving the meaning [*sens*] of the words "truth" and "justice" that is at stake. We can write all the pages and give all the impassioned speeches we like, but whenever we imagine that murder is the solution to the world's misery, we renounce both truth and justice: "I have never believed in the power of truth itself. But it is at least worth knowing that when expressed forcefully truth wins out over falsehood. This is the difficult equilibrium we have reached. This is the distinction that gives us strength as we fight today."[33]

As stated above, *Letters to a German Friend* is articulated around four oppositions. The first concerns the logic of the license to kill. The second discusses two conceptions of the nation [*la patrie*]. The premises around which the discussion is articulated, specifically, truth and lies, may be unexpected but are nevertheless of the highest importance. Anyone who tries to think or rethink the history of the twentieth century knows that the question of "murder" and the question of the "nation" [*patrie*] are indissociable. They are indissociable because it is in the name of the nation—its salvation, its integrity, or its defense—that murder becomes the object not only of consent but of all sorts of appeals, invocations, and encouragements: to kill for the nation, to die for the nation, or to leave others to die or be killed in its name. They are indissociable because, in the same vein, the murderers' first and last justification of their victims' execution is to call them "enemies of the nation." In the logic of murderous consent, the word "nation" (I will return to this with Karl Kraus) has functioned (and continues to function everywhere in the world)—whether in street demonstrations [*tribune*] or in courts [*tribunaux*], whether on the radio or in the newspapers (as propaganda)—like a "magic word." It was used everywhere and continues to be used to separate humanity into two groups: compatriots and the others.[34] Does this mean that we must take leave of the term "nation" and ban it from our vocabulary because of the suspicion it arouses? And if not (it could not be otherwise for Camus and so many others whose countries were occupied, over the course of the century, by foreign troops), how can we make distinctions between its multiple invocations? Where are its nuances?

Camus tries to answer these questions—and would be compelled to answer them again because of his position on the war in Algeria some fifteen years later. It is no coincidence that I just evoked propaganda, a fabrication of lies. To the "German friend" who claims to place Germany before truth, Camus responds: "But, as I have already told you, if at times we seemed to prefer justice to our country, this is because we simply wanted to love our country in justice, as we wanted to love her in truth and in hope. This is what separated us from you; we made demands. You were satisfied to serve the power of your nation and we dreamed of giving ours her truth." He later clarifies: "What is truth, you used to ask? To be sure, but at least we know what falsehood is; that is just what you have taught us. What is spirit? We know its contrary, which is murder. What is man? There I stop you, for we know. Man is that force which ultimately cancels all tyrants and gods."[35]

There are two ways of loving the nation. One depends on lies (for example, the fabrication of a threat or the designation of a scapegoat) and accommodates itself to the injustices that it sanctions, beginning with the persecution of the scapegoat that is its target. The other subjects our attachment to the nation to the demands of truth and justice. But how do we recognize the difference between truth and lies, justice and injustice? We recognize it through what Camus unflinchingly calls the "undeniably human."[36] What is "undeniably human"? At the risk of getting ahead of myself, I will advance the following response: the term refers to the relational character of existence; it is tied to that which grounds (or should ground) all moral and political relations. It is nothing other than the attention, care, and aid demanded, independently of all appearance, by the mortality and vulnerability, not only of our compatriots *in particular*, and of others *in general*, but of each and every other *singularly*. This is where we must seek truth and justice. Action, speech, and calculation that forfeit the undeniably human, in the name of the nation, its "security," "integrity," supposed rights, or some other reason, are never far from falsehood and injustice. If Camus had lived longer, he would no doubt have noted with consternation (and as justifying rebellion) that even the most secure democracies forget this: "Words always take on the color of the deeds or the sacrifices they evoke. And in your country the word 'fatherland' assumes blind and bloody overtones that make it forever alien to me, whereas we have put into the same word the flame of an intelligence that makes courage more difficult and gives man complete fulfillment."[37]

What Camus says of the nation in the second letter opposes two conceptions of Europe, as we find in the third letter. What I said above about the nation could be said about the entire continent, about speech that invokes and constructs a European identity, and about actions that claim to shape it. For many reasons, Europe's history (beginning with the history of its name, the signifier "Europe") cannot be separated from a range of "murderous consents." First, European nations have entered into conflict with one another in the name of opposing visions of Europe (which are, in reality, appropriations of the ideal that is Europe). Rarely do European nations hesitate to identify their own interests with those of the entire continent, making Europe (that is, the way that its capricious frontiers must be remapped to suit their interests) a pretext to take up arms. Moreover, nothing in the self-constructed idea of Europe has prevented it from killing people on every continent in the world in order to impose its domination.[38] It has never seemed illegitimate to European leaders to consent to massacring indigenous populations so as to allow Europe to wield influence and project glory across the oceans and seas.

The signifier "Europe" remains a difficult word for us today. It is subject to all sorts of appropriations, simplifications, and denials, such as those that deny the evidence of past murders and profess at best only moderately repressed consent. This was the case in 1944 when Germany seized Europe and made Europe speak on its own behalf. Two visions of Europe opposed one another, Camus reminds us. The first (which claims fidelity to a European "spirit" or "conscience") extends the sense of belonging from the nation to the whole of the continent, while the second (which dreams of expansion) imposes on Europe its own ambitions. One vision of Europe erases borders in order to assert "mutual complicity," the sharing of projects and the landscapes that Freud evokes with nostalgia in 1915, while the other breaches borders and erases them in order to expand an empire:[39]

> And there too we were not speaking the same language; our Europe is not yours. . . . when you let yourselves be carried away by your own lies, you cannot keep yourselves from thinking of a cohort of docile nations led by a lordly Germany towards a fabulous and bloody future. I should like you to be fully aware of this difference. For you Europe is an expanse encircled by seas and mountains, dotted with dams, gutted with mines, covered with harvests, where Germany is playing a game in which her own fate alone is at stake. But for us Europe is a home of the spirit where for the last twenty centuries the most amazing adventure of the human spirit has been going on.[40]

Within Europe—that is, within the relationship between the nations that constitute Europe—the question of ownership or, more explicitly, of appropriation is decisive. Of these two opposing visions, one embraces all forms of murderous consent while the other rejects them. The former has no objective other than the unilateral expansion of its domain, a strangle-hold on available resources, and territorial expansion, whereas the latter pursues a shared disappropriation, a placing in common, the transferal and exchange of intellectual work, and cherishes the free passage from one landscape or cityscape to another. In other words, we can think of Europe as the site of a competition or a race for power, or we can think of it in terms of circulation and translation. When Camus writes that he sometimes thinks of his country as speaking "in the name of Europe," this does not mean that he invests it with some sort of universal mission. Rather, he is affirming that what is said in one country, and in one language, far from belonging to a singular community or addressing itself to only one fragment of Europe's population, speaks to "the heart of all Europe's inhabitants."[41]

As suggested above, one of the most remarkable features of Camus's *Letters* is their progressive expansion from the nation to Europe and from Europe to the world. In the fourth and final letter, we are therefore left with the world, with what confers or does not confer meaning [*fait sens*, "confers meaning," "makes meaningful," "provides direction"] on the world.[42] Rather than two ideas or visions of the world, Camus opposes two ways of being-in-the-world. Between them a barrier emerges, grounded in the belief (or disbelief) or faith (or absence of faith) in the possibility of endowing the world with meaning. We must not allow ourselves to be misled as to the nature of this endowment. Finding meaning in being-in-the-world does not imply imposing it by force or making ourselves the masters of some totality in our effort to escape nihilism. It means finding a reason in one's belonging to the world to think that "not everything is allowed" or, better yet, to make this reason (which distinguishes and draws the boundary between "good" and "evil") the foundation of belonging itself. In the final analysis, beyond the idea of nation and our vision of Europe, it is the meaning of being-in-the-world that divides us—and it is our way of *responding to it* that determines our relationship with both the nation and Europe.

This meaning is not given; it has to be created. And it can be created only by inventing a relationship or a connection to others to which Camus gives several names: "solidarity," "mutual complicity," or, in *The Rebel*, "fidelity to the human condition."[43] These names take hold (we must constantly remind ourselves of this) only if they tolerate no exceptions or exclusions. The absence of meaning is "destiny" or "fatality" only for those who refuse to believe in the possibility of its invention (like that of the dialogue that Camus discusses in *The Rebel*). Murderous consents proliferate where the refusal to believe is orchestrated, where it is proclaimed and repeated over and over again that it is senseless to believe in this possibility. Violence always begins with this kind of denial. In other words, there is no exit from the vicious circle of murderous consent unless a contrary "conviction" confers meaning on belonging to the world. This is the "undeniably human." The ambition of Camus's writing is to turn this conviction into insurrection, to rise up against all the forces that are mobilized to prove the contrary and that fight to maintain or introduce divisions in the unity of the world:

> I continue to believe that this world has no ultimate meaning. But I know that something in it has a meaning and that is man, because he is the only creature to insist on having one. This world has at least the truth of man, and our task is to provide its justifications against fate itself. And it has no justification but man; hence he must be saved if we want to save the idea we have of life. With your scornful smile you will ask me: what do you mean by saving man? And with all my being I shout to you that I mean not mutilating him and yet giving a chance to the justice that man alone can conceive.[44]

The "Casuistry of Blood"

What we must find (or rediscover) is the path to an insurrection. Each of the authors I discuss in the following chapters embodies, on many fronts, ways to forge such a path. This applies to Levinas and Grossman,[45] Kraus and Butler,[46] even Anders,[47] and in a more oblique but equally decisive sense it is also true of Freud.[48] I return here to Camus's "Thought at the Meridian," in which he explains the philosophy that appeals to this meaning [*sens*] of rebellion, which is always, as we saw, the creation of a singularity: "If, on the other hand, rebellion could found a philosophy it would be a philosophy of limits, of calculated ignorance, and of risk. *He who does not know everything cannot kill everything.*"[49] A philosophy of *limits*, calculated *ignorance*, and *risk*: however we describe or define these three terms, they provide the necessary conditions for an insurrection against injustice and misery and prevent it from turning against itself in the form of "murderous consent." These conditions chart Camus's path of rebellion. Three things enable these conditions: the mutual limitation of justice and freedom; the examination of the reasons for violence; and the commitment to life, "beyond nihilism."[50]

By reading Camus's *Letters to a German Friend* we observe how the conception of the nation, Europe, and the world paves the way to murder, but we also discern ways to conceptualize (and desire) justice and ways to conceptualize (and desire) freedom that are distinguished by their condemnation of murder. We cannot count all the crimes that have been committed in the name of justice and freedom. Caligula dreamed of justice in order to free himself from the rule of law and treat freedom as absolute. Absolute freedom, we recall, only compounded injustice and misery in the world, leaving the emperor with the hopeless realization that his freedom was not the right freedom. Blinded by Caligula's dream of absolute—unconditional—justice, freedom suppressed law. Caligula's freedom could not tolerate the voice of law when it confronted and opposed his conception of what is "just." It became nothing more than an insane soliloquy that knew no outcome other than murder (first, that of citizens, then his own). For Camus the despots and dictators of the twentieth century follow Caligula's example. It always plays out the same way: whenever freedom (henceforth absolute freedom) suspends law in the name of justice, it leads to murder. Moreover, it is not only tyrants who consent but also all those who, in similar circumstances, subscribe to the suspension of law, directly or indirectly—even if far away and immune from danger themselves.

This does not mean that all law is legitimate, nor does it suggest that the law does not participate in the organization and justification of murder. Countless laws, both past and present and from around the world, remind us of the law's murderous potential. But it does mean that justice cannot do without law. Moreover, when we appeal to some principle of justice, the fulfillment of that principle requires some degree of *negotiation* with existing law. It is one thing to rebel against the law to transform it, but it is another to act as though the law does not exist and to *make do without it* for some unspecified period, always longer and more unspecified than we initially thought or hoped. Negotiation assumes that we recognize a bond or some collectivity that comes to terms or fails to come to terms or may no longer come to terms with the law but that nevertheless exists. Negotiation recognizes that there is *more than one voice* in this collectivity, which justice cannot ignore. Inversely, the suspension of negotiation implies the exercise of an absolute freedom, unconcerned by any of these voices, assuming it is not working to silence them—in which case, there is no longer any opposition to murder when it appears as a solution:

> In particular, it [a revolutionary action that wants to cohere with its origins] would preserve as an absolute law the permanent possibility of self-expression. This defines a particular line of conduct in regard to justice and freedom. There is no justice in society without natural or civil rights as its basis. There are no rights without expression of

those rights. If the rights are expressed without hesitation it is more than probable that, sooner or later, the justice they postulate will come to the world. To conquer existence, we must start from the small amount of existence we find in ourselves and not deny it from the very beginning. To silence the law until justice is established is to silence it forever since it will have no more occasion to speak if justice reigns forever. Once more, we thus confide justice into the keeping of those who alone have the ability to make themselves heard—those in power.[51]

The second condition to which Camus's subordinates rebellion (and which also supposes limits) concerns the reasons for violence. It takes us back to the path of paradox with which our discussion began. On the one hand, no insurrection against misery and injustice can decree in advance that it will renounce violence. On the other hand, any recourse to violence contradicts (and jeopardizes) the reasons for the insurrection. Here again, we can oppose two forms of violence. The first form alleges that historical necessity (concerning the nation, Europe, or the world) precludes the possibility of respecting limits. It grounds the necessary absence of limits in some or other knowledge claim (for example, the end of history). According to this form there is nothing to lose because there is no belief that there is something that can be broken or disrupted. The moral and political relationships that ground what Camus calls our *"fidelity*[52] to the human condition" are foreign to it. It is a violence that knows no doubt, no worry, no trembling. Consent to violence prevails as a matter of course—and, as Ionesco shows in *Rhinoceros*, it is all but impossible to oppose its propagation and extension. We know what the consequences are when it assumes extreme forms: the feeling of irresponsibility and impunity that is characteristic of the criminal, indifference with regard to victims, the "banality of evil"—these are not only the prerogatives of the past.

Opposed to this first form is a second kind of violence that knows—and this is the only thing it claims to know—what it is breaking. It does not seek legitimacy in the ends of history any more than it evokes a vision of the future. The person who becomes resigned to violence feels this second sort, always provisionally *and against his or her will* [*à son corps défendant*], as an "effraction." This term is essential, as is the appeal to the body (*à son corps défendant*) and thus to life. Unlike the violence that is justified by history, the "effraction" posits the foundational anteriority of nonviolence and the vital relationships that nonviolence grounds. Murder is not originary—and it is important that we not forget what murder destroys.[53] The difference is laden with consequences. First, if the possibility of "legitimate violence" is at issue here, it must not be systematic. There is not, nor can there ever be, any possible justification for mass murder. If anything characterizes mass murder, as Vasily Grossman reminds us in *Life and Fate*, it is the inverse of legitimate violence. It is the desired, calculated, and organized ignorance and denial of the *effraction* that is each and every act of violence and each and every murder, singularly. The second consequence is that responsibility is restored. If a person who kills is conscious of the effraction, if he knows what is fractured, he can no longer find a secure alibi, a doctrine, or some reason of state that allows him to evade his responsibility. Third, consenting to violence (assuming rebellion cannot avoid it) can only be temporary and occasional—short of definitively rejecting the reasons that justify it. On this point, Camus's warnings are forceful and in marked contrast to all the intellectual digressions and blunders of his century: "Authentic acts of rebellion will only consent to take up arms for institutions that limit violence, not for those which codify it. A revolution is not worth dying for unless it assures the immediate suppression of the death penalty; not worth going to prison for unless it refuses in advance to pass sentence without fixed terms. If rebel violence employs itself in the establishment of these institutions, announcing its aims as often as it can, it is the only way in which it can be really provisional."[54]

The last condition to which Camus subjects rebellion relates to this central theme of its limits. Rebellion must *serve life*. The decisive opposition here passes between moderation [*mesure*] and disproportion [*démesure*, "outrageousness"]. Where is the dividing line? What enjoins us to respect moderation? When, how, and why do we lose ourselves to disproportion? Here again, we can read the entire history of the twentieth century—beginning with the history of literature and its political engagements—in the light of such questions. Disproportion not only exceeds moderation but also forgets about it or even abandons it. Disproportion strays beyond the bounds within which moderation is still a possibility or is even borne in mind. What, then, is moderation in rebellion? It is found in words that are central to Camus's thought: "solidarity," "mutual complicity among men," "fidelity to the human condition." These words designate the reasons for insurrection. We rebel because some law, decree, evolution in the law, institution, organism, administration, or government is "disloyal" to the human condition. We judge it as such because it goes against what we believe are the requirements of solidarity and the requisite signs of complicity that bear witness to it—in other words, because we are convinced that it increases misery and injustice. Inversely, disproportion is the loss of our moorings. It taints all rebellions that lose their attachment to their initial purpose. Insurrection is out of joint when it forgets its need to increase solidarity in the world and "complicity" among people.

But what are *solidarity* and *complicity*? They are the modalities of living-with that define communal life.[55] They prescribe the nature of the moral and political relationships that should compose the fabric of our existence. At stake in solidarity and complicity is life itself. This is why Camus writes that rebellion "takes the part of true realism" and that "if it wants a revolution, it wants it on behalf of life, not in defiance of it."[56] When rebellion falls prey to disproportion, this relationship is inverted. It turns into murderous consent. It loses the generosity that it can retain only if it remains moderate and dedicated, not to a future or past life, but to the *present appeal of the living*, an appeal that can come from anywhere, at any moment. Just as every tomorrow is a new day, every day renews humanity's demand for solidarity and complicity. Rebellion comes to the rescue not of abstract life but, indeed, of what is most irreplaceable and most singular in the life of the living. It is the movement of life itself, allowing each individual life to invent its own singularity and share it with others. The example that Camus gives is eloquent and could evoke many others on many fronts. It is that of Catholic prisoners under the Franco regime who refused Communion because priests loyal to the regime had made it obligatory for all prisoners:

> This insane generosity is the generosity of rebellion, which unhesitatingly gives the strength of its love and without a moment's delay refuses injustice. Its merit lies in making no calculations, distributing everything it possesses to life and to living men. It is thus that it is prodigal in its gifts to men to come. Real generosity toward the future lies in giving all to the present.
>
> Rebellion proves in this way that it is the very movement of life and that it cannot be denied without renouncing life. Its purest outburst, on each occasion, gives birth to existence. Thus it is love and fecundity or it is nothing at all.[57]

This is not an easy undertaking. It sometimes imposes choices, decisions, and interventions that run contrary to the charted course of history. The war in Algeria would foist such an ordeal on Camus himself. His positions widened the gap created by the publication of *The Rebel* and the polemic that ensued with Breton, Jeanson, and Sartre. He became estranged from his contemporaries, deeply engaged in the ideological struggles of the postwar era. In April 1958 Camus published his writings on Algeria in a volume entitled *Actuelles III: Algerian Chronicles*. The first of these essays was written on the eve of the Second World War. Already they stand out because of their uncompromising denunciation of France's colonial policies, which perpetuated oppression and misery in Algeria.[58] The book's preface contains most of the questions that have set out my central theme up to this point. The two forms of violence and their symmetrical effect form the backdrop. Not only do they systematically and deliberately shatter any possibility of "dialogue" and understanding, making peace impossible, but they appeal to theoretical justifications, intellectual authority, and radical positions that induce many forms of murderous consent. The two forms (relevant today, especially since 9/11, the "war against terrorism," the war in Iraq, and Abu Ghraib) are terror, on the one hand—the terror of bombs blindly striking innocent victims—and torture, on the other hand. Camus reminds us that these two forms of murderous consent engender each other mutually in the illusion that they justify one another. One might say that the objective of torture is to prevent future attacks, and the objective of bombs is to combat oppression (which torture prolongs and aggravates), and that bombs are indeed the only possible response to repression and the disregard of popular demands. Camus, in terms that resonate with his analysis in *The Rebel*, refuses to be trapped by this doubly aporetic alternative. Once again it is a matter of drawing a "red line." As soon as we justify terror or torture, we accept *in principle* that lives may be mutilated and sacrificed. We must not lie to ourselves: this is the "triumph of nihilism,"[59] to which we are contributing as well as applauding.

> I have said repeatedly that, if criticism is to be effective, both camps must be condemned. I therefore concluded that it was both indecent and harmful to denounce French torture in the company of critics who had nothing to say about Melouza or the mutilation of European children. By the same token, I thought it harmful and indecent to condemn terrorism in the company of people whose consciences found torture easy to bear. . . . Each side thus justifies its own actions by pointing to the crimes of its adversaries. This is a casuistry of blood with which intellectuals should, I think, have nothing to do, unless they are prepared to take up arms themselves.[60]

The "casuistry of blood"—we are at the heart of the matter. It is (or could be), in the final analysis, another way of designating what I have been analyzing, with Camus, as murderous consent. Not only does such casuistry hearken back to the darkest pages of our history, but it continues in our time. It continues to rip apart "communities," to contort our sense of "belonging," and, in some given space (a neighborhood, a street, a courtyard, an apartment building, or a school), to engender violence and provoke words and gestures that inflict irreparable harm. But more than that, this casuistry (this distinction, this *discrimination* between cases) also divides the world by "criminalizing" some and "decriminalizing" others. It establishes an inconstant and biased relationship toward injuries, suffering, injustice, and death. If the misfortune of some, by leaving us outraged and revolted, bolsters our solidarity in Camus's sense of the term, its impact on others can leave us indifferent, at best, and even delighted, at worst. On either side of the line of separation that it inscribes—real, imaginary, or symbolic—it *counts* differently the dead and the wounded.[61] Dreams of unity and complicity among the living are thus cast aside by history. Without a doubt this is what I ultimately mean by "murderous consent." We see both how life is implicated with it and how it contributes to breaking the world apart.

In his acceptance speech for the Nobel Prize, which he received on December 10, 1957, Camus endeavored to describe the challenge confronted by his generation, by those born on the eve of the First World War, battered by the Second World War, and trapped in the Cold War. Camus and his contemporaries were exposed to the temptation of nihilism. The challenge was to invent "an art of living in times of catastrophe." At no time could they be content to enjoy peace. More than that, they had to prevent (or try to prevent) "the world from destroying itself." The challenge gave meaning to their rebellion: "to re-establish . . . a little of that which constitutes the dignity of life and death."[62] It was everyone's responsibility to comprehend that this dignity was at once singular and collective, that it was invested in one's own life as much as in the lives of others (all others)—and that there exists no greater *responsibility*. Addressing this challenge is not only the task of writers, even though literature can make a contribution. As the French Resistance showed, at issue was a collective mastery of these moments of fragile and fugitive truth that enable rebellion to render some meaning to being-in-the-world:

> Each generation doubtless feels called upon to reform the world. Mine knows that it will not reform it, but its task is perhaps even greater. It consists in preventing the world from destroying itself. . . . In a world threatened by disintegration, in which our grand inquisitors run the risk of establishing forever the kingdom of death, it knows that it should, in an insane race against the clock, restore among the nations a peace that is not servitude, reconcile anew labor and culture, and remake with all men the Ark of the Covenant.[63]

2

Life

He had found the only right path for a writer to take in such times: not to participate in destruction and murder, but—following the great example of Walt Whitman, who served as a hospital orderly in the Civil War—to be active in works of assistance and humanity.

—**Zweig,** *The World of Yesterday*

What happens when the *bonds* of solidarity and the fabric of complicity, in which Camus placed hope, are torn? What does this rupture weaken and damage? To answer these questions we must first interrogate in greater depth the *vital* nature of these bonds. In other words, we must first try to understand not only how the fabric of relations binds us to *all others* but also how its fissures (the interruptions or eclipse of the responsibility that binds us to the vulnerability and the mortality of the other) are a part of the "nature" or the "essence of life," at least "human life." If it is true that all life, however it defines its belonging, is protected by the ideals and the institutions that constitute a common good for humanity, and if it is true, more importantly, that no one can elude murderous consent, then the paradox of murderous consent is that our common good turns against life itself. Rather than merely accept, encourage, and promote the destruction of life, the fabric of relations that should prevent such annihilation assists it. All wars, all acts of violence, whether civil or between states, trample on the ideals of humanity, even as those who are responsible for the abuse proclaim these same ideals as their own. Nothing (no civilizational ideal) that safeguards life is immune from being invoked and exploited so as to effect this kind of reversal.

This was the bitter conclusion, as expressed in his *Reflections on War and Death*, that Freud reached in 1915 after the first of four long years of mutual devastation by Europe's nations. The first thing that caught Freud's attention, and caused him alarm as a "European scholar," was scholarship's own participation in this reversal, that is, the partisan subordination of knowledge and the authority of knowledge (as human ideals) to the specific aims of war making: "The anthropologist [had] to declare his opponent inferior and degenerate, the psychiatrist [had to] diagnose him as mentally deranged."[1]

Stefan Zweig, in *The World of Yesterday: Memories of a European*, a retrospective on the war, came to this same conclusion regarding literature, though twenty-five years later. Zweig recalls how, from one day to the next, his contemporaries were setting fire to what they had previously cherished. They were rejecting, on both sides of the frontier, what they had previously shared with their neighbors, eradicating with a single, belligerent stroke of the pen all that united them in times past: the exchanges, the mutual influences, reciprocal translations. Once war broke out, they could not find words harsh enough, or declarations grating enough, to deny any distinction to the culture of their new "enemies." Their own cultures, meanwhile, were exalted as the apogee of civilization. They exploited the *creative* force of language, time and time again, to further a work of destruction. Abandoning all critical distance, all recourse to reason, all appeal to "dignity," they rushed to put their intellectual stamp on the flimsiest rumor that would spur hatred of the enemy. To support their political and military authorities, they wove their talents into a whip that these same authorities would use again and again, after the initial enthusiasm for conflict had begun to fade, to preserve death's "heroic" character and keep alive the flame of murderous consent:

> Solemnly the poets swore never again to have any cultural association with a Frenchman or an Englishman; they went even further, they denied overnight that there had ever been any French or English culture. All that was insignificant and valueless in comparison with German character, German art, and German thought. But the savants were even worse. The sole wisdom of the philosophers was to declare the war a "bath of steel" which would beneficially preserve the strength of the people from enervation. The physicians fell into line and praised their prostheses so extravagantly that one was almost tempted to have a leg amputated so that the healthy member might be replaced by an artificial one. The ministers of all creeds had no desire to be outdone and joined in the chorus, at times as if a horde of possessed were raving, and yet all of these men were the very same whose reason, creative power, and humane conduct one had admired only a week, a month, before.[2]

Literature and scholarship, however, were merely exemplifying what was manifestly (still today) a more general disorientation.[3] Literature and scholarship were merely marching in lock step with what characterizes beings when implicated in and embarked on *any* war (there are no exceptions) and the violence of murderous consent that war implies. "Implicated," "embarked"—these words do not overstate the dereliction of responsibility. They tell us, in each and every case, that we had (we always have) to compromise, to make an impossible deal regarding principles or rules that we thought were settled, and to choose among conflicting "values." But what does it mean to be "disoriented" in the face of violence? What signposts did we miss, what directions were we searching for— assuming that we are not forced to accept violence or justify or, perhaps, in the end, even support it, even before it breaks out? My reading of Camus tells us that this kind of disorientation is hardly exceptional. It applies to anyone who is no longer sure where he is or how things are or where he is going because he has been led to suspend, in specific circumstances, all concern for the care, the aid, and the attention that the vulnerability and the mortality of the other still, everywhere, demand of him. Disorientation consists in entering into a contradiction with *oneself*, in finding oneself lacking coherence with the *self* in which one could once securely recognize oneself, that is, the self formed of shared ideals, of a shared education, and, in a word, of everything that we ordinarily consider to be the "legacy" of civilization, and of everything that would seem to *found* and guarantee life with others (broadly defined) as *living-with*.

Does this mean that the foundation and the guarantee provided by this legacy are an illusion? Are the various forms of murderous consent, in which our lives are caught up or carried away, telling us that this guarantee and this foundation are fundamentally tenuous? And what do we mean by this word "illusion"? What does it mean that *we* have illusions? *Who* is the subject and what is the object? Life itself? If this is so, we are investing murderous consent with even greater heuristic significance: murderous consent is the reminder that the very guideposts on which life relies for orientation can convey (and perpetuate) an illusion. Thus, we find ourselves without orientation from the very moment that war dispels—and *because* war dispels—our illusions regarding these guideposts. To see more clearly the place that murderous consent occupies in life—its "vital foundation"—I turn to Freud to learn more about this "loss of illusions."

"The Whole World Stood Open to Us"

Freud devotes the first half of his essay *Reflections on War and Death* precisely to this loss of illusions. The first illusion to which he assigns importance concerns an experience that every war rekindles: cruelty. What is the question? It is, first and foremost, that of an untenable demarcation or frontier. As war rages, it quickly becomes impossible to believe that Europe (hastily identified with the "highest degree of civilization") will be *exempt from cruelty*. It becomes impossible to believe that Europe will be protected by the wealth of knowledge and wisdom that it had accumulated over the centuries against practices and acts that *everything* about the idea that we entertain of civilization compels us to consider "cruel." By this I mean practices and acts that seem to proceed from the simple desire to do evil for evil's sake and that seem, despite all possible justifications, to spring from some pleasure that we derive from causing pain. It is an illusion to imagine that, between peoples who share similar ideals (the same ideals that Europe, the embodiment of *Civilization*, tried to impose on others), extreme forms of violence (those that respect nothing about life and for which the lives of others count for nothing, lives whose destruction the perpetrators of violence enjoy imagining and watching) might be unthinkable. Freud summarizes the disillusionment with "European civilization," that is, with Europe's constructed image of itself, and with the responsibilities that it had once acknowledged as its own, in a single, decisive sentence: "We expected that the great ruling nations of the white race, the leaders of mankind, who had cultivated world-wide interests, and to whom we owe the technical progress in the control of nature as well as the creation of artistic and scientific cultural standards—we expected that these nations would find some other way of settling their differences and conflicting interests."[4]

The disillusionment, in other words, is that of civilization's inability to institute stable norms of conduct that would protect it from the recurrence of the kind of cruelty, whether individual or collective, that war always produces. The question bears not only on the protection that civilization should provide but on its orientation and the understanding that we have of both the one and the other. The question bears on the way life matters to the self. But what, then, is this illusion? It is simply the fact of believing, in spite of all the violence in the world, that what life protects itself against is extraneous to life. It is something incidental, random, or accidental. It is the belief that the desire to murder or the acquiescence in murder, which we observe in all murderous consent, does not belong to the essence of life. The illusion is our failure to see that life defends itself against itself. It is our failure, for this very reason, to see that the protection of life against cruelty and against all those forms of extreme violence to which life could never conceivably consent remains, however necessary, fragile and retractable.

This is the lesson we must retain: the work of civilization consists in protecting life by rising up against it. Civilization is simultaneously *for* and *against* life. But what does it mean that civilization is opposed to life, and what does its protection consist of, and how are the two indissociable from one another? It means that protection and opposition are not limited simply to resisting the three primordial drives—incest, cannibalism, and the pleasure-desire to murder—that Freud had described, several years earlier, in *Totem and Taboo*. Civilization does not come to the aid of life simply in this negative, restrictive, or repressive way. If civilization must assign restrictions (so as to prevent humans from destroying each other by giving free rein to their drives), it must also support life by expanding it. It is up to civilization to make of life an extensive living-with, to which, in principle, no limit can be assigned in advance. Civilization orients life by favoring, organizing, and instituting that which ties life to other lives. It recognizes, in and through its works, that the impetus to live (what Freud would later call the "life drive") is borne by the "with." This is why we cannot think of life as ordered by civilizational gains without bringing this drive to light, without discerning its symptoms, and without specifying its criteria. In so doing we provide ourselves with a yardstick with which to measure the disillusionment of war and all forms of murderous consent that accompany it.

Freud, not without a certain nostalgia, evokes several aspects of disillusionment in the first pages of his essay. The terms he uses to convey *what had been lost* in war resonate with those that Stefan Zweig, shortly before taking his own life, employed in *The World of Yesterday* to express his alarm at a similar loss—that of belonging to a world that is confined, solidified, hardened, and finally stifled by the criminal weight of stigmas and murderous identifications. The *with* should suggest or connote, on the contrary, something different. The *with* evokes a dream or causes us to mourn by reminding us that the verb *live*, which *with* complements in its essence, should not be confined within the bounds of determinate communities. It evokes the living dynamic (admittedly relative) of being-in-the-world. What does it consist of? It consists of the possibility, forever present, of maintaining or breaking the ties that attach each of us (or not) to a country (or countries), to one or several peoples, to a space or to a plurality of spaces—a possibility therefore based on the freedom to feel oneself bound or free to enter, to exit, or to return. Two phenomena describe this possibility, as Freud and Zweig observe when, within a twenty-five-year interval, the frontiers of Europe are brutally closed not once but twice. The first is the freedom to circulate and establish one's residence. This freedom signifies—*as much today as in the past* (we must continually remind ourselves of this)—the legitimate extension (legitimate because in conformity with life in its essence) of that set of relations (with beings, places, creations) whose variability constitutes the moving and therefore dynamic fabric of existence. It is appropriate, in today's context, to read their respective testimonies side by side:

> Trusting to this unity of civilized races countless people left hearth and home to live in strange lands and trusted their fortunes to the friendly relations existing between the various countries. And even he who was not tied down to the same spot by the exigencies of life could combine all the advantages and charms of civilized countries into a newer and greater fatherland which he could enjoy without hindrance or suspicion. He thus took delight in the blue and the grey ocean, the beauty of snow clad mountains and of the green lowlands, the magic of the north woods and the grandeur of southern vegetation, the atmosphere of landscapes upon which great historical memories rest, and the peace of untouched nature. The new fatherland was to him also a museum, filled with the treasure that all the artists of the world for many centuries had created and left behind. While he wandered from one hall to another in this museum he could give his impartial appreciation to the varied types of perfection that had been developed among his distant compatriots by the mixture of blood, by history, and by the peculiarities of physical environment. Here cool, inflexible energy was developed to the highest degree, there the graceful art of beautifying life, elsewhere the sense of law and order, or other qualities that have made man master of the earth.[5]

> We were able to devote ourselves to our art and to our intellectual inclinations, and we were able to mold our private existence with more individual personality. We could live a more cosmopolitan life and the whole world stood open to us. We could travel without a passport and without a permit wherever we pleased. No one questioned us as to our beliefs, as to our origin, race, or religion. I do not deny that we had immeasurably more individual freedom and we not only cherished it but made use of it as well.[6]

We see that the expansion of life, in conformity with the drive that presses humanity to unite and gather together, is exemplified by the lands of exile, the countries of immigration, and the cosmopolitan cities. There are assuredly historical reasons behind the existence of such places. But they also teach us that it is not in the nature of life to remain compartmentalized, as war demands, behind protective walls, barbed-wire barriers, or other ramparts, whether real, symbolic, or fantastical. If the notion of civilization has a meaning that exceeds the simple repression of drives, it is in the breaching of such barriers (cultural, linguistic, political, and religious) and in the displacements that such breaching implies. The world prior to the war, evoked by Freud, and the "world of yesterday" recalled by Zweig, designate in the end a crucible of plural affiliations. Those affiliations should have provided people with the opportunity or good fortune to stem the spread of murderous consent (but this was often far from the case). At a minimum, geographical space was still largely unbounded, and there were places that kept hope alive that the opportunity would endure. We recall especially, among all the lands of exile, Ellis Island, the gateway to America, and what it must have represented for millions of men and women of all origins and religions from around the world—Irish peasants, Polish nationalists, German liberals, Armenians, Greeks, Turks, Jews from Russia and the Austro-Hungarian Empire, and Italians from the Mezzogiorno. Georges Perec, in his collection of immigrant testimonies, recalls this opportunity: "During the first half of the nineteenth century, a tremendous hope galvanized Europe. For peoples that were crushed, oppressed, downtrodden, enslaved, or butchered, for classes that were exploited, starved, afflicted by epidemics, or decimated by years of scarcity and famine, a promised land came into existence: America, a virgin land open to all, a land of freedom and generosity where the castoffs of the Old World could become the pioneers of the New and build a society free of injustice and prejudice."[7]

Of the two phenomena that illustrate the expansion (or decompartmentalization) of the living-with, understood as the movement of life, the second is the "disappropriation" of culture, or to put it another way, the availability to be shared of the "works," "ideals," "realizations," and "conquests" of "Civilization," however relative these might be. To argue that it is in the nature of life to expand, to extend the network of relations that attach life to the world, is to argue simultaneously that the "life drive"—at least as Freud understands this term—is committed to placing "civilization's works" in common, that is (and here we should understand this expression in its strongest sense), to constituting a *common heritage* for humanity. No community, however defined, should be able to lay claim, exclusively or jealously, to some or other work of human creativity. The expansion of the living-with is *mediated* by the cultural realizations that we make available for sharing (works of art, technologies, clothing and cooking styles, calendar dates such as feast days, rituals, celebrations, and commemorations that we are *invited* to attend). This mediation should not be conditional. No authority (whether religious or political) should be able to jeopardize or prohibit it. It is no accident that the powers that restrict their nationals' freedom to circulate, close frontiers, and erect walls to prevent them from traveling are generally those that intervene with equal brutality to control the circulation of ideas, to censor the books and films imported from outside, to close the libraries and the bookstores, and to purge, confiscate, or burn all that is foreign.

> The new fatherland was to him also a museum, filled with the treasure that all the artists of the world for many centuries had created and left behind. . . . We must not forget that every civilized citizen of the world had created his own special "Parnassus" and his own "School of Athens." Among the great philosophers, poets, and artists of all nations he had selected those to whom he considered himself indebted for the best enjoyment and understanding of life, and he associated them in his homage both with the immortal ancients and with the familiar masters of his own tongue. . . . and yet he never reproached himself with having become an apostate to his own nation and his beloved mother tongue.[8]

Such is the common sense of expansion. Expansion makes of the variety and the diversity of the relations implicated in the living-with the principal reason or motive to invent a singularity that resists assimilation by, or the promotion of, the culture of some "national identity," just as it resists being enclosed in some or other allegiance to an authority that claims the right to monitor it or circumscribe it because it is seen (in a way that is always fictitious and fantastical) to embody that identity.

And yet expansion remains, even for Freud, partial and conditional. I examine below the illusion, which Freud seeks to decrypt, that accompanies expansion. Its illusory character—that is, the fragility of the gathering whose loss we mourn in times of war—is tangible, in a way that Freud, even at the core of his analysis, was perhaps unaware of. Freud can conceptualize this gathering, this living-with, only among so-called "civilized" peoples." The "humanity" that he has in mind is that which, in 1915, was still claiming to embody *Civilization* alone. Cruelty, in other words, is a surprise and a disillusion only to the extent that it concerns the violence that these so-called "civilized" peoples inflict on one another. Surprise and disillusionment do not extend to the violence that these same peoples might inflict on the rest of the world or to the violence that such "alterities" might inflict on themselves. The world before the war, the world of exchange and transformation (but also the world of conquest and colonial domination)— the world that Freud, like Zweig, idealizes—repressed violence and cruelty in a way that was only partial, in both senses of the term, with the result that this world accommodated itself with ease to the violence and cruelty that occurred across the seas and oceans, far from Europe's frontiers.

If it is true that the freedom of circulation, the freedom of residence, the exchange, the borrowings, and the translations are the fabric of this world, it is also true that these same goods were, at that time (and today are still), very unequally distributed. We need only read the memories that André Gide retained of his travels to Chad and the Congo, and the polemics that they incited a mere ten years following the publication of Freud's essay, to realize the limits of this expansion and the level of cruelty to which it consented in its relations with the rest of the world. In one digression of *Travels in the Congo*, which would hardly qualify as an inflammatory anticolonial tract, Gide feels compelled to share reports of the cruel treatment inflicted on the region's inhabitants according to the wishes or orders of the colonial administration, as reported to him by its perpetrators:

> On October 21 last (six days ago that is) Sergeant Yemba was sent by the administrator of Boda to Bodembéré in order to execute reprisals on the inhabitants of this village (between Boda and N'Goto). . . . When they arrived at Bodembéré, the reprisals began; twelve men were seized and tied up to trees, while the chief of the village, a man called Cobelé, took flight. Sergeant Yemba and the guard Bonjo then shot and killed the twelve men who had been tied up. Then followed a great massacre of women, whom Yemba struck down with a matchet [machete]; after which he seized five young children, shut them up in a hut, and set fire to it.[9]

The relative, selective, and partial [*partial*] repression of cruelty was no less apparent in the United States. While the hospitality, however conditional, that the American government was prepared to grant to the persecuted peoples of Europe and elsewhere was a sign of hope, the United States nevertheless was conspicuous for its enduring policy of segregation, notably in the southern states, which denied rights to people who had been freed from slavery with much difficulty mere decades previously. Although abolition was supposed to put an end to cruel and unusual treatment, the white population of the South was prepared to encourage and promote nearly any effort to find a substitute, including, within the realm of legality, the discriminatory recourse to the death penalty, which remains in force in our day. Cruelty thus continued to manifest itself in the form of mutilations, lynchings, and summary executions, always in the name of a certain conceptualization of justice or the "superiority of a given civilization." Ernst Bloch, in the beginning of his book *Natural Law and Human Dignity*, reminds us: "When the white power holders and Babbitts of the Southern states in America began to feel the urge toward justice, blacks began to shudder, and with good reason."[10]

In other words, the notion that European or Western civilization could claim to have domesticated violence or to have banished cruelty from its history in some hypothetical golden age was and remains an illusion. It emerged, like so many similar idealizations of culture (and so many idealizations of a similar order), from that same form of blindness and deafness—the will not to see or hear—that has forever made the bed of murderous consent.

There Is No Such Thing as "Eradicating" Evil

It was of course an illusion to imagine that the gathering and the expansion of the living-with were limitless, as if they had not constantly been interrupted by exclusions and suspended by exceptions that were seen as self-evident. The possibility of cruelty was never completely absent. That is why the disillusion produced by war merely recalled in a new light this capacity to cause suffering, which subsists at the heart of all life as one of its irreducible dimensions. The war might have been more ferocious and deadly (given perfections in weaponry), and it might well have ignored "the prerogatives of the wounded and of physicians," that is, the care and aid that the wounded could rightly expect from physicians.[11] But the war's cruelty should not be considered exceptional and, even less, accidental. The subsistence and irreducibility of cruelty define the enigma that Freud explores in his essay, in view of the multiple violations that war seemed to justify. From one day to the next, as Zweig and so many others attest, not only did cruelty "return," but it was applauded, encouraged, desired. Acts and practices that expressed repulsion and even hatred of others were again commonplace. Mass populations endorsed such acts and grew accustomed to them. The possibility that this would occur must therefore have already existed.

But what is it exactly that we become accustomed to in war? What does cruelty consist of? The answer applies to all conflicts and to all of human history: we become accustomed to seeing people die. Even the term "sacrifice" is infused with this habituation, supposing as it does that there are reasons of a higher order against which all objections and protests against death are vain. Because we are compelled by necessity, it is in fact not merely the death of the enemy that we should desire but the death of those close to us, family and friends, that we should accept. We are supposed to consent to both the one and the other.[12] Such is the inextricable nature of *cruelty*. Cruelty inflicts on us a twofold relation to death that thwarts and even contradicts that of everyday life. In war it is not only cruel to consent to the suffering of others (in all the forms that such consent assumes, from the most active to the most passive) but equally cruel to deprive oneself of the right to cry out in revolt, openly and publicly in any case, against death. War places all expressions of opinion and emotion under surveillance. It compels us to mourn in silence.[13] If the cry of revolt dares contest the apologia of sacrifice, then the affects, as manifested by "troop morale" or morale on the home front, are liable to disparagement as cowardice, defeatism, or demoralization, if not outright collusion with the "enemy." The military, political, and ideological forces that are implicated in the pursuit of war, as we have seen again and again, will not fail to deploy all means necessary to control or influence our affective reactions to war's disastrous results.

How are we to understand that great masses of men and women could accept the sacrifice of lives close to them, family, children, friends—not to mention the lives of the enemy? There is no narrative, no testimony, that eludes this question. What is the source of this *force* that enables life to turn against life, this force that leads to the abdication of *everything* that made the expansion of life as living-with possible? How are we to understand that, given only the support or authorization of military, political, and/or religious leaders, nothing restrains the great masses of these same men and these same women from committing, despite themselves (but what does this word "despite" mean?), "acts of cruelty, treachery, deception, and brutality, the very possibility of which would have been considered incompatible with their level of culture?"[14]

It is only because we have not found the answer to this question, Freud tells us, that we are disillusioned by the atrocities of war, whether endured or inflicted. Our confusion is a function of our ignorance, or denigration, of the *forces* that compose life. Freud reminds us, moreover, that our distress bears on two points. It bears, first, on the fact that our institutions, beginning with the state itself, prove powerless to prohibit such an abdication—assuming that they are not working actively to enable or provoke it. However solid the foundations of these institutions, they never provide a strong guarantee against the return of the acts we enumerated above. No political regime escapes this observation, including the most "exemplary" democracies that so readily invoke the respect of human dignity. No one is safe. No one is assured of living in a state that will not lose itself in calculations about its survival and what it calls *its* security and, when pressed by "threats" that offer an alibi, will not provide such cruel practices with new legitimacy. This is the first of our disillusions: as long as the state is sovereign, as long as it considers its sovereignty the foundation of all the commitments and sacrifices that it imposes on us, it is always able, as war proves over and over again, to organize and accommodate such practices, even in the name of peace and justice. Hence, we are dealing not only with the disillusionment of war but also, indissociably, with the disillusionment of peace as armed peace.[15] There have been so many witnesses to this double disillusionment. The witnesses are often veterans, whose heroic actions the community seeks to commemorate, but who are forever unable to find satisfaction in what society offers as compensation for the sacrifice it has exacted from them. Returning from Vietnam, Iraq, Afghanistan, or Chechnya, they have often borne, and still do today, a burden of doubt regarding the reasons for the horrors and deaths to which their society consented. Zweig, in a grim assessment of the consequences of the first global war, cannot find words strong enough to express such doubts:

> But it was only outwardly and in a political sense that radical change was averted; a tremendous inner revolution occurred during those first post-war years. Something besides the army had been crushed: faith in the infallibility of the authority to which we had been trained to over-submissiveness in our own youth. . . . it was only after the smoke of war had lifted that the terrible destruction that resulted became visible. How could an ethical commandment still count as holy which sanctioned murder and robbery under the cloak of heroism and requisition for four long years? How could a people rely on the promises of a state which had annulled all those obligations to its citizens which it could not conveniently fulfill? . . . To the extent that it was wide-awake the world knew that it had been cheated. Cheated the mothers who had sacrificed their children, cheated the soldiers who came home as beggars, cheated those who had subscribed patriotically to war loans, cheated all who had placed faith in any promise of the state, cheated those of us who had dreamed of a new and better ordered world and who perceived that the same old gamblers were turning the same old trick in which our existence, our happiness, our time, our fortunes were at stake.[16]

It is true that cruelty is indissociable from the thirst for power of those who authorize or legitimate it.[17] But an equal sense of bewilderment takes hold of *us*—for what Freud and Zweig say of the First World War could be said of all wars (despite the fact that there will always be some degree of deceit and mystification regarding some or other exceptional conflict). It is the same sense of bewilderment and even terror before the spectacle of the *limitless* violence of which individuals are capable, once they are *freed* by our institutions from the prohibition of murder. It is an undeniable fact that nothing is more disorienting than the effects produced by this release.

Indeed, if evil and cruelty recur so often and so repeatedly, and seem so reproducible, if they appear to be characterized primarily by a terrible "banality," it must be because the object of this release—the pleasure/desire to destroy—never left life. This is what we are forced to admit. It is our conviction that we have a relation toward evil and cruelty that evolves progressively, that evil and cruelty can recede or be eradicated through education, culture, civilization, religion, art, literature, that is shaken: "there is no eradicating evil."

Among the Great War's many testimonies and narratives there is one that is particularly apposite because it evokes this release that turns life against itself in terms that seem to reprise, almost word for word, Freud's analyses. It is the long letter that a certain Jerphanion writes to his friend Jallez, which appears in *Prélude à Verdun*, the fifteenth volume of Jules Romains's saga *Men of Good Will*. The letter occupies an entire chapter, the title of which, "How We Manage to Get through It" (Comment on s'arrange pour vivre ça), could be read as the tragic summation of the problematic that I seek to elucidate here:

> Generally speaking, our attitude to death and its trappings is symptomatic of a really remarkable change in outlook. It makes one realize, looking back, how much quiet efficiency went, in the old pre-war days, to keep the living from being obsessed by the idea of mortality, from finding themselves suddenly face to face with its material evidence. Sanitary precautions were admirably organized, so admirably that we never really gave the question a moment's thought. In the world of our present existence they are badly handicapped by circumstances—have, in fact, been literally overthrown. . . . I've noticed that the men are not content with having gained a familiarity with death which hardens them and renders them less susceptible to being shocked, if, indeed, shocked at all, at the idea of doing things that in the old days would have sickened them. Such an attitude is an inevitable result of the deadening effects of war on human sensibilities. But their moral deterioration goes much further than that. In many cases they seem actually relieved at being freed from the particular attitude of respect of human life in which most of them have been brought up. That is something quite different from a mere deadening of sensibility. It is an active satisfaction in loosening the bonds of sentiment, and it worries me very considerably.[18]

We must still try to understand the reasons behind this "release." These reasons are "vital" in the sense that they cannot be conceptualized as extraneous to life, that is, as accidental or circumstantial. The works of Freud, particularly *Totem and Taboo*, *The Future of an Illusion*, and *Civilization and Its Discontents* (the last two written after the war), cast a distinctive light on the question of murderous consent. Freud's thought compels us to confront once again the question of the forces, which we must recognize as forces, that lurk at the heart of life. Only by acquiring an awareness or knowledge of such forces, a knowledge toward which we have been inching in these pages, can we put *our* disillusion in proper perspective. For Freud these forces are "the most profound essence of man." They are the drives that impel life: "Psychological, or strictly speaking, psychoanalytic investigation proves, on the contrary, that the deepest character of man consists of impulses of an elemental kind which are similar in all human beings, the aim of which is the gratification of certain primitive needs. These impulses are in themselves neither good or evil. We classify them and their manifestations according to their relation to the needs and demands of the human community. It is conceded that all the impulses which society rejects as evil, such as selfishness and cruelty, are of this primitive nature."[19]

If we follow Freud, we must acknowledge that cruelty, the pleasure-desire to murder, and the delight in doing evil for evil's sake and in destroying the relations that make up existence belong to these primal drives. We either have forgotten or no longer want to concede this fact. The illusions of education, the ideals of culture, and the accomplishments of civilization conceal it from us. We have forgotten or no longer want to acknowledge the reality of a drive whose desire and satisfaction civilization has repressed. Psychoanalysis no doubt abstains from judging such drives. It refuses to formulate any moral pronouncement regarding them. But nothing prevents us from seeking a point of view, a perspective, determined by what "human community" requires, from which to interrogate these drives. In many ways, what I am seeking to think through in these pages under the moniker "murderous consent" attempts to define this perspective. If it is true that murderous consent means the suspension of responsibility for the care, the assistance, and the attention that the vulnerability and mortality of the other demand, and if it is true that this eclipse opens a chasm in our belonging to the world, then we must begin our analysis with this fault or flaw, since it affects the possibility for life to realize its necessary expansion.

Life, in effect, does not remain subservient to these "primal drives" without reshaping them in important ways—inhibitions, reorientations toward other goals, fusions, inversions or mutations of their object—the study of which is one of the principal tasks of psychoanalysis. But life also inherits the accomplishments, from time immemorial, of preceding generations. This does not mean that drives disappear. The fact that there is no "eradication of evil" attests to their continued presence. Indeed, it is not in life's power to suppress these forces that are the "malign drives." It can only convert them. It is therefore this conversion, fragile and reversible, that we must examine if we want to understand what makes possible, from the perspective of life, the historical recurrence and persistence of murderous consent, as signified by war, among other things, in all periods of human history despite the progress of *Civilization* [*la* civilisation].[20] War, Freud tells us, is the work of two factors, one endogenous and the other exogenous. The first (endogenous) hearkens back to the vital need, examined earlier in this chapter, that makes of all life a living-with, a shifting fabric of relations, that ties us to others. It is, in other words, "the love needs of man interpreted in the widest sense," without which the very idea of "civilization" would have no meaning. In the "ordinary" course of life, it is this need (life's erotic component) that outstrips the pleasure of destroying and causing suffering so as to ensure one's existence.[21] But it succeeds only if buttressed by a second factor (the exogenous factor), which consists of the heritage of civilization, that is, of the constraints and rites that education transmits to the individual, replicating, always singularly, the course of humanity. Without this contribution—without the communal assimilation and internalization of interdictions—nothing could guarantee that the gathering and expansion of life as living-with could durably provide orientation to the movement of life.

But it is this same contribution that, in more ways than one, makes for the worrisome fragility of the gathering and expansion of life. It is true that war gives us the impression that culture and civilization have failed, since it resuscitates a kind of violence and cruelty that we happily thought had been definitively repressed. But it is the solidity and the tenability of this conversion that should be questioned—beginning with the restrictive system in which it is inscribed. In a word, renouncing the satisfaction of our drives, no matter the tradition in which such renunciation is embedded, protects us only in a very *partial, unstable, insufficient,* and very *temporary* way from the spread of murderous consent, to which humanity would seem everywhere to be historically preordained. The fragility is twofold. It derives first from the fact that cultural acquisition is reversible, and its claim to innateness is much weaker than we like to think. Beyond forbidding us the satisfaction of our drives, education also seeks to minimize the existence and power of such drives, if not deny their existence altogether. Religion and morality thrive under the supposition that it is both possible and desirable to eradicate our inclination toward evil and cruelty. Nothing is more contrary to morality than the recognition that life's drives are irreducible. That recognition denies morality any response to evil and cruelty other than ratcheting up the restrictions and intensifying the repression, thus forcing life, and habituating life, to be cruel toward life itself. Religion and morality combat the drives (the inclination toward cruelty being among them) using practices that are themselves "inhuman"— awaiting the slightest historical opportunity (war, for example) to release life to turn its drives outward in violation of all morality's and religion's principles.[22]

No authorization frees or precipitates violence more powerfully than that of morality and religion. But there is more. Fragility also stems from the fact that the "adaptation to culture," which occurs through assimilation and the internalization of restrictions, is always *selective*. No matter how "protective" it might be, there is no education that does not leave some room for cruelty. There is no education that does not tolerate and even encourage exceptions to its own prohibitions. To the extent that we call education an *acquisition*, it is tributary to the prejudices that discriminate between people regarding to whom the prohibitions apply and to whom they do not apply. For this reason, the prohibitions are dependent on the authorities who reproduce and impose them. Although this acquisition is performed by what Freud calls the *superego*—that part of the psychic apparatus that presides over the repression of drives—the *destiny* of cruelty is vulnerable to the forces (religious, political, and/or ideological) that participate in its constitution and that seek to exercise control over it, sometimes through violence.[23] If these forces do not regard a certain cruel and inhuman treatment of some category of individuals as illegitimate, however that category might be defined (by faith, "origin," "class," "race," etc.), then *nothing* can prevent such treatment. The strictest and most repressive educational systems have never found it difficult to inculcate the extreme violence that the authorities condone against subjected segments of the population. It never seemed illegitimate to the children of white masters, brought up to respect religion (and property), to mistreat, mutilate, or kill the slaves of their family plantations. Nor did their education and cultural capital ever prevent the men and women of some nation or other, or of some fantasized community, from showing the most extreme cruelty toward those whom the weight of tradition and the transmission of hatred exempted from the prohibition of cruelty.

Such is the twofold foundation, both *vital* and *cultural*, of murderous consent. It is attributable to the fact that "primitive states can always be restored." Stefan Zweig testifies to the possibility of such regression in the first pages of his memoirs, written as if under an ominous cloud: "I was forced to be a defenseless, helpless witness of the most inconceivable decline of humanity into a barbarism which we had believed long since forgotten."[24] But it is also attributable to the fact that regression is a force, and as such, it is manipulable. Its destructive power is never more terrifying than when commandeered by religious or political authorities who, leveraging prejudices sustained by education and mobilized by some circumstantial propaganda, define a community's appropriate target. Freud's conclusion seems to toll the knell of our illusions:

> These discussions have already afforded us the consolation that our mortification and painful disappointment on account of the uncivilized behavior of our fellow world citizens in this war were not justified. They rested upon an illusion to which we had succumbed. In reality they have not sunk as deeply as we feared because they never really rose as high as we had believed. The fact that states and races abolished their mutual ethical restrictions not unnaturally incited them to withdraw for a time from the existing pressure of civilization and to sanction a passing gratification of their suppressed impulses.[25]

But this analysis leaves us midstream. If we try to think through the possibility of radical evil and cruelty in these terms, we still do not reach the essential point that concerns our "attitude toward death." I asked above, to what does war accustom us? Narratives and testimonies, like Jules Romains's *Verdun, the Prelude and the Battle* or Jean Giono's *To the Slaughterhouse*, leave no doubt. We have already encountered it: we get used to people dying, everywhere and all the time. It is our entire being-in-the-world that undergoes, not only the brutal irruption, but the perdurance of the "spectacle" and experience of death. We have to keep this fact in mind. Otherwise, we have said nothing meaningful about war. On both the front lines and in the rear, war intrudes on people's awareness massively and on a daily basis.[26] The apprehension and presence of death constitute, more acutely than ever, the foundation on which our relations to others are formed, both those near to us and those farther away. We fear death, both ours and theirs, as night, though without assurance, follows day. This is the temporal signification of all *armed* conflict: when it begins, while it endures, and when it ends, it means, above all else, this sense of unease. It is death's presence in life, understood as living-with. Death's presence is apparent in forms as diverse as the camaraderie of combatants, their feeling of "brotherhood," and the waiting and anguish of their families in the rear.

"Generations of Murderers"

Freud's *Reflections on War and Death* forges several paths that help us understand this presence of death in life. It confronts the reader with an immediate and considerable challenge, related to the diversity of conflict and its multiple justifications, as well as to the many qualifiers that are often appended to some or other attitude toward death. As I wish to show here, none of these challenges has lost its relevance, as Derrida observed in an address to a conference of psychoanalysts, published under the title "Psychoanalysis Searches the States of Its Soul: The Impossible Beyond of a Sovereign Cruelty": "If there is still war, and will be for a long time, or, in any case, the cruelty of war, excruciating, massively or subtly warlike, it is, inversely, no longer certain that war, and especially the differences between individual wars, civil wars and national wars, will continue to correspond to securely rigorous concepts. We need a new discourse on war. We await today new 'Reflections on War and Death' and a new 'Why War?' (I refer to writings by Freud), or at least new readings of this kind of text."[27]

The problem is this: there is something about our relation to death that is being signified by violence—and by war, in an exemplary way—that we have not yet come to understand. With every new testimony, with every new narrative, we run into the same enigma: how can we accept seeing our attitude toward death—how to avoid it—in time of peace be so utterly convulsed, and even rejected altogether? Freud himself underscores the importance of such tribulation. As war inflicts on us its inventory of the dead, it is clear, he says, that "we cannot retain our previous attitude toward death." And yet, "we have not found a new one."[28] We are defenseless, unfamiliar with what is happening to *us—absent*—as if the exotic cruelty of "death en masse," every war's wages, was a dream. How then, despite all this, do we come to habituate ourselves to this convulsion?

Freud's analyses enable us to make a decisive advance specifically on this point. The conceptual step he takes is as perilous as that attempted by Rousseau, who, confronted by a comparable difficulty, put forward his hypothesis of the state of nature. Freud, in a similar conceptual leap, reprises analyses he had proposed three years earlier (1912), in *Totem and Taboo*, to argue that the violence and the atrocities of which men and women are the victims in times of war take us back, as regards our relation to death, to paths already trodden by primitive humanity. He buttresses his analytical efforts with an archeology of the drives that govern life. He places the reader in a double register of description and narration. Psychoanalysis, as Freud insists again and again, declines commerce with the ethical. It does not express moral judgment regarding our drives or offer prescriptions. And yet it frequently clears paths that lead in the direction of judgment and prescription. In making of "murderous consent" the trial of ethics (and of politics as enjoined by ethics), as I do in this book, I am aware that we must begin with the *vital* basis of our relation to the death of others if we want to follow these paths.

How does Freud conceptualize this "basis"? The most rational hypothesis, he says, is to suppose that humanity's attitude toward death has forever been contradictory. It has always been split between the flight or denial inspired by the idea of our own death and the lack of compunction, even the enjoyment, that we have felt regarding the physical elimination of the person who we imagined was a rival or who seemed to threaten our lives or the lives of those who are close to us: "The death of another person fitted in with his idea, it signified the annihilation of the hated one, and primitive man had no scruples against bringing it about. He must have been a very passionate being, more cruel and vicious than other animals. He liked to kill and did it as a matter of course. Nor need we attribute to him the instinct [drive] which restrains other animals from killing and devouring their own species. As a matter of fact the primitive history of mankind is filled with murder."[29]

In terms employed in this book, this means that murderous consent has always been part of our relation to the death of others. The pleasure-desire to murder belongs to the essence of life. But it is only one component of this relation. Here is the force and originality of Freud's analysis. Even though the experience of the death (or putting to death) of the other is part of life, it is not the origin of the *thought* of death. Freud makes this very clear: "primitive man probably triumphed at the side of the corpse of the slain enemy, without finding any occasion to puzzle his head about the riddle of life and death."[30] If this is the case, it is because there is space for another relation, no less essential, but doubtless more complex and certainly more ambivalent: the space created by the death of "loved ones." We remember how, in the beginning of this chapter, the expansion of life as union, as gathering (living-with), emerged as a constitutive element of the essence of life. Now, however, we see that the relation to the death of the other belongs *equally* to this expansion. In other words, we cannot consider it to be originally and definitively a captive of murderous consent.

It would be an illusion to believe in the absolute separation of these two components. If the death of those near to us was a determining factor in the formation of our "thought" of mortality, it is also the case that the feelings that such death engenders are themselves ambivalent. As much as we loved them, and however strong the pain we felt at their disappearance, our relation to our loved ones was not free of a hostility that may have made them appear to us as "strangers and enemies."[31] There is no relationship that is entirely free of cruelty. According to Freud, we must attach importance and much attention to this ambivalence because it is the source of morality's first commandment, "thou shalt not kill." The emergence of this commandment was anything but simple. The proscription of murder became firmly established only because, in mourning our loved ones, we remembered our ambiguous desire to see them dead: "The first and most important prohibition of the awakening conscience declared: Thou shalt not kill. This arose as a reaction against the gratification of hate for the beloved dead which is concealed behind grief, and was gradually extended to the unloved stranger and finally also to the enemy."[32]

When we contemplate the "progress" of civilization, when we proclaim that we share the confidence that is placed in it, it is this proscription that we want to believe in, against and despite the litany of history's many disappointments. But it is this same proscription that every war puts in question, no matter how "just." This is what we have to remember, with regard to and against all the professions of allegiance, the concessions, and the complaisance that press us to believe the contrary. Freud refused (or claimed to refuse) to advance moralizing prescriptions concerning our attitude toward cruelty and violent death. But he did emphasize the fact that there is nothing that disturbs us more, and that is more painful to observe (how could it be otherwise?), than the ease with which, once war is declared, "civilized man no longer feels [any interdiction] in regard to killing enemies."[33] This is what we must realize. This is what helps us dispel our illusions *otherwise*: all relations are based on a more or less precarious "balance," always more fragile than we want to imagine, between the ancestral temptation of murder and the will to pursue the expansion of the living-with, or the bonding-with [*se lier avec*], in compliance with murder's prohibition. Though the will to shatter bonds never completely disappears, the balance, in times of peace, tips in favor of that which gathers together. In time of war, on the contrary, it tips toward that which destroys. When I speak of "regression," this is what I mean. "To regress" is to suspend the force that gathers, thus benefiting that which fragments, and opening the door to the pleasure-desire to murder. Psychoanalysis therefore enables a clearer perception of "that which is lost." By inciting us to recollect our historical parentage, it helps us understand what otherwise we could only have understood as the disillusionment of our disillusionment:

> Such a powerful inhibition can only be directed against an equally strong impulse. What no human being desires to do does not have to be forbidden, it is self-exclusive. The very emphasis of the commandment:

Thou shalt not kill, makes it certain that we are descended from an endlessly long chain of generations of murderers, whose love of murder was in their blood as it is perhaps also in ours. The ethical strivings of mankind, with the strength and significance of which we need not quarrel, are an acquisition of the history of man; they have since become, though unfortunately in very variable quantities, the hereditary possessions of people of today.[34]

This is the meaning of war. It reminds us of the primitive human in *ourselves*, whose memory we have not preserved, even though "if we are to be judged by our unconscious wishes," we have constantly been "nothing but a band of murderers." In so doing, war consigns "the later deposits of civilization" to oblivion and forces us to confront the question: if it is true that nothing of this primitive ancestry (the cruelty, the taste for murder, not to mention the pleasure of destroying most of the relations that compose existence) has ceased to dwell within us secretly, or, in other words, if the possibility of war (and its atrocities) is so rooted in life that we cannot eradicate it, is there any chance at all of resisting it with some "force" such as that of reason or the calculability of interests or feelings? Or are we just indulging in more wishful thinking, in one more (though hardly the least significant) moral illusion that stems from our ignorance of life? Freud has no answer to this question. But he does ask, in concluding his essay, that we radically revise our attitude toward death (the legacy of civilization), which only intensifies the attitude that is inflicted on us by war. Freud claims, rather enigmatically, that humanity, by conforming to civilization's heritage, lives "beyond its means." He asks therefore that we "give death the place to which it is entitled both in reality and in our thoughts."[35]

This implies, first of all, that we acknowledge the ambivalence of our feelings when we lose people who are close to us, despite the fact that everything in our "civilized" lives, from education to religion to politics, encourages us to deny that ambivalence and to repress the hostility that such ambivalence harbors. What does "living beyond our means" signify if not imagining that civilization gives us *sufficient means* to prevent ourselves from lapsing back into "barbarity"? But Freud offers no recourse other than psychoanalysis itself. We remain powerless before the question of what supplementary "means" we might try to think up. What do we do once we have acknowledged the swings in our relation to death? First of all, whose death are we talking about? What mortals are in question? And, finally, what are we to make of this unequivocal maxim, *si vis vitam, para mortem*—if you want life, prepare for death—which is at odds with every illusion we might harbor (including the illusion of disillusionment)?[36]

What Opposes War

Freud did not leave these questions entirely without response. Just months before Hitler assumed power, Freud returned to the topic of war in his reply to a question that Alfred Einstein had addressed to him on July 30, 1932: "Is it possible to control man's mental evolution so as to make him proof against the psychoses of hate and destructiveness?"[37] The exchange is interesting in that it adopts from the outset a cosmopolitical perspective. At issue for both thinkers is the possibility of securing respect for the rules of international law and avoiding the subordination of the law's opposition to violence by state interest and claims to sovereignty.[38] According to Einstein, who had just resigned from the League of Nations' International Commission on Intellectual Cooperation, only an independent international agency endowed with coercive power could prevent that subordination, assuming that this agency does not itself become an instrument of powerful nation-states. Nevertheless, however indispensable such an organization might be, the law needs more than the force of arms. It needs another, but different kind of force, the force to create and maintain, over time, the attachment to the community that is constituted by those who wish to abide by rules. This is Freud's first point. If it is true that all law—and therefore international law—presupposes the existence of a "community of interests" endowed with a power of its own, then we must acknowledge that this community cannot win respect unless the feelings that bind together those who are attached to it are formed, preserved, and even reinforced. "Thus the union of the people must be permanent and well organized; it must enact rules to meet the risk of possible revolts; must set up machinery insuring that its rules—the laws—are observed and that such acts of violence as the laws demand are duly carried out. This recognition of a community of interests engenders among the members of the group a sentiment of unity and fraternal solidarity which constitutes its *real strength*."[39]

If we envisage law, not from the perspective of a bounded community, but as pertaining to the world as a whole (as the fear of war incites us to do)—if, in other words, we admit that humanity cannot deal effectively on a smaller scale with the destructive rage that it has displayed over the course of its history—then this means that we can conceptualize belonging to the world only on the basis of such an attachment. We have to discover—and this book pursues no other aim than this—what *binds* us, each of us singularly, to the community of mortals. All our reflections on the frictions and fractures that affect such a bond, moreover (which jeopardize the *with* that defines each life in its singularity), imply precisely this approach: we must find a balance between the force that gathers and the violence that divides. If we refuse to do this, because we maintain that there is no such force, or that this balance is illusory, then we are treating hostility as inevitable and war as fate. Such is the conclusion, scarcely concealed, that emerges from the American political scientist Samuel Huntington's theory of civilizational clash. By venturing to deny the existence of a bond that transcends the ties uniting members of the same civilization, Huntington's theory gives attention to nothing that might restrain them from the path of destruction. It gives attention to nothing that might extract them from the spiral of murderous consent in which they are confined by the dogma of civilizational difference.[40]

How might we understand such a bond? It assumes what Freud calls an *identification*, which secures, and guarantees, the preservation of union and cohesion between members of a group. The question then becomes whether such identification is possible (and possible for what) in a way that does not simply displace this bond and reproduce elsewhere the violence that it is supposed to constrain. All wars in effect duplicate this experience: there is no identification that is not potentially murderous, to the extent that it is exclusive. This seems obvious, and yet only rarely, when we assert some or other feeling of belonging, do we actually admit it. Or, to put the problem more radically, we do not, as a matter of course, recognize the destructive power that animates the force of attachment that binds us to a community of culture, language, religion, or "destiny." We have the greatest difficulty understanding that war is part of the bond. War is even, as all forms of nationalism and cultural identification [*communautarisme*] prove, one of that bond's most effective mediums and assets. It is the arm that no (political and/or religious) authority, in the exercise of his or her power of control over the modalities of such identification, has ever failed to wield in order to retain or reinforce the legitimacy of their power.

If we can speak of "manipulation," it is only in a very partial way. Those whom we would expect to contest this "function" of war do not contest it. On the contrary, it is acclaimed and encouraged as the necessary condition for the renewal or restoration of an identification that is lost or imperiled. Stefan Zweig's recollection of the first days of war in 1914 helps us understand its implications and ramifications. His account contrasts two periods. In the first, he describes the mobilizing enthusiasm of a feeling of newfound unity. No one is immune from it, even the committed pacifists, the most circumspect, the most clear-sighted, as if, in a kind of collective blindness, nothing could oppose the wave of reckless consent to the atrocities that war heralds:

The first shock of the news of war, the war which had slipped, much against their will, out of the clumsy hands of the diplomats who had been bluffing and toying with it, had suddenly been transformed into enthusiasm. There were parades in the street, flags, ribbons, and music burst forth everywhere, young recruits were marching triumphantly, their faces lighting up at the cheering—they, the John Does and Richard Roes who usually go unnoticed and uncelebrated. . . . A city of two million, a country of nearly fifty million, in that hour felt that they were participating in world history, in a moment which would never recur, and that each one was called upon to cast his infinitesimal self into the glowing mass, there to be purified of all selfishness. All differences of class, rank, and language were flooded over at that moment by the rushing feeling of fraternity.[41]

But the unity, the union, the mobilization, the fraternity are ambivalent. They harbor more obscure origins and motivations. After acknowledging the seductive power of mass mobilization, Zweig is at pains to correct its meaning. The force of being-together, of a living-with that is carried away by (and gathered for) a common cause, is never without ambiguity. The fact that mothers no longer have a genuine right to weep for their dead children, given the legitimacy of the "sacrifice" of their lives for the fatherland, is already a sign. By confiscating public demonstrations of mourning so as to control them, political power tries to mask the unpardonable cruelty of death.[42] Zweig evokes the words of Freud in *Civilization and Its Discontents* in order to emphasize the dissimilarity between such demonstrations and the idealized image of warrior enthusiasm:

But it is quite possible that a deeper, more secret power was at work in this frenzy. So deeply, so quickly did the tide break over humanity that, foaming over the surface, it churned up the depths, the subconscious primitive instincts of the human animal—that which Freud so meaningfully calls "the revulsion from culture," the desire to break out of the conventional bourgeois world of codes and statutes, and to permit the primitive instincts of the blood to rage at will. It is also possible that these powers of darkness had their share in the wild frenzy into which everything was thrown—self-sacrifice and alcohol, the spirit of adventure and the spirit of pure faith, the old magic of flags and patriotic slogans, that mysterious frenzy of the millions which can hardly be described in words, but which, for the moment, gave a wild and almost rapturous impetus to the greatest crime of our time.[43]

And yet neither war nor the consent to cruelty nor the various forms of killing can be regarded as the last word regarding identification. It is significant that Freud, in his letter to Einstein, tries to resolve the paradox of identification by invoking, if not idealizing, those forms of expansion that transcend belonging in the strict sense of national belonging. He evokes in turn the Panhellenic ideal and Christendom. Yet neither of these excludes the possibility of internal divisions. Indeed, both presuppose an excluded third, the alterity relative to which they are defined and toward which violence is not prohibited. This is the limit of all cultural identification (whether by "origin," "ethnicity," "race," or "civilization" or by religion, be it Christian, Jewish, or Muslim): it cannot preserve those who seek refuge in it from the deadlock of murderous consent.

We must therefore look elsewhere for the basis of this *other* identification, assuming there is one. This other identification would have to be located, to reprise the terms of the Derridean aporia, *beyond* cruelty.[44] Freud, in his reply to Einstein, is aware that he has to throw caution to the wind. He has arrived at a point in his analysis where it would seem, at least provisionally, that no common idea, unifying ideal, or integrating set of institutions with which people could identify is capable of halting or even resisting the course of violence. He is compelled therefore to introduce into his explanation the theory of drives developed by psychoanalysis (which he nevertheless has no hesitation in calling a mythology). He references the analyses that he developed in *Beyond the Pleasure Principle* and *Civilization and Its Discontents*, around which we have been circling throughout this chapter on life, according to which there are two broad families of drives: "those that conserve and unify," which will be called erotic or sexual, and those that "destroy and kill," which will be called "aggressive or destructive drives."[45] He emphasizes—this is the decisive point—their inexorable complementarity, the bond that unites them: "Each of these drives is every whit as indispensable as its opposite and all the phenomena of life derive from their activity, whether they work in concert or in opposition. It seems that a drive of either category can operate but rarely in isolation; it is always blended ('alloyed,' as we say) with a certain dosage of its opposite, which modifies its aim or even, in certain circumstances, is a prime condition of its attainment."[46]

Our search must begin with this bond—especially since it is working in all human actions that exhibit "a blend of eros and destructiveness."[47] Even as violence rages and it seems as if nothing that enables life as living-with can be saved, some element of living-with still subsists. Just as there can be no eradication of evil, neither can evil triumph. As we seek, if not to eradicate evil or the possibility of war but to attenuate its destructive effects, beginning with all the renunciations and consents that accompany it, we must direct our attention to the *composition* of these drives. The variations we see draw a map of the world. The weight of educational systems, of living conditions, of the precarity of life (which is so often a struggle for survival), all affect the redirection outward of the death drive, as if life itself depended on it. When security is lacking, when the sacrifices demanded by civilization are not meaningfully compensated, or when their distribution is flagrantly unjust, Freud himself recognizes that the human tendency toward aggression will outstrip all forms of idealization.

How, then, do we oppose war? How do we modify the composition of drives? Is it even possible to *compose* them otherwise? The solution depends on what Freud calls, again, the mythology of drives, a mythology that, in turn, gains an increment of legitimacy from the solution it enables, if there is one. To the question, frequently asked, of why we should accord any credit to this "mythology," we might reply that it allows, for good or evil, and for want of anything better, an understanding of life that does not leave unresolved the problem of cruelty, as raised by Nietzsche in his *Genealogy of Morality*. If it is true that cruelty belongs to the essence of life, this does not mean (and this is Freud's lesson) that there is no force in life that can oppose its power.[48] To state it more boldly—again and always in opposition to the heroic and bellicose exaltation of death in the name of some allegedly superior sense of sacrifice—to oppose war is not to turn life against itself.

What is the solution? Freud says that it consists in "mobilizing" the drive of Eros against the drive to destroy, with which it is both complementary and antagonistic. It consists in forming bonds composed either of a relationship (of an erotic nature) with the object of one's love or of an identification. We saw that the latter is more often than not exclusivist and, for this reason, potentially murderous. It withdraws into attachments that are partisan, "ethnic," social, cultural, religious, etc. Freud in fact draws parallels between the primitive horde of *Totem and Taboo* (marked by murder) and the modern crowd, which is particularly susceptible to the instrumental manipulation of identification (see his 1921 essay *Group Psychology and the Analysis of the Ego*).[49] As suggested above, if we want to find a solution to war in *some* identification, then it must be sought in forms of attachment that cannot be reduced to some targeted deployment of cruelty. Can the "mythology of drives" help us advance in this direction? To summarize, if it is true that these identifications are shared sentiments that summon and provoke "important common traits," then what sentiments and traits are we talking about?

In the last pages of his letter to Einstein, Freud wonders why we remain, in our great majority, repelled by war, even though it possesses indisputable biological roots, and why we refuse to consider it and accept it "as another of life's odious importunities."[50] It would have made things simpler. What, then, is the source of this force that, both with and despite life, retains, contains, within us, the limitless upsurge of murderous consent? We keep coming back to this question. The ultimate response (which sounds almost like a testament) comes in two parts. The first part adheres to the path of psychoanalysis: "Because every man has a right over his own life and war destroys lives that were full of promise; it forces the individual into situations that shame his manhood, obliging him to murder fellow men, against his will; it ravages material amenities, the fruits of human toil, and much besides."[51]

What is meant by "has a right over his own life" and by "shame his manhood"? We cannot separate this question from the problem of identification. We cannot detach it, in other words, from the ways in which we *identify*, which induce, ineluctably, the negation of the right to life and the deprival of dignity, because the ways in which we identify place lives (our own and that of others) in the hands of those who do not care about rights and dignity, that is, in the hands of those for whom the consideration of rights and dignity is of no account. The "great patriotic wars" and the sacrifice that the military authorities, for various reasons, demand *without measure*, as well as the many narratives that such wars have inspired, bear testimony to this fact. More generally, it is what happens every time identification gets away from us, or plays into the hands of powers that hold life under their control (and will do anything to maintain that hold) and that claim the authority and defend their power to make use of life. There are—and this is what we must bear in mind—ways to identify that hold lives captive and force them to renounce everything to which *they are otherwise attached*, in the name of interests that are not theirs. Hence the question: under what conditions do we dispute such ways of identifying?[52] Is there something that we are capable of sharing with others that is not, from the start, like the way we are dragged into war and that is not synonymous with this captivity? All life is living-with. The right to life means that the limits of this "with" are not given, are not circumscribed in advance, or predetermined by some or other affiliation but, rather, remain open, variable, and forever the object of an invention (that is, of a responsibility) that is singular. Therefore, it is this circumscription, this predetermination, this fatality of allegiance and its murderous consents that this *other* identification, whose outlines remain to be delineated, must shatter.

This initial gloss, however, which reads rather like a cry from the heart, is not Freud's last word. There is yet another reason, more essential in his eyes, that explains our indignation in the face of war, even though our indignation remains (we cannot remind ourselves of this enough) partial and selective: "I pass on to another point, the basis, as it strikes me, of our common hatred of war. It is this: we cannot do otherwise than hate it. Pacifists we are, since our organic nature wills us thus to be."[53]

What is the nature of this basis? What is its *organic nature*? The answer lies in that which, *in* and *from* life, enables an identification that resists our fascination with, and temptation by, violence. It relates back to the psychic transformations that are brought about by cultural and civilizational progress. Despite the regression that war, *without exception*, always signifies, one cannot deny that life has incorporated some resistance to cruelty and has repressed [*interiorisé*] and displaced its aggressive tendencies, if only by turning such tendencies against themselves. Thus, what was once a source of pleasure has become, over centuries, *unbearable*. And yet—this is the paradox—this same culture draws its force from no source other than that which binds it to death. If it is true that culture is borne by the drive to life (the expansion of the living-with), and that this drive to life in turn assumes a relation to death oriented by the mortality of the other, then this implies that the life drive's relationship with the death drive breaches the narrow horizon of a security that is the more murderous as it becomes more exclusionary and bounded. If the "with" means something, it is first and foremost in this breach that we must look for it. Life opens up and expands the more it makes *its* responsibility the care, aid, and attention that the vulnerability and the mortality of the other demand. Life shuts down and withdraws the more it makes concessions at the expense of this demand. This is the "organic" sense of the incorporation of culture. Such responsibility is also the only possible path toward an identification that is not murderous. In fact, this path is (or will be) less murderous only to the extent that we find (or will learn how to find) in this responsibility (and in the impossibility of allowing even the slightest compromise regarding the signs, testimonies, and engagements that this responsibility enjoins) the common attribute that can sustain the feeling that both this path and this responsibility are shared by all. When culture loses itself in war, when it justifies or endorses murder in war, it stumbles and turns against itself. This is why, despite all history's denials, Freud's conclusion allows a glimmer of hope to subsist that belongs to the essence of life: "How long have we to wait before the rest of men turn pacifist? Impossible to say, and yet perhaps our hope that these two factors—man's cultural disposition and a well-founded dread of the form that future wars will take—may serve to put an end to war in the near future, is not chimerical. But by what ways or by-ways this will come about, we cannot guess. Meanwhile we may rest on the assurance that whatever makes for cultural development is working also against war."[54]

3

Freedom

Murder is made of the pleasures of the Earth. All life is cruel because we are not sensitive enough, never considerate enough of oneself, of others.
—Nicolas de Staël, letter to Pierre Lecuire, December 3, 1949

There is no greater obstacle to the possibility of a cosmopolitan being-in-the-world than our *discriminating* relation to the vulnerability and mortality of others. To be a "citizen of the world" means that we do not divide the living and the dead between a here and a there, or between proximity and remoteness. In other words, the care, assistance, and medical help that the living demand, and the mourning and tears that the dead enjoin, know no borders. But such a transcendence of our affiliations is less than obvious. In our lives with others, the hierarchy of our responsibilities is not limited to those nearest to us. Rather, it engenders circles and distinctions: family, friends, fellow citizens, Europeans, and others. The question of cosmopolitanism has to do, first of all, with the nature of such distinctions, their extension, and their legitimacy. But this hierarchy already draws a line of separation between those who think that our responsibility stops at the border of the nation-state (and who demand protection on these grounds) or an association of states transformed into a fortress and those who are incensed by all discriminations and expulsions (of "others" or "foreigners") and who believe that nothing can justify the use of borders to demarcate our responsibilities.

And Still No Help

The forms of vulnerability in the world are numerous.[1] The most obvious are war and plague (epidemics such as AIDS, malaria, and tuberculosis).

The most recurrent, extensive, and disturbing form of vulnerability, however, is famine. It is estimated today that more than a billion people suffer from hunger and five million children die from hunger each year. The causes of famine are many: climate (as in Somalia, Eritrea, Ethiopia, and Kenya in our day, caused by drought and the loss of livestock), economics (the emphasis on export farming to the detriment of subsistence and family farming, extensive speculation on raw materials, the development of biomass fuels, and, finally, the rural exodus that is itself aggravated by the economic crisis), and the media (indifferent and not mobilized). Finally, of course, there is politics (support of land acquisition by multinationals, diminution of international aid, and refusal to treat the explosion in mortality as pressing—the refusal, in sum, to mobilize *without restriction* the means required to save threatened populations).

While Europe imposes production quotas to boost agricultural prices, others, beyond Europe's borders, *die* of hunger on a massive scale. A "national" catastrophe—a spectacular accident or a growing epidemic—makes the front pages of newspapers for days if not weeks. Only exceptionally do the anonymous and everyday deaths of millions of men, women, and children attract any attention. All thought of cosmopolitanism, all declarations of commitment to cosmopolitanism, inevitably stumble over this observation. Famine inscribes an irreducible fault line in our relation to the world. It epitomizes the axiom according to which the world is without meaning if we make exceptions to the assistance we bring to the vulnerable and mortal other. In other words, because there is no more extreme form of abandonment than consigning others to ineluctable death, famine divests globalization [*mondialisation*] of any possible meaning [*sens*: "meaning," "direction," "orientation"]—other than consent to mass murder.[2]

We must always bear in mind what "famine" is and what it means. Vasily Grossman helps us here, not only in his epic novel *Life and Fate*[3] but in the shorter book entitled *Everything Flows*, written when Grossman, exhausted, was convinced that the manuscript of his masterpiece had been lost forever. His depiction of the organized famine imposed on Ukraine in 1932 reads like a moral and political testament:

> The villagers were left on their own; the State withdrew from them. People began wandering from house to house, begging from one another. Poor begged from poor; the starving from the starving.[4]

> It seems that he chose to kill all these people, that he starved them deliberately. They didn't even help the children. So was Stalin, then, worse than Herod? Did he really take away people's last kernels of

grain—and then starve them? "No," I say to myself, "how could he?" But then I say to myself, "It happened, it happened." And then, immediately: "No, it couldn't have!"[5]

The whole village died. First it was the children that died, then it was the old people, then it was the middle-aged. At first people dug graves for them, but then they stopped. And so the dead were lying on the streets, in the yards, and the last to die just remained in their huts. It went quiet. The whole village had died. Who was the last to die, I don't know.[6]

Levinas, using one of his Talmudic readings (as he did on several occasions in the 1980s) to stress the importance he accorded to Grossman's work and how deeply it moved him, summarized in the following terms the horrors of Stalinist reality[7] as portrayed by *Life and Fate*: "In its writing, at once cold and inspired, the Stalinian reality, in all its horror, was blended with the Hitlerian horror. Its style, wedded to its essence, attests to *a world that is no longer a place. An uninhabitable world* in the abyss of its dehumanization. The breakdown of the very basis of European civilization. An uninhabitable world of people who have been degraded, stricken in their dignity, delivered to humiliation, suffering, death."[8]

What is a world that is no longer a place? What is an uninhabitable world? Is there any chance that our world could become a bit less uninhabitable—that is, could today's world, not just Europe or some set of rich countries (spared the scourge of famine), but the world as such become a place again? And would this not define the aim of a politics that takes the world as its object, that is to say, a "cosmopolitics"? The scenes that Grossman describes in *Everything Flows* do not belong to the past. Villages in which peasants die of hunger, cities in which the famished wander the streets until they succumb to starvation, and the forces that consent to their extinction (when they are not actively contributing to it) are not absent in today's world. The world is shared between those who, because of their insatiable appetite, pay no heed to the hunger of others and those who are worn out and left to die because of this same appetite. No cosmopolitics can ignore this. Cosmopolitics is nothing if not an insurrection against this state of affairs and its supposed "fatality."

The question of hunger is omnipresent in Levinas's work. Beginning with his 1963 preface to *Difficult Freedom*, he reminds us that our duty to feed the hungry, *wherever they are* in the world, is inescapable. It is even our first obligation. Far from the pious discourses that play with words so as to offer refuge in the convenient idea that our greatest need is "spiritual nourishment," Levinas insists that there is nothing more "spiritual" than feeding the hungry. The world, in other words, cannot find meaning [*sens*] in the dream or achievement of some hypothetical spiritual unity, any more than it can find meaning in the universality of science. The world is not given to us as an object of knowledge. Rather, the world *attests* to the *impossibility* of justifying any conditions, limitations, or exclusions whatsoever that might be placed on the care and assistance that we must provide to others—that is, on our responsibility as enjoined by their vulnerability and mortality. No argument or calculation, whether economic, geopolitical, or strategic, and no ideological reason can prevail over this imperative:

> Thanks be to God, we are not going to offer up sermons on behalf of dubious crusades undertaken to "link arms as believers" and unite "as spiritualists" in the face of the rising tide of materialism. As if we should present a front against this Third World ravaged by hunger; as if the entire spirituality on earth did not reside in the act of nourishing; as if we need to salvage from a dilapidated world any other treasure than the gift of suffering through the hunger of the Other, a gift it none the less received. "Of great importance is the mouthful of food" says Rabbi Johanan in the name of Rabbi Jose b. Kisma (Sanhedrin 103b). The Other's hunger—be it of the flesh, or of bread—is sacred; only the hunger of the third party limits its rights; there is no bad materialism other than our own.[9]

In other words, we must interrogate our ambivalence toward hunger. On the one hand, it must be thought with reference to pleasure, as underscored in *Totality and Infinity* and in a lecture in the series God and Onto-theo-logy entitled "Don Quixote: Bewitchment and Hunger."[10] On the other hand, it is one of the extreme forms that is everywhere assumed by the vulnerability of the other. Grossman reminds us that hunger erases all singularity. It melds the famished into a forsaken and anonymous *mass* of the dying, for whom there awaits no assistance. On occasion, hunger can be wrested from the imperatives of survival. In this case, the need for nourishment is no longer the price of survival but of the variable, selfish, and ultimately solitary demand for "contentment." Despite the rules and rites of conviviality, family banquets and meals are a circumscribed and exclusive sharing of nourishment. The comforts of a circumscribed being-among-ourselves [*entre-soi*] are always predicated on the limits that define that circumscription: the supervised partaking of finer feelings, the self-centeredness of families, communities, and, ultimately, nations. On other occasions nourishment is tied to conditions of survival that have turned precarious. Its symptom is the anxiety of not finding, from one day to the next, enough nourishment—the bare minimum—for oneself and one's loved ones, to the point of exhaustion.

In *Everything Flows* the question of nourishment's pleasure precedes the examination of the conditions of tyranny and the evocation of famine in Ukraine. It is a decisive moment in Grossman's analysis of servitude. Nicolas Andreievitch leads a comfortable life, on an upward trajectory, but filled with compromises. He takes stock of his life as he waits to greet his cousin Ivan Grigoryevich, who has been liberated from the camps. He recalls the letters of encouragement he did not write, the phone calls he did not make, the acts of assistance and signs of compassion that he kept to himself, and also the condemnations he endorsed—in other words, all the forms of resignation before violence and murderous consent that weave the fabric of a life exposed to terror. A painful observation interrupts his examination of conscience with the sonority of a fermata in a musical score: "Yes, his whole life had passed by in obeisance, in a great act of submission, in fear of hunger, torture, and forced labor in Siberia. But there had also been a particularly vile fear—the fear of receiving not black caviar but red caviar, mere salmon caviar."[11]

Terror is tied to the extremes of hunger. At one end, the promise of food, joyful, bewitching, and even paralyzing, fortifies subservience. Terror turns the guarantee (or security) of nourishment into an instrument that, along with fear, promotes the "dehumanization" that Levinas discusses.[12] On the other end, in the camps, terror turns hunger into the most urgent and inaccessible condition of subsistence and survival—and turns organized or sanctioned famine into the cruelest form of extermination. Two extreme modalities of *living-with* have hunger in common. Neither has lost its relevance. Starving others, resigning ourselves to famine, or justifying it so as to continue enjoying earthly—in a certain sense, the world's—nourishment or to enjoy it in greater abundance, in complete security and tranquility, remains the highest form of dehumanization.

But these extremes cannot be superimposed onto one another—the ultimate meaning of hunger does not come from the enjoyment of appeasing or satisfying it. Before hunger is *appetite*, it is *privation*. Levinas reminds us of this in a very difficult passage of "Don Quixote: Bewitchment and Hunger." If there exists a way of being-in-the-world, a way of deriving pleasure from the fruits of the earth that enchants, lavishes, or thrills us because it encloses us in the pleasure of being while shutting out the voices of the starving—"the afflicted and the needy," as countless narratives attest—then we can without exaggeration call this pleasure bewitching. It enables us to plug our ears and close our eyes, to hear nothing and see

nothing. We need pay no attention to the hunger that leaves our pleasure untouched or to the famines that might expose our pleasure to the
vulnerability and mortality of others. But if we set out from the notion of
privation—of hunger as privation—we get the opposite result. What happens then, and what happens to us (which is the condition of all cosmopolitan thought and politics), is "a movement that goes towards the other
man, and that is from the outset responsibility":

> How to get outside the circle that encloses Don Quixote in the cer-
> tainty of his enchantment? How shall we find a nonspatial exterior-
> ity? Only in a movement that goes towards the other man, and that
> is from the outset responsibility. At a very humble level, in the hu-
> mility of hunger, we can see taking shape a non-ontological transcen-
> dence that begins in human corporeality. . . .
>   . . . Here, in the *conatus essendi*, hunger is astonishingly sensitive
> to the hunger of the other man. The hunger of another awakens men
> from their well-fed slumber and their self-sufficiency. We cannot won-
> der enough over the transference, which goes from the memory of
> my own hunger to suffering and compassion for the hunger of the
> other man. This is a transference in which an untransferable respon-
> sibility is expressed, and with it the impossible evasion that individ-
> uates even him who, sated, does not understand the hungry one and
> does not cease escaping his own responsibility without also escaping
> himself.[13]

Nothing is more illusory than to console ourselves with the idea that
pleasure is the first and last word as regards the human condition. If this
were the case, if our living-with encountered its limits in interest understood as enjoyment, cosmopolitics would be impossible, and even inconceivable. It is the most common and banal argument against cosmopolitics.
However much we might acknowledge the unity of the human race, it will
object that "belonging to the world" is meaningless and cannot provide us
with a principle of politics, since we cannot possibly share interests *with
everyone*. Secure in this knowledge, in this understanding of the world, and
of the place we occupy in it, even if it were "uninhabitable," we can only
conclude, according to this argument, that the calculations, strategies, and
wars that partition pleasure are inescapable.

The force of Levinas's rejoinder is his refusal to acquiesce in this logic
of imprisonment. He testifies to the singular gestures of care and assistance
and expressions of compassion that rebut this logic. Before examining the
conditions of cosmopolitan politics, it is incumbent on us to be heedful of
the singular accounts that attest to the impossibility of shirking the call of

the starving. Responsibility is no chimera. We see it in the unforeseen manifestations, foreign to all reason, that Celan calls "radical individuation." Because the appropriation of the world that dilates the pleasure of earthly nourishment cannot be achieved without resorting to force, it happens that some of these manifestations are acts of resistance. Only in resistance can singularity exist. It is no accident that Levinas, in his discussion of Grossman's novel, displays the greatest feeling in his evocation of Ikonnikov's profession of faith. Ikonnikov, a singular, marginal character, stands out from the others by an act of refusal that bestows on the novel an almost unparalleled, transcendent light. Interned with other Russians, he refuses at the risk of his life to take part in the construction of new gas chambers. Shortly before his execution, he hands personal notes over to one of his companions, the old Bolshevik Mostovskoy, that will later provoke a long conversation, one of the novel's key passages, on the similarity in logic and principle between Nazism and Stalinism. Levinas reads and revisits these pages constantly because he encounters the following observation, which returns us to the problem of hunger:[14] "I saw whole villages dying of hunger; I saw peasant children dying in the snows of Siberia; I saw trains bound for Siberia with hundreds and thousands of men and women from Moscow, Leningrad and every city in Russia—men and women who had been declared enemies of a great and bright idea of social good. This idea was something fine and noble—yet it killed some without mercy, crippled the lives of others, and separated wives from husbands and children from fathers." Hunger returns, but so does its obverse, the gestures that seek to assist the hungry and thirsty:

> Yes, as well as this terrible Good with a capital "G," there is everyday human kindness. The kindness of an old woman carrying a piece of bread to a prisoner, the kindness of a soldier allowing a wounded enemy to drink from his water-flask, the kindness of youth towards age, the kindness of a peasant hiding an old Jew in his loft. . . . This kindness, this stupid kindness, is what is most truly human in a human being. It is what sets man apart, the highest achievement of his soul. No, it says, life is not evil!

The conclusion garners Levinas's full attention:[15] "Human history is not the battle of good struggling to overcome evil. It is a battle fought by a great evil struggling to crush a small kernel of human kindness. But if what is human in human beings has not been destroyed even now, then evil will never conquer."[16]

Such gestures of assistance validate [*rendre droit*] the responsibility enjoined by the vulnerability and mortality of the other. They invert the meaning of hunger by making the plea for nourishment the initial appeal that is addressed to us *from everywhere* by the other in its transcendence. To call oneself a "citizen of the world" means, first and foremost, refusing to subordinate this appeal to any border or self-styled authority. Cosmopolitanism presents itself as a disavowal of this tyranny of choice and preference. It does not distinguish between those who must be saved and those who must wait and hope for a miraculous deliverance.

And yet, while these gestures attest to the possibility of another relation to the world, unresponsive to power, they do not yet constitute a politics. As a testimonial to humanity they are essential. But they carry little weight against the tyranny of famine, its scale, and the mass deaths that it heralds. The political, economic, geopolitical, strategic, industrial, and/or military forces that consent to famine, on this ground, are sovereign in their murderousness. I should add, with regard to pleasure, that it was not absent from Europe's relations with its alterities, as defined, understood, imagined, fantasized, as well as dominated and generally exploited by Europeans. We should remember, without demanding "repentance," that the food that reaches Europeans from the Americas, Africa, and Asia will, in time, become indispensable to the satisfaction of their hunger. Levinas underscored this fact twenty-five years ago in his essay "Peace and Proximity," in which he evokes the contradictions of the European conscience. We must welcome the peace that Europeans have enjoyed, even if its terms move us to form reservations and concerns about the durability of selfishness: "A peace that is enjoyed therein as tranquility assured by solidarity— the exact measure of reciprocity in services rendered between counterparts: the unity of a Whole in which each finds his or her rest, place, or basis. Peace as tranquility or rest! The peace of rest between beings having a firm footing or resting on the underlying solidity of their substance, self-sufficient in their identity or capable of satisfying themselves seeking satisfaction."[17]

Inversely, we must remember that Europe, haunted by its past, "its millennia of fratricidal struggles, political or bloody, of imperialism, scorn and exploitation,"[18] is tired, and its predominance is contested. Two observations are important in this regard. First, peace has spread to all of Europe following the fall of the Berlin Wall, though not without violent jolts in the Balkans, but the unity of this *Whole* (which is one of comfort and satisfaction) still continues to fissure. Not in the sense that new wars have been declared, but, first and foremost, because hunger has returned to Europe (assuming it ever disappeared)—hunger: the last stage of precariousness, which affects a growing fraction of Europe's population, reduced to mendacity, without shelter and without resources. Second, what Levinas calls Europeans' "bad conscience" is a symptom. Bad conscience makes it impossible to enjoy the world with peace of mind, to appropriate and exploit its riches without anxiety, to ignore misery and hunger. Levinas tells us that Europe is haunted by its consciousness of the inadequacies, the faults, and the failures of the peace that it is enjoying. I might add that this bad conscience could constitute the lever for cosmopolitan action and thought, understood as *being-in-the-world otherwise* [*être-au-monde autrement*]:

> There is the anguish of the responsibility incumbent upon each one of us in the death or suffering of the other. The fear of each for himself in the mortality of each does not succeed in *absorbing* the gravity of the murder committed and the scandal of indifference to the other's suffering. Behind the risk run by each for himself in a world without security looms the consciousness of the immediate immorality of a culture and a history. Have we not heard, in the vocation of Europe, before the message of truth that it bears, the "Thou shalt not kill" of the Decalogue and the Bible?[19]

At issue is a different understanding of peace, a peace that no longer identifies itself with "the bourgeois peace of the man who is at home behind closed doors," a peace that cannot and does not want to stop at Europe's borders, forgetting or ignoring the speech or speechlessness of the starving.[20] Any idea of peace, any plea for peace, or any politics that makes peace its first principle is illusory if it tolerates famine, if it becomes habituated to this extreme form of the vulnerability and mortality of the other. *Peace otherwise* cannot be satisfied with an understanding of the world that marks distinctions between individuals according to criteria of belonging, such as gender, "class," "race," or "ethnicity," that are capable of engendering a thousand and one explanations, reasons, and ultimately justifications (economic, climatic, geopolitical, or other) for the "inevitability" of famine. The world of famine exists, not as an object of understanding, calculation, or, even less, a dream of power, but in the *limitless* extension—beyond all frontiers—of our responsibility. Only this extension makes the world, as world (and not as some island of relative security), *habitable*. No doubt, this is not peace in the political sense of the term. But it is the ethical condition of such a peace. Without it, peace is just a mask for this supreme form of nihilism that is *all* murderous consent.

"Everything Inhuman Is Senseless and Useless"

How can we possibly escape murderous consent—and the tyranny, in all its masks, that forces us to it? Famine reduces freedom to powerlessness in at least two ways. First, as we have seen, famine is an element in the arsenal of weapons that tyrants count on to subdue freedom. It cultivates fear (of want) and in the end suffocates all resistance. It reduces to slavery those who do not know what to do, what to say, or what commandment to obey in order to feed themselves. Famine turns most of those whom it spares into spectators, passive witnesses, and even accomplices in the abandonment that it reveals. What is each and everyone's freedom worth if it proves incapable of assisting the hungry—if freedom proclaims that it is powerless, that famine is not its concern or responsibility, but instead the fault of a climate, of governments, of globalization, in short, of an assortment of forces, which freedom admits, with good (or bad) conscience, has overtaken it? What is freedom worth if it always capitulates to these same forces, accepting servitude here or renouncing, forgetting, or abandoning there whatever these forces single out? What is a freedom that knows that it is enslaved to the protection and security of borders, which it closes, and of ramparts, which it raises, against the hunger of others? Thus does famine, with fear and all the forms of self-centeredness that accompany it, call into question the certitudes of the free citizen. It disturbs or suspends both his assurance and her comfort. It forces us to think about what "being free" means by subjecting it *to conditions.*

No one more than Levinas has taken the measure of the imperative character of this conditionality and its consequences. To think of freedom otherwise, without lying to ourselves about servitude—in other words, without forgetting, neglecting, or minimizing any of the thousand and one forms of enslavement of which the preceding decades have offered (and continue to offer) multiple examples—we must begin by removing freedom from its pedestal. This is Levinas's radical first lesson in *Freedom and Command*, published in 1953, just after the Second World War: "That one can create a servile soul is not only the most painful experience of modern man, but perhaps the very refutation of human freedom. Human freedom is essentially unheroic. That one could, by intimidation, by torture, break the absolute resistance of freedom, even in its freedom of thought, that an alien order no longer hits us in the face, that we could accept it as though it came from ourselves, show how desirable is our freedom."[21]

The observation is incontrovertible. If we must conceptualize freedom as resistance to tyranny, then experience proves that there is nothing irreducible about freedom. On the contrary, there is nothing that tyranny cannot force us to say or think, no crime that it cannot oblige us to accept or even to perpetrate against those whom it subjects to its law. Tyrants can let some people entertain the illusion that they are free to think what they want, to accept what they want, and to act how they want. But the beings they address are no longer free, they are not in command of freedom, and the conscience on which they are imposing obedience is not free. Tyrants do not, in reality, *address* anyone. Tyranny's other, Levinas reminds us, is always first and foremost a "material exposed to violence."[22] Tyranny rejects no means or methods to obtain such a reduction, from the simplest to the most extreme: from fear to famine and torture. No doubt Levinas found a good many additional accounts of this in *Life and Fate*, beginning with the avowals, the confessions, and the denunciations wrested from prisoners by terror in the basement of the Lubyanka, the Gestapo's prisons, and elsewhere.

Surely, we have to make distinctions and measure the increments that separate the various forms of submission. Again, we cannot put everything on the same level, beginning with terror's administrators and terror's victims, even though Stalin's regime regularly mixed them up every few years or so. To be exposed to, annihilated by, and ultimately compromised by violence are not the same thing as approving, encouraging, organizing, and ordering it. Nevertheless, the lines that divide the one from the other in these situations are never clear. The question of murderous consent cuts across such lines, especially when it gets mixed up with the question of freedom. The very idea of *consent* is in tension with freedom because it nurtures basic questions that are rarely aired, questions that we must now acknowledge. What does *murderous consent* say about freedom? Is it freedom's radical perversion? Or should we concur with Levinas that it is the effect of tyranny, hence the "refutation" of freedom?

To say that the idea of "refutation" characterizes the work of Vasily Grossman's books, not just *Life and Fate* but also *Everything Flows*, would be an understatement. The discussion it demands fills the final pages of the latter work, which Grossman completed on the eve of his death. It is a kind of dialogue from beyond the grave, for two reasons. The central character, Ivan Grigoryevich, addresses the wizened figure of the woman, racked by illness, whom he is about to lose but with whom he had begun to rediscover a taste for life after returning from the camps. What he confesses to her, what he would have wanted to narrate at greater length had she lived, is his hidden torment, his spectral recollection of a strained conversation he had with a cellmate after returning from an interrogation. At issue in this exchange between the two destitute prisoners is the question, what is life about? Is it about perpetual violence, or is it about the progressive movement toward freedom? For Ivan Grigoryevich, "human history is the history of freedom, of the movement from less freedom to more freedom; [it is] my belief that the history of life—from the amoeba to the human race—is the history of freedom, of the movement from less freedom to more freedom." But Aleksey Samoilovich, his companion in misfortune, counters with an entirely different story, with despair and obstinacy:

> That's just a comforting lie. The history of life is the history of violence triumphant. Violence is eternal and indestructible. It can change shape, but it does not disappear or diminish. Even the word "history," even the concept of history is just something people have dreamed up. There's no such thing as history. History is milling the wind; history is grinding water with a pestle and mortar. Man does not evolve from lower to higher. Man is as motionless as a slab of granite. His goodness, his intelligence, his degree of freedom are motionless; the humanity in humanity does not increase. What history of humanity can there be if man's goodness always stands still?[23]

In a few sentences, Samoilovich says that violence is the essence and history of life (of life in general). We understand why Grigoryevich's memory is a nightmare: the most radical and terrifying justification of murderous consent issues from the mouths of the condemned. It is not the state that imposes the greatest servitude; it cannot be ascribed to some particular era, continent, or culture more than any other; life's greatest servitude is to life, itself, to the cruelty of life. Only its shape changes. People do not consent. Rather, they are, first and foremost, enslaved by the violence of life. We may try to eliminate violence, but it resists, indestructible. We therefore have no reason to be outraged by famine, torture, incarceration, and murder or to imagine that it could be otherwise. To do so would go against life itself, which is by essence murderous. This understanding, this vision of crime, is simultaneously a temptation and a blindness. It is the temptation of nihilism (which we rediscover here and which recalls Camus's thinking). The blindness obliges us to see the death drive in action everywhere (taking us back to Freud). Grossman himself is not far from acquiescing in both when, at the end of a long chapter on the various types of informers, he concludes in despair:

> Maybe it is human nature itself that has engendered informers, stool pigeons, writers of denunciations, collaborators with the security organs? Perhaps informers are born from the secretions of glands, from the pap slopping about our intestines, from the noise of gas in our stomachs, from mucous membranes, from the activity of the kidneys? Perhaps they are born from blind instinct—from the noseless, eyeless instinctual drives for nourishment, self-preservation, and reproduction? . . . The hot steam of State terror breathed upon

mankind and little grains that had been sleeping swelled and came to life. The State is the earth. If the earth has no grains lying hidden inside it, neither wheat nor tall weeds will grow from it. Humanity has only itself to blame for human filth. . . . But why is all this so painful? Why does our human obscenity make us feel such shame?[24]

Violence, riveted to the life of the body, seems indefinitely replicable. Yet, in Grossman's novella, it does not have the last word. The last word belongs to Ivan Grigoryevich, who utters it twice, stubbornly, like a testament, as one declaims a profession of faith in response to those who are exacting a disavowal, or perhaps as one might whisper a prayer: "everything inhuman is senseless and useless."[25] Meaningless; useless. Why? Precisely because "life itself is freedom." What is inhuman is not the work, the fruit, or the effect of freedom. What is inhuman is the ransom of its destruction—and this ransom is impossible. To be sure, we must recognize, with Levinas, the oppressive weight of tyranny, and it never weighs more oppressively than in the mass and variety of the murderous consents that it organizes. Because murderous consents are imposed, they knock freedom off its pedestal. And yet, Grossman tells us, freedom endures as the essence of life. Does this mean that Levinas and Grossman are in disagreement? Or would it not be more accurate to say that, if one questions freedom while the other *saves* it from the inhuman, it is to invite us conjointly to think of freedom *otherwise*?

"Everything inhuman is senseless and useless." In only a few words, Grossman brings together all that he thought he had lost—and that should have constituted the principal lesson of his confiscated manuscript, *Life and Fate*. This is the great paradox of this epic book. We find all the various forms of the inhuman in this great fresco, which, by confronting Nazism and Stalinism, offers unparalleled testimony to the mutilation of life that is inflicted by terror and to the violation of the relationships that form the fabric of life, both inside and outside barbed wires. But all the forms of inhumanity that the book lays bare are concentrated in a brief chapter at the heart of the book, a recapitulation that evokes the multiple forms of "consent" that are implicated in the destruction of the human:

> Most people, however, are horrified at mass murder, but they hide this not only from their families, but even from themselves. These are the people who filled the meeting-halls during the campaigns of destruction; however vast these halls or frequent these meetings, very few of them ever disturbed the quiet unanimity of the voting. And it wasn't merely tens of thousands, or hundreds of thousands, but hundreds of millions of people who were the obedient witnesses of

this slaughter of the innocent. Nor were they merely obedient witnesses: when ordered to, they gave their support to this slaughter, voting in favor of it amid a hubbub of voices. There was something unexpected in the degree of their obedience.[26]

All the forms of the inhuman are laid out—but they attest, not to the perversion of human nature, but to the violence of coercion. Again, life itself is not, in essence, violent. What we must understand, Grossman tells us, is the nature of the forces that engender submission. First, there is the preservation instinct, activated by fear (and hunger), followed by the "hypnotic power" of ideology (its lies and the culture of the enemy that it implements), and finally the terror exercised by the systematic organization of murder, as a tool of government.[27] Against all simplifications, all unfair characterizations, all references to basic psychology, these forces remind us that "man does not renounce freedom voluntarily."[28] This is the conclusion that Grossman wants us to retain. It "holds out hope for our time," he writes, "hope for the future."[29] This is the paradox. It is from the depths of the most unendurable horror that he proclaims and reaffirms the intrinsic link between life and freedom. This reaffirmation punctuates the book's most painful passages—specifically, Chapters 45–49, which describe the progression of a line of women and children toward the gas chambers. Freedom, Grossman tells us, is what engenders the singularity of all life. It promises the uniqueness and originality of the universe and of each person's identification with it. It restores meaning to death, which murderous consent denies: the extinction of a spark of freedom and, with it, the collapse of an irreplaceable universe.

> When a person dies, they cross over from the realm of freedom to the realm of slavery. Life is freedom, and dying is a gradual denial of freedom. Consciousness first weakens and then disappears. . . . The stars have disappeared from the night sky; the Milky Way has vanished; the sun has gone out; Venus, Mars and Jupiter have been extinguished; millions of leaves have died; the wind and the oceans have faded away; flowers have lost their colour and fragrance; bread has vanished; water has vanished; even the air itself, the sometimes cool, sometimes sultry air, has vanished. The universe inside a person has ceased to exist. This universe is astonishingly similar to the universe that exists outside people. It is astonishingly similar to the universes still reflected within the skulls of millions of living people. But still more astonishing is the fact that this universe had something in it that distinguished the sound of its ocean, the smell of its flowers, the rustle of its leaves, the hues of its granite and the sadness of its au-

tumn fields both from those of every other universe that exists and ever has existed within people, and from those of the universe that exists eternally outside people. What constitutes the freedom, the soul of an individual life, is its uniqueness.[30]

In these pages, which give Grossman's book, along with many others, the power of a requiem, freedom is known only in its extinction, that is, in the meaning [*sens*] of the death of others. It emerges less from the analysis of the singular relationship of each person to his or her own end (the anxiety of the condemned) than it does from the evocation of the death of others. To its readers, the book recalls what lives condemned to violence and engulfed by terror really are. For Grossman, the issue is not one of asserting the rights of a sovereign subject, blessed with the goods of the world, to demand and defend her *own* freedom. The issue is not one of just institutions (a different state) that would better preserve the freedom in question. It is about proclaiming, as freedom, if not the responsibility that is evoked by the mortality and vulnerability of others—even if exemplified by Ossia Ossipovna's care for David, the child whom she leads by the hand to the death that awaits him—then at least the meaning of the life of every other. If Grossman reminds us of this by evoking the victims of terror, it is because none of the infinite forms of cruelty that can be exercised against *one* life can deprive life itself of this meaning. This is why "everything inhuman is senseless and useless."

But is this how we always experience the freedom of others, particularly in wartime? Is *their* freedom not also the "license to kill" that executioners accord themselves or that is accorded to them precisely in the name of freedom, as they understand it? Behind the freedom guaranteed by institutions there always lies hidden the possibility that, at certain times or under certain circumstances, freedom may turn against others and veer toward tyranny. Knocking freedom off its pedestal demands not only, as Levinas would have it, that we recall the servitude that haunts it—even if we deny, like Grossman, that servitude can prevail—but also that we evaluate the possibility of its reversal, its metamorphosis into a license to destroy. The experience of the freedom of others is therefore not univocal but divided or torn between the meaning that it derives from its confrontation with the mortality and vulnerability of the other and the meaning that it assumes in the perception of the other as enemy or adversary. Nowhere is this division or rupture more clearly demonstrated than in the ordeal of war.

Levinas presses this point in *Freedom and Command*. In war, violence is directed against a being whose freedom is itself perceived as potential or effective violence. What violence sees in the other is not the breath of a life, the site of an irreplaceable universe, but rather a freedom that is frightening and that must be contained—it is the reciprocal possibility of murder:

> Violence applied to a free being is, taken in its most general sense, war. War surely does not differ from labor solely by virtue of the greater complexity of forces that have to be overcome, or by virtue of the unforeseeable character of those forces and of their composition; it differs also by a new attitude on the part of the agent with regard to his adversary. Is not the adversary himself recognized to be a freedom? But this freedom is an animal freedom, wild, faceless. It is not given to me in its face, which is a total resistance without being a force, but in my fear and in my courage which overcomes it.[31]

What is this freedom without a face? To what is it reduced? To what do *we* reduce it? First and foremost, to the force that it makes manifest. This is why freedom is never assailed directly but only in its weak spots. Levinas echoes Camus and the heroine, Dora, in *The Just Assassins*, who reminds Kaliayev just how difficult it is to kill while looking one's adversary or victim in the eye—unless they have already been effaced by blind hatred.[32] War deploys many diverse calculations and strategies whose goal is to *eclipse* from the freedom of the other, now designated as "enemy," the mortality and the vulnerability of the other as expressed in the face.[33] War as a rule sees in the other only an active "substance" that it must "treat," "neutralize," or "eliminate"—all terms that express this reduction. We will see below how the discourse and imagery of war, how the deceptions and lies of propaganda, produced and marshaled by the belligerents to nurture a conjoint culture of fear and the enemy, participate in this eclipse.[34]

This eclipse is a shackling [*enchaînement*]. It shackles the perception of the other to an expression that completely ignores mortality and vulnerability. It encloses the other in physical, physiological, physiognomical, or biological ruminations or in some other characterization such as "race" or "class." Every culture of the enemy proceeds in this way: it "treats" [*traite*] the other by seizing on the traits [*les traits*] that can feed, spread, and justify hostility and cruelty. Levinas was not mistaken when he pointed out, in 1934, in an essay entitled "Reflections on the Philosophy of Hitlerism," that the true Nazi ideology—its appeal to the "mysterious urgings of the blood," its incessant invocation of an original past and a tragic legacy, "for which the body serves as its enigmatic vehicle"—stems precisely from such a shackling.[35] This eclipse compresses and inserts the universe—the universe in which everyone escapes determinism and invents her own singularity and individuality—into ways of being, living, and thinking that are supposed to distinguish and synopsize the diversity of "racial belongings," their "force" and their "weakness." Twenty years later, it would result in a definition of violence and tyranny made more tragic by the full shock of the war:

> In other words, what characterizes violent action, what characterizes tyranny, is that one does not face what the action is being applied to. To put it more precisely: it is that one does not see the face in the other, one sees the other freedom as a force, savage; one identifies the absolute character of the other with his force. . . . Violence is a way of acting on every being and every freedom by approaching it from an indirect angle. Violence is a way of taking hold of a being by surprise, of taking hold of it in its absence, in what is not properly speaking it. . . . Violence, which seems to be the direct application of force to a being, in fact denies that being all its individuality, by taking it as an element of its calculus, and as a particular case of a concept.[36]

Two kinds of freedom are thus opposed to one another. The first is the obsessive, blinding freedom that is concentrated in the force that it expresses—this same force, history shows, produces domination and submission and generates a desire for murder that bloodies it. Second, there is freedom understood primarily as the *freedom of others*, which exists only by virtue of the vulnerability and mortality that is expressed by the face. This second freedom also *commands*, but in a completely different way from war. Because the first kind of freedom attacks the second kind indirectly (it assumes that it has the same intentions), it inscribes it in a whole that is circumscribed in advance and encloses it in a belonging that it presumes and claims to know. This second freedom labels the face; it categorizes it, whether morally, economically, socially, "ethnically," nationally, or "racially." All murderous consent assumes a knowledge of this order. Below I will examine the strategies that organize the production of this knowledge. The second kind of freedom, by contrast, only hews to that of others in its suspension of judgment. If, as Grossman contends, the freedom of others is given in the singularity of the universe, whose death signifies extinction, then respecting this freedom requires that nothing of this universe be judged, defined, or determined in advance. Its irreplaceable and incomparable character cannot be effaced by what we imagine we know about it.

For Levinas, this suspension (which inverts the meaning of freedom) recognizes [*rend droit à*] what he calls "the absolute nakedness of the face"— which means that it is, as such, "absolutely defenseless . . . , without covering, clothing or mask."[37] Foreign to all categorizations, the freedom of the other is imperative before it is indicative. It does not *first* inform us of its force or weakness. Freedom cannot be correlated with some *identity* that protects some while exposing or abandoning others. It suffices that it *be*, independently of *what* it is, to enjoin the responsibility of all: "The face is the fact that a being affects us not in the indicative, but in the imperative, and is thus outside all categories."[38]

Below I will try to grasp the many consequences of this exteriority, even if not exactly in Levinas's own terms. Specifically, I will ask if it might not open up a different, double understanding of the world—not as an object of knowledge or mastery but as a two-pronged responsibility, intensive and extensive. How is the world given to us? First, intensively, it is that which bears the freedom of others. Every free being—that is, every being—is, in and of itself, the world. Second, it is the extension, beyond all categorizations—that is, without borders—of the attention, the care, and the assistance that are enjoined by the vulnerability and mortality of others, in that each death signifies, each and every time, the extinction of the world. But before discussing this twofold perspective that may provide an additional foundation for cosmopolitanism, we must still measure how thinking of freedom as subordinated to the face turns murderous consent into the impossibility of killing.

"The Other Is the Only Being That We Can Be Tempted to Kill"

Of the many characters whose fates cross one another in Grossman's masterpiece, none commands Levinas's attention more than Ikonnikov, and no passage inspired him more than the ramblings of this fool of God. At the heart of this confession is a narrative that accords great attention to the question of murder and that subsequently will haunt the novel. Ikonnikov tells the story of a woman who saw a detachment of German soldiers enter her village to carry out a punitive retaliation. After taking away her husband along with some twenty other villagers and ordering the women to dig a pit at the edge of the forest, the Germans set up camp in her home to have a feast. In the course of their drinking binge, one of the soldiers shoots himself in the stomach with his machine gun. Soon thereafter, the soldiers leave the house to complete their assignment. The woman stays alone with the injured soldier:

> Then they were called outside. They signed to the woman to look after the wounded man. The woman thought to herself how simple it would be to strangle him. There he was, muttering away, his eyes closed, weeping, sucking his lips. . . . Suddenly he opened his eyes

and said in very clear Russian: "Water, Mother." "Damn you," said the woman. "What I should do is strangle you." Instead she gave him some water. He grabbed her by the hand and signed to her to help him sit up: he couldn't breathe because of the bleeding. She pulled him up and he clasped his arms round her neck. Suddenly there was a volley of shots outside and the woman began to tremble.

Afterwards she told people what she had done. No one could understand; nor could she explain it herself.

Ikonnikov comments: "This senseless kindness is condemned in the fable about the pilgrim who warmed a snake in his bosom. It is the kindness that has mercy on a tarantula that has bitten a child. A mad, blind, kindness."[39]

Levinas does not pay a lot of attention to this narrative, but he does offer several comments on the gestures of kindness that Ikonnikov relates—a spontaneous solicitude, irreducible to any calculation (of interest or risk) or to any identification, as illustrated above using the appeasement of hunger and the quenching of thirst and the assistance provided to the starving and thirsty. Recall that Levinas cites testimonies in *Life and Fate* to an "uninhabitable world," "a world that is no longer a place." And yet, as Levinas tells us, this plunge into the abyss of disaster is not the novel's final word. It is, moreover, no accident that he evokes this fact in a Talmudic reading entitled "Beyond Memory," which evokes the "war of Gog and Magog too strong for memories, pictures, texts."[40] The reason he feels compelled to read Grossman's book is this: between its lines (which are those of fundamentally radical evil), it traces a path that extirpates humanity from the endless spiral of murderous consent. It finds yet another testimony—at the margins of political and religious institutions, at the margins of one's engagement in a good cause, but one whose exclusive vision of the good is jeopardized by murder—to which he clings in his work as if to a life preserver: *the paradoxical testimony to the impossibility of killing*: "But we must listen. From one end to the other of that inhuman apocalypse, from out of its depths, there can be heard the muffled stirrings of a persistent, invincible humanity. The 'I' of men, forced by suffering back into the shackles of the self, breaks forth, in its misery, into mercy. . . . Through the inhuman, extraordinary promptings of mercy survive, from one human uniqueness to another, independently of, and as if in spite of, structures—political or ecclesiastic—in which they were always exhibited."[41]

In the novel, numerous passages intertwine the inhuman plot of intrigue with a countertestimony that, as in the scene cited above, accompanies or refines the "impossibility of killing" through the care enjoined by the mortality and vulnerability of others. The assistance that resists mortality and resists vulnerability—all forms of *medical assistance*—therefore resists human despair. Two mother figures, who mirror one another across the chapters separating them, illustrate such resistance. The first is Anna Semyonovna, the mother of one of the novel's main characters, the physicist Shtrum. Semyonovna writes Shtrum (Chapter 18) one last letter from behind the barbed wire of the Jewish ghetto, knowing that she is doomed. She relates, first and foremost, all the most abject forms of murderous consent: the "gloating spite" of those who rejoice at "the end of the Jews,"[42] the neighbor who takes advantage of the situation to throw her out of her own home, calling her an "outlaw," those who argue over who will acquire her possessions, and, finally, the people who vilify Jews in public rallies just to please the Germans. Inversely, however, there is her patient who comes to help her carry her belongings to the ghetto, prompting Semyonovna to confess that she "began to feel once more that I was a human being."[43] Particularly important are her visits to the sick, the ongoing treatments, and the promises of recovery, despite the certainty of death. Finally, there is what she reads in their eyes: "I'm used to looking into people's eyes for symptoms of diseases—glaucoma, cataract. Now I can no longer look at people's eyes like that; what I see now is the reflection of the soul. A good soul, Vityenka! A sad, good-natured soul, defeated by violence, but at the same time triumphant over violence. A strong soul, Vitya!"[44]

The second mother figure is Semyonovna's daughter-in-law, Lyudmila Nikolaevna. When Nikolaevna learns that her son is gravely injured, she travels a great distance to visit him in the hospital. Throughout her journey, she recites softly, over and over, the prayer that is said in all wars, past, present, and future (one need only change the name): "Don't let Tolya die!" Like Anna Semyonovna, over the course of her voyage she experiences irreconcilable feelings, of *sharing misfortune* and of indifference toward suffering, of the human and the inhuman, of compassion and brutality. On the one hand, there is that which transforms our relation to the fragility of others, our fears for the lives both of those closest to us and of those more removed, into collective individuation (the "we" of misfortune). There is, first, the care that is given, the speech that frees, the listening that comforts, and, with every passing encounter, the soothing transformation of a suffocating anxiety into a growing confidence. "She talked to a sick old woman about Marusya and Vera, and about her mother-in-law who had died in occupied territory. Her grief was the same grief that breathed on this deck, a grief that had always known the way from the military hospitals and graves of the front back to the huts of peasants, huts without numbers standing on patches of waste ground without a name."[45]

On the other hand, however, there is also the "inhuman behavior"[46] of the woman who throws the lost blind man to the ground as he tries to hold on to her, begging for help to get on a bus. There is the hatred for the man abandoned to helplessness and handicap, worn down and humiliated by the "merciless world of the sighted," and there is the way the sick person is treated by the healthy, the indigent by the privileged, the weakest by the closed world of those who are only slightly less impoverished. There is the weariness and the indifference of bystanders who have no time for and make no effort to help the blind man back up. What emerges from this misery that isolates us and directs us all toward the hopeless busyness of our own survival is the hostility of all these worlds that have been subjected to the hardening of the very lives that bear them: "It was as though everyone Lyudmila had gathered together, with hope and love, into one great family of labour, need, grief and kindness, had conspired to behave inhumanly. It was as though they had made an agreement to refute the view that one can always be sure of finding kindness in the hearts of people with dirty clothes and grimy hands. Something dark and agonizing touched Lyudmila, filling her with the cold and darkness of thousands of miles of desolate Russian steppe, with a feeling of helplessness amidst life's frozen wastes."[47]

Lyudmila arrives too late, however. Grossman shows her roaming the hallways of the hospital, meeting with the surgeons who operated on her son, the nurse who treated him and closed his eyes, and the staff sergeant who buried him. She feels the malaise of those who are faced with a death they could not prevent, the deafening torment of having failed to do what was needed, the weight of guilt that hangs over one's responsibility to assist, care, and provide treatment when one is foiled, when all one can do is grapple with the impossible mourning of loved ones. For all the men and women she meets, and who render an account of themselves, the ordeal is one of disruption—disruption of the comfort and assurance of their being-in-the-world. The ordeal causes a breach in their universe; it upends, rattles, and makes *their freedom* blameworthy. If, as Grossman says, the irreplaceable singularity of freedom is to bear, in one's own way, the universe, then freedom cannot be separated from the way that each of us experiences the death of the other, speaks to those whose death awaits or to loved ones who sense its arrival, to be present and attentive or to remain indifferent: "Everyone feels guilty before a mother who has lost her son in a war; throughout human history men have tried in vain to justify themselves."[48]

A close reading of these pages reveals that each of the characters who are exposed to Lyudmila Nikolaevna's mourning are prevented from enjoying and appropriating the world, however modestly and unsatisfactorily, by the mother's pain and their own memory of her son. This impossible mourning and the degree of suffering that it manifests subject them to an ordeal of radical alterity that perturbs the (*their*) "meaning [*sens*] of the world."

This prohibition, *ordeal*, or *mutation* is what Levinas repeatedly scrutinizes as the requirement for what he names ethics. And it brings us back to the question of murder. Often—and justifiably—we call Levinas the theorist of the "impossibility of killing." But he is just as much the philosopher of the double possibility of murder and its temptation. The essential point lies in the improbable articulation of these three terms (impossibility, possibility, and temptation). If it is true that the epiphany of the face of the other overturns the "power, by essence murderous of the other," and imposes, "'against all good sense,' the impossibility of murder," then we should remember that it is a question primarily of a becoming, a transformation, if not a victory.[49] When Anna Semyonovna and Lyudmila Nikolaevna walk through the streets of the ghetto or in Saratov, it is sometimes the "caricature" rather than the epiphany of the face that is given in their encounters. When the peasant from Ikonnikov's story recounts that she gave a murderous soldier something to drink, she knows not how or by what means she was able to suspend both her perception of his murderous power and her temptation to strangle him. But she does know that neither the power nor the temptation could be easily denied.

How are we to understand this articulation? Must we say, like Freud, that it follows from the tension and complementarity of an erotic drive that brings people together and a death drive that pushes them apart? Levinas goes down a different path completely. If murder is the attempt or the temptation of a "total negation" of the other, then these drives exist only on the basis of an underlying relationship. It is because the relation with the face of the other is completely other that it resists all appropriation, refuses all possession, and defies "my power of power" [*mon pouvoir de pouvoir*: my power to be able, my ability to be able, my ability to do]. In other words, *it is because the face expresses the impossibility of killing* that murder is possible. This is the paradox. The face of the other invites negotiation and signifies for me a relation that is irreducible to the power [*pouvoir*: power, ability] to know or enjoy, since her radical alterity and her infinite transcendence command, "You shall not kill," closing the door on all subjugation (as Grossman would say), yet opening the door to the possibility of absolute negation. How is this conceivable?

At issue is the indissociable connection of the face to its caricature. Regarding the first, we must recall that under the influence of some or other "thought" or affect (hate, anger, fear), it is always possible to construct an image or representation or idea (always finite) of the face. The idea substitutes for the face, taking hold of it and attacking it surreptitiously, masking the features, signs, and symptoms of the face in its "nudity." The face of the other is deformed by what we want to see (or show) in it, to remember and understand of it. But it does not cease to be a face. No caricature can prevail over its transcendence. The infinite that the face expresses is indestructible . . . *unless it is killed*. This is how the caricature is connected to, and may even be the first phase of, murderous consent. It accustoms us to see in the face of the other nothing more than a palpable appearance, susceptible to all sorts of distortions and interpretations. It inflicts features that can always lead to an *impossible* reduction, for faces resist such subjugation— however caricatured, the transcendence that they express remains fundamental [*première*], and hence unbearable, to murderers.

> The face at the limit of holiness and caricature is thus still in a sense exposed to powers. In a sense only: the depth that opens in this sensibility modifies the very nature of power, which henceforth can no longer take, but can kill. Murder still aims at a sensible datum, and yet it finds itself before a datum whose being cannot be suspended by an appropriation. . . . To kill is not to dominate but to annihilate; it is to renounce comprehension absolutely. Murder exercises a power over what escapes power. It is still a power, for the face expresses itself in the sensible, but already impotency, because the face rends the sensible. The alterity that is expressed in the face provides the unique "matter" possible for total negation. I can wish to kill only an existent absolutely independent, which exceeds my powers infinitely, and therefore does not oppose them but paralyzes the very power of power. The Other is the sole being I can wish to kill.[50]

Sometimes "caricature" entails dissolving the other into the threat that it is supposed to represent. It is a favorite recourse in the "culture of the enemy," which paves the way for all sorts of murderous consent. The caricature attaches itself to names, diminutives, and epithets that engender an idiom of hate.[51] But the names, insults, and affronts are never enough. They commit the people who utter them to spiral in their own powerlessness to make the infinite finite. This is why transcendence, in Levinas's thought, is consonant with freedom, an equation that Grossman treats as an act of faith. The weak and limited meaning [*sens*] of the caricature and other murderous characterizations, as vain as they are formidable, echoes the judgment found in *Life and Fate*: "everything inhuman is senseless and useless."

And yet, caricatures can be effective when it comes to promoting the acceptance, justification, spread, and generalization of murder as one turns hatred into a shared feeling. A particularly bitter passage of *Everything Flows* relates the reprehensible story that Anna Sergeyevna tells Ivan Grigoryev-ich concerning her active participation in the "dekulakization" of the early 1930s, prelude to the great famine. She recounts the groundwork provided by propaganda, the slow penetration of names and injurious epithets into the marrow of cognition; in other words, the construction of a collective representation—kulaks—whose only object was to efface the singularity of their lives, fusing them into a common representation, into a material malleable and appropriate for tyranny's violence, so as better to destroy them:

> Everything about the kulaks was vile—they were vile in themselves, and they had no souls, and they stank, and they were full of sexual diseases, and worst of all, they were enemies of the people and ex-ploiters of the labor of others. . . . All these words had their effect on me too. I was only a girl—and during meetings and special briefings, from films, books, articles, and radio broadcasts, from Stalin him-self, I kept hearing one and the same thing: that kulaks are parasites, that kulaks burn bread and murder children. The fury of the masses had to be ignited against them—yes, those were the words; it was proclaimed that the kulaks must be destroyed as a class, every ac-cursed one of them . . . I too began to fall under this spell. It seemed that every misfortune was because of the kulaks; if we were to an-nihilate them immediately, then happy days would dawn for us all. No mercy was to be shown to the kulaks. They were not even human beings; goodness knows what they were—some kind of beasts, I sup-pose. And so I became an activist.[52]

To be an "activist" meant at least three things as regards the perception of the "kulaks"—three things that constitute, in truth, the common de-nominator of all discrimination and persecution, wherever they have been (and still are) produced in the world. First, it meant that, by the power of naming and designating, the victims were dissolved into and equated with their representation—they were captured in a few words and a few features, of which every activist was obliged to become a zealous publicist. This im-plies, second, that, in the frantic course of collective passion, the various elements that composed the caricature incorporated a dimension of threat. Every "culture of the enemy," as we have seen, rests on a "culture of fear." The face of the peasant, the neighbor, or yesterday's guest could be dis-torted into a "kulak" only when it was regarded or perceived no longer as itself but rather as hostile to the well-being of all, as a real nuisance—*as if the possibility of murder first came from the victim.* And yet, third, the face was basic [*primaire*]—and as long as it was present, in its own singularity, before the eyes of the activist, it discredited the caricatures. Because the infinite freedom expressed by the face was irreducible to the violence that was attached to it, *it offered resistance*—it opposed the efforts to destroy it with a force that spurs Grossman to write, "everything inhuman is sense-less and useless." In the final analysis, the murderous brigades pushed back against this "resistance" (of the eyes and the gaze). It provided (it was), for-ever, the reason for escalation, both verbal and physical. Such resistance explains why *regardless of culture*, still today, there is no limit to the rage of propagandists when they call for murder. The moment that their victim's face reminds terror's bureaucrats and their subordinates that killing is im-possible, the moment that the face imposes its transcendence as an obsta-cle to their reductions, they must steel themselves against the injunction not to kill—to *eclipse*, in other words, the responsibility that is *still* evoked by the vulnerability and the mortality of the other.

Levinas shows over and over again that if ethics conserves a meaning, it is entirely due to the way that we confront this test of the persistence and resistance of the face, the irreducibility of a core transcendence and freedom, in which opens up an inappropriable world and which is always offered singularly. From this perspective, it is not by chance that Levinas discovers in Grossman's book a substantiation of his own investigations into the impossibility of killing, though his core ideas were already consigned to paper. But this impossibility does not efface the possibility of or the temptation to murder, any more than it prevents me from perceiving others as a (as *my*) potential murderer. It lives-with one and the other—haunted by the certitude (where are concentrated the memories of past wars and the apprehension of future conflicts) that "the other is the only being that we can be tempted to kill."[53] This spectrality of murder is conveyed, first of all, by the memory of all the victims of war in the last century, both civilian and military. And we cannot dismiss this spectrality as long as the fear of death reemerges and perdures in some form or other.

In other words, we would risk missing a crucial point if we forgot that the temptation to murder is indissociable from its impossibility—if we re-fused to recognize more explicitly that they cohabit in the vision of the face to the extent that the face is always liable to become (or be turned into) a mask or grimace. The face remains inviolable only as long as it proffers itself in its nudity—that is, without protection—unadorned and unarmed. Real or fictitious, weapons blind us. When we perceive or imagine the face as armed, we see no longer the face but the weapon, just as happens with words when, instead of offering up the world, they become lost in shouts, commands, and insults. There is no getting outside ourselves in these conditions. There is no experience of the infinite—only gestures, attitudes, and speech that drive us back into the selfish and constraining sensation of the fragility of our own existence. This is why Levinas writes, in one of the first texts of *Difficult Freedom*, entitled "Ethics and Spirit" (1952), that the "impossibility of killing is not real, but moral":

> [The] vision of the face in which the "You shall not kill" is articulated does not allow itself to fall back into an ensuing complacency or become the experience of an insuperable obstacle, offering itself up to our power. For in reality, murder is possible, but it is possible only when one has not looked the Other in the face. The impossibility of killing is not real, but moral. The fact that the vision of the face is not an *experience*, but a moving out of oneself, a contact with another being and not simply a sensation of self, is attested to by the "purely moral" character of this impossibility. A moral view [*regard*] measures, in the face, the uncrossable infinite in which all murderous intent is immersed and submerged. This is precisely why it leads us away from any experience or view [*regard*]. The infinite is given only to the moral view [*regard*]: it is not *known*, but is in *society* with us.[54]

His analysis affects how we understand what we are trying to grasp under the term "murderous consent" by making two essential points. First, murderous consent is always about accepting compromises, at least in the beginning, if not accepting the outright impossibility of what Levinas calls a "moral gaze" [*regard moral*], which is always more than a simple gaze [*simple regard*]. When we *consent* to murder, whether actively or passively (though passivity is always more active than we think), we proceed voluntarily to delete the face. We let the effective possibility of murder override its moral impossibility. We help crime chart a course with the help of "ordinary" suspicions, bullying, vexations, a tolerance for humiliation, and the encouragement of persecution, abandonment, indifference, and forgetting. We allow crime to exercise power over "what escapes power," which is the infinite.[55] Ultimately, we subscribe to *the eclipse of this same infinite*.

The second point follows the first. Suppose, as I have tried to show, that all murderous consent divides or fractures being-in-the-world, that it opens a breach or inscribes a rift in the "worldization" [*mondialisation*] of the world. We can only conclude that this fracture, breach, or rift is not without some relation to the eclipse of the infinite. The abyss opened in being-in-the-world by our every consent to the infringements on and exceptions to our responsibility, as enjoined by the vulnerability and mortality of the other, proceeds from a *temporary and selective* obfuscation of the infinite. What the image of the *eclipse* is telling us is that the denial of responsibility never applies to everyone and never applies permanently. No one can definitively evade the epiphany of the other in the face. Even the cruelest, most ruthless executioner, in his spare time and in his circle of friends and family, can manifest the attention, care, and assistance that he denies his victims. It is this ambivalence that is the stuff of terror, lies, and servitude. This is why a single eclipse, a single exception of this kind, is enough to engender a world in which there subsists only the absence of meaning [*sens*].

Levinas writes that the infinite is "in *society* with us." We share it among ourselves. It is an object of "exchange" ["*commerce*"]—which is not to say that it lends itself to calculation. From what precedes, we see that the challenge is to know to whom this *us* refers and, furthermore, how this "society" manifests itself and how far it extends. And since the infinite assumes infinite responsibility, how can we dispute the (geographic, geopolitical, civilizational, religious, and other) limits that power places on its extension? Or rather, how do we conceptualize the "society of the infinite" without running up against borders that ipso facto empty it of any possible meaning?

"To See the Face Is to Speak of the World"

Levinas summarizes the proposal and ambition of *Totality and Infinity* in that work's first pages: "The effort of this book is directed toward apperceiving in discourse a non-allergic relation with alterity, toward apperceiving Desire—where power, by essence murderous of the other, becomes, faced with the other and 'against all good sense,' the impossibility of murder, the consideration of the other, or justice."[56] "Against all good sense!" We recall that Mostovskoy came to this same verdict when he called "senseless" the "babbling" of Ikonnikov," the "feeble spirit" who made his confession to him, when Ikonnikov sought to oppose the violence of history with "everyday human kindness"—"an unwitnessed kindness," "a kindness outside any system of social or religious good."[57] For Ikonnikov, the source of history's violence is the cruelty of fate that disposes the aspiration for good to sow the seeds of misfortune and turn destructive as soon as it tries to transform the world. This is the origin of violence: there is no idea of the good that will not put its universal calling at the beck and call of some particular interest and, in so doing, wind up confusing the transformation of the world with its "appropriation." No political doctrine, no religion, eludes the law of this reversal. The consequences are terrible: the desire to impose on the world some particular vision of the good can never be pursued and never be accomplished (this is its law) without "shedding the blood of old people and children":[58]

> This doctrine caused more suffering than all the crimes of the people who did evil for its own sake. . . . In great hearts the cruelty of life gives birth to good; they then seek to carry this good back into life, hoping to make life itself accord with their inner image of good. But life never changes to accord with an image of good; instead it is the image of good that sinks into the mire of life—to lose its universality, to split into fragments and be exploited by the needs of the day.[59]

From *the contamination of the world* by violence as good turns against itself there arises an ambiguity that weighs upon the *idea of the world* as such. This takes us back to my initial question, but in a new form: "Is there any possibility of making the world habitable [*habitable*]?" Can we conceptualize and speak of such a world without radically revising the meaning that we generally accord to the word "inhabit" [*habiter*]? In other words, is there any possibility that the world might signify something other than the divided and bruised object of conquest and appropriation? Such unease regarding the meaning of the world is inscribed on the front cover of *Totality and Infinity*.[60] What, in fact, is the world? It is, to start with, nothing more, but nothing less, than the place where the I finds the means to secure its autochthony—its "abode" or "house," with which it identifies (because it is at home) and where it exercises its power.[61] If we assume that the world confronts the I with some degree of alterity or strangeness, it is rapidly overcome—that is, it is reduced to one and the same. The world is what "offers itself to or resists possession."[62] The paradox therefore is this: if the task and the concern of "inhabiting" refer back to this autochthony, their only effect is to exacerbate the struggle to ensure, extend, and protect this same inhabiting by means (appropriations, expropriations, extortions, expulsions, exclusions, etc.) that generally have the effect of making the world *uninhabitable*. The various forms of murderous consent that populate the history of this *possession*, whatever they might be, always bring us back to this paradox. When the forces implied by possession go to the trouble of searching for a justification, they always look for it in their *right* to organize as they wish the world as habitat. The other never emerges as anything but a potential rival or enemy.

Is this the last word regarding the "meaning of the world"? Levinas's whole project in *Totality and Infinity* is to find a way to prove the contrary. Doing so entails the possibility of a turning back (the reversal of the reversal) [*un revirement (le retournement du retournement)*] that restores to the world its radical alterity. This supposes, at the very least, that the world is no longer reduced to the privileged but competitive (thus belligerent and murderous) instrument for expanding the I. But how could the world be *given* otherwise? First and foremost, *by offering itself to others.* If goodness has a meaning, it is found in this offer or gift. Is such an offer or gift even *possible?* Levinas replies in the opening pages of his book:

> Desire and goodness concretely presuppose a relationship in which the Desirable arrests the "negativity" of the I that holds sway in the Same—puts an end to power and emprise. This is positively produced as the possession of a world I can bestow as a gift on the Other—that is, as a presence before a face. For the presence before a face, my orientation toward the Other, can lose the avidity proper to the gaze only by turning into generosity, incapable of approaching the other with empty hands. This relationship established over the things henceforth possibly common, that is, susceptible of being said, is the relationship of conversation.[63]

In our reading of Camus, we already discovered the extent to which language provides resources with which to radically oppose murderous consent. More specifically, Camus reminds us that all consent of this order assumes an abdication, if not an abandonment, of language—assuming language has not already been contorted into a weapon of destruction. In *Totality and Infinity*, the question of murder and that of language (as well as discourse) are indissociable. It is because I share the world with others through the words that I address to them that "power, by essence murderous of the other, becomes, [where] faced with the other and 'against all good sense,' the impossibility of murder, the consideration of the other, or justice."[64] The epiphany of the face cannot manifest itself in the mute and distant contemplation of its transcendence. We must always be concerned that such an attitude might be confused with the "aestheticization of the other" ("sacralization" or "idealization") and turn all too quickly into an aversion. The epiphany, on the contrary, supposes exchange. Levinas writes over and over again that it cannot occur "outside the world." In other terms, the epiphany places the possession of this same world in question only to the extent that, through language, it offers the world to others.

The profound intention of language is therefore ethical. It is the condition of possibility of an exchange and thus of the epiphany of the face. But, as we will see below, it is also the reason that there is no murderous consent that does not assume the manipulation of language—in other words, that does not suspend (we do not speak to victims; we confront them with threatening silence) or wrench language from its purpose or its fundamental vocation (by the force of a cry, an injury, or an appeal to murder).[65]

And if our attention to the vulnerability and the mortality of others, and the care and assistance that vulnerability and mortality demand, assume an "offering of the world" through language, then it is truly this *offering* that violence, when it is substituted for speech, interrupts. This is why "to see the face is to speak of the world."[66] The epiphany of the face subjects us to the law of an exchange such that the words that are spoken in recognition of it [*lui rendent droit*] also—at each and every instant—reveal the limits of our own power. *To speak* of the world is not to reap the benefits of my knowledge of it singularly. Nor is it to use such knowledge to assert my own worth—it is to give the world as *shared*. In other words, being in the world does not mean possessing it but, rather, sharing it.

But the epiphany of the face is not just an invitation to speak of the world; it is also a call to responsibility. The moment the other invites me to speak of the world, it entrusts me with its vulnerability and mortality. The other proclaims them to be a constitutive dimension of the *sociality* that we share. Whoever makes an offering of the world does so in defiance of arms (one's own and *all other* arms) to the extent that the vulnerability and mortality of the other are imposed upon him. If this offering *produces* the idea of the infinite, it also produces the responsibility that is entailed by the specter of violence. The exchange that affirms the impossibility of murder remains haunted by the possibility of evil, of wounds, and of assaults that can do harm to him whom the face *introduces* into the world. For if, in this exchange, the I were to mischaracterize, ignore, or neglect such possibilities, closing his eyes and plugging his ears, then he would condemn the exchange to indifference and selfishness. As commonplace as they may be, such evils are recalled by everyday greetings, in many languages: "Comment ça va?" "Wie geht es dir?" "How are you?" When we are short on words that express worry or inquire about the lives of others, we know that what is missing in the relationship is an opening onto the infinite. The solicitude being expressed necessarily refers us back to the transcendence of the other, whereas certitude—the claim to know everything or know enough or not be concerned—declines to undertake this examination. This is to say that the "impossibility of killing"—along with the attention, care, and assistance that acknowledge this impossibility—must inhabit all speaking of the world, like its shadow, in a manner worthy of this sociality.

But what is this speech, and what does it say? The world that speaks belongs to no one—and certainly not to the person who says it does. If "to see the face" and "to speak of the world" are one and the same, it is because the world that is being offered in speech, always singularly, is commensurate with the irreducibility of the face, singularly—it yields, it submits to the injunction of its uniqueness [*unicité*]. The world opened by speech, in exchange [*commerce*], is always *received* from the other. This is why, inversely, murder and all the forms of consent that accompany it always imply a *nonreception* [*sont toujours des fins de* non-recevoir; "dead on arrival"]. Murderous violence wants to hear nothing about the world of others and has nothing to say about it. Its existence is so minimal in the eyes of the murderer that execution is only the completion, the ultimate confirmation, of a destruction that took place long before. In the dungeons of Lubyanka, in the torture chambers and interrogation rooms of all regimes, the verdict preempts the execution over and over again. Execution is already inscribed in the privation of freedom that relies not so much on imprisonment, or the privation of space, as it does on the negation of the world. Executioners never talk about the world. On the contrary, they signify, over and over again, to their victims: "You are nothing to me!" "Your world does not exist!" "There is no world in you—or for you!"

At the end of *Life and Fate*, Shtrum and his friend Chepyzhin, both learned men, are reunited in a troubling conversation about freedom, life, and the world. Chepyzhin enthusiastically relates to Shtrum his new conviction that freedom is the great principle governing the organization of all life and that the entire evolution of the living world follows an upward movement, from a little bit of freedom to greater and greater freedom, eventually enabling humanity to master the universe. But Shtrum expresses reservations regarding the Promethean vision of humanity that undergirds such confidence. A few questions suffice to send the whole experience of Grossman's book—and, with it, the experience of war in the twentieth century—spiraling into cross-examination:

> You say life is freedom. Is that what people in the camps think? What if the life expanding through the universe should use its power to create a slavery still more terrible than your slavery of inanimate matter? Do you think this man of the future will surpass Christ in his goodness? That's the real question. How will the power of this omnipresent and omniscient being benefit the world if he is still endowed with our own fatuous self-assurance and animal egotism? Our class egotism, our race egotism, our State egotism and our personal egotism?[67]

Does this mean that the essence of life is not freedom? We saw above that this would not be Grossman's response. Rather, it means that life and freedom matter less than the idea of the world implied by such thinking. Chepyzhin's doctrine of freedom proposes and announces a world that is neither more nor less than the corollary [*corollaire*] of the power of some demiurge [*puissance démiurgique*], exploited by humanity to transform matter into energy so as to produce living matter. As doctrine it wagers that such a transformation will serve life, understood as freedom: "The universe will come to life. Everything in the world will become alive and thus free. Freedom—life itself—will overcome slavery."[68] But Shtrum objects that this vision, however brilliant, is not compatible with human imperfection—that the world it promises will not bring about the "evolution of kindness, morality, mercy."[69] It is no coincidence that, at this time, the reality of the concentration camps, to which the entire novel bears witness, supports Shtrum's objection. Cut off from the world, the camps introduce a rift in the optimistic vision of a *world to come* that, regardless of what Chepyzhin says, cannot make sense [*faire sens*], not as long as some singular life believes its *right to the world*—that is, its freedom—is being contested. This is what the voices whisper as they rise from the cold night of the camps: the world cannot exist otherwise than as intensive extension. It holds together—this is the lesson of *Life and Fate* and perhaps of Varlam Shalamov's *The Kolyma Tales* as well—only if it extends the universe that each and every life expresses intensively and singularly, through speech, from one person to another. And, in the face of and against all threats of violence, it is fruitful only to the extent, forever tenuous, that it sustains itself as a sharing of singularities.

In a 1956 text entitled "On the Spirit of Geneva," later reprised in *Unforeseen History*, Levinas had already tied the possibility of murder to the *meaning* [*sens*] of *the world*: "All that satisfies us and all that kills us come from our fellow man, their generous or bad will that triggers disasters if only by failing to foresee them. The certainty that our misfortunes come from our neighbors, that there is responsibility for everything, the right to accuse and judge—perhaps this is civilization. A world that has sense."[70] Lucidly, and concurrently with Günther Anders,[71] he scrutinizes the implications of nuclear weapons, which pose a threat to the world that is incommensurate with traditional political conflicts. Though their architects are human, their force is superhuman. They surpass the capacity of humanity, if it stays locked in its habitual political struggles, to control them. Nuclear weapons thus demand that humanity transcend the bounds of egoist, sovereign, nation-state politics. In other words, they demand a *new* consciousness of the world [*une* autre *conscience du monde*], which Levinas does not hesitate to call (here is the word that is important for us) a "cosmopolitics." Because the dangers with which it is concerned are of a cosmic order, it is, first of all, a physics [*physique*] of that order. Its foundation is in the certainty that, henceforward, people can physically destroy the totality of what surrounds us, and themselves along with it. The solidarity and fraternity that distinguish the "Spirit of Geneva" are a response to a "care for the world" that is primarily concerned with nature's ability to turn on itself—that is, to turn on life—according to the will of people. But the fear that undergirds this spirit does not ground a moral responsibility. It challenges only superficially the power calculations of states. The strong and the wicked take delight in agreements that focus on the physical to the detriment of the moral, as Levinas pointedly observes. This kind of cosmopolitics is ambivalent. Its ambiguity is expressed in the smiles of those who discuss and decide, from their summits, the future of the world. Levinas concludes: "This broad, stiff, stereotyped smile is troubled. Men still don't know which is better: to lean on the columns of the temple of the unjust and take the risk of 'dying with the Philistines' or to think of the innocent who will be buried in the ruins."[72] "To think of the innocent" is to submit thought and the "organization of the world" to care for the vulnerability and mortality of others. This is why the possibility of overcoming the trouble that shows through this smile depends on a world *otherwise* [*du monde* autrement]. Such a world, against all murderous calculation, is opened up by the double test of the infinite that is responsibility toward life (the life of others), a responsibility that is conceived of as an intensive, as well as extensive, freedom, and not as an exclusive one.

We must take up one last text: the four painful pages of extreme intensity in "Nameless," where, in 1966, Levinas returns to the experience of the concentration camp. He reminds us first in an introductory way (to better inform those who have a tendency to forget) that "bloodshed has not ceased" since the end of the Second World War and that "racism, imperialism, and exploitation remain ruthless in our day."[73] But he then specifies that, unlike yesterday's victims, for whom nothing evoked the possibility of a livable world and who therefore died in the camps feeling that *the world itself had collapsed*, today's victims know that *the world endures*, even if it seems to have abandoned them. A demand for justice persists. Voices are raised to make it heard. Institutions and associations try to secure it, even as antagonistic forces remain very active. How can we use this "tumor in the memory," this "gaping pit," which is the spectral memory of the concentration camp, to serve those who today have been forgotten and who continue to die *alone in the world* and in despair?[74] We can do so by reminding our contemporaries, especially those who would rather be free of their vertigo, of "three truths."

The first truth, Levinas emphasizes, is the fragility and the very relative nature of the "achievements (or goods) of civilization." "To live humanely" was possible *otherwise*, despite and contrary to the disappearance of everything that ordinarily grounds our belonging to the world. Because life no longer had access to the peaceful enjoyment of such goods, life bore witness, under constraint, to the fact that it was no longer shackled to the comfort and security with which the executioners identified it. Thus, life resisted the "dehumanization" that they had contrived and administered. But to this first "truth" (confirmed by so many witnesses), we must quickly add a second: where war imposes its law, where "human security" is entirely absent, where life is rendered extremely fragile, and where we can no longer count on anything, our highest responsibility (embodied in all forms of resistance) is to believe, despite the violence, in the possibility that peace shall return—and to work, by virtue of that belief, to make possible the impossible. Inversely, we could say, murderous consent always begins when the decree that something is impossible becomes an excuse for abandoning people to the triumph of misery, murder, war, and all other forms of destruction.

The third "truth" is the keystone that holds up the edifice as a whole: the world cannot hold (and we cannot hold on to it) without the resources of what Levinas resolves, in "Nameless," contrary to all "objectivism" and all "realism," to name "interior life." But what kind of life *can* this be? Not the life of sanctimonious or revolutionary thought. What should have taken a stand against the disintegration of the world (and *must* still take a stand against it), Levinas tells us, is that which resisted (and still resists) chaos, which was (and still is) "the obligation to lodge the whole of humankind in the shelter—exposed to all the winds—of conscience."[75] Here, all the threads come together, so much so that, from book to book, it is this obligation that unremittingly stalks the author who dedicated *Otherwise than Being; or, Beyond Essence* "to the memory of those who were closest among the six million assassinated by the National Socialists, and of the millions on millions of all confessions and all nations, victims of the same hatred of the other man, the same anti-Semitism."[76] The "humanity" that is its object is twofold. It is, first, the humanity of each of us, which we feel, in all perilous situations, as an extension and augmentation of our responsibility. It is, second, the humanity of every vulnerable and mortal other who, in peril, begs for assistance. The image of shelter [*cabane*] expresses well the fragility of what takes a stand against the tempests of history and the disaster of the world when they sweep individuals away like straw. It is essential that, instead of walling ourselves up in a fortress, the shelter remain open to all those whom the winds carry its way.

4

Truth

Optimist: Are you then in a position to establish a tangible connection between language and the war?

Grumbler: Yes: those who speak a language that is the most congealed into set phrases and stock terminology have the tendency and the readiness to find, in accents of conviction, blameless in themselves everything that they find blameworthy in others.

—**Karl Kraus,** *The Last Days of Mankind*

"Natural" catastrophes (tsunamis, earthquakes, volcanic eruptions), unlike war (or perhaps famine), never fail to spark the media's admiration for the surge of solidarity, embracing the entire international community, that they engender. It is as if something of the *unity of the world* is being restored and revealed in the aid that "*other* peoples" or their "representatives" bring to the victims whose bodies have been injured or whose lives have been destroyed. This "something," which the normal course of events tends to efface, is the feeling of belonging to the world, a "being-in-the-world" that discovers its amorphous foundations in the renewed awareness that, beyond all differences of culture and religion, a *shared vulnerability* binds us all to one another. Vulnerability, understood as a "can-be-injured" [*pouvoir-être-blessé*], in our own lives as in the lives of those close to us (that is, in the affective, moral, and political relations that compose the fabric of our lives), is an inescapable dimension of human existence. It constitutes the foundation of the *living-with* that defines life with others, individually, and that, therefore, in times of catastrophe, knows no (or almost no) frontiers.

But not all causes of violence are natural. Famine, misery, war, deadly assaults, and political oppression also figure among the sources of, and among the reasons for, human insecurity and vulnerability. Vulnerability and insecurity thus have the effect of increasing, extending, and "universalizing" our interdependence. Our exposure to being attacked *from anywhere* "worldizes" [*mondialise*, "globalizes"] the world. It is this exposure that makes our world a shared world. If *everything* can increase the fragility of life, then *nothing* that happens in the world can be met with indifference, as shown by the growing importance assumed in our century by the threat of terrorism, the risk of nuclear proliferation, and, in a different domain, the production of greenhouse gases and global warming. All these phenomena make their presence known to us through the rumors, the hearsay, and the echoes of the world, but more specifically, through the images and the discourses that are made available to *us* or inflicted on *us*. If it is true, as is said now and then, that these three phenomena—terrorism, nuclear proliferation, and climate change—weave the fabric, torn and conflictual, of a shared involvement and a shared belonging to the world, the "with" of living-with (expressed by the word "shared") ultimately derives its meaning from our *sharing* in vulnerability.

The Geographies of Vulnerability

And yet nothing is less apparent or more ignored, and even denied, than this *sharing*. We must keep two things in mind. First, the universality of our vulnerability, however inescapable in a globalized world, is infinitely variable. It is, stated otherwise, unequally distributed. Judith Butler evoked this inequality following the attacks of September 11, 2001, when she pressed her fellow citizens, justifiably traumatized by the aggression, not to be blinded to the multiple forms of insecurity that beleaguer other populations and other peoples around the world: "What this means, concretely, will vary across the globe. There are ways of distributing vulnerability, differential forms of allocation that make some populations more subject to arbitrary violence than others. But in that order of things, it would not be possible to maintain that the US has greater security problems than some of the more contested and vulnerable nations and peoples of the world."[1]

Second, there is in this sense a *geography* of vulnerability, a mapping of which overlaps that of famine, misery, war, epidemics, political violence, or oppression. There can be no disputing that the inscription of frontiers that separate wealth from poverty, hunger from opulence, access to care from scarcity of care, instruction from illiteracy, and "democracy" from dictatorship and authoritarianism ground the "reality" of our world. They fracture and partition it. They inscribe a yawning chasm at the heart of our being-in-the-world. That chasm is ultimately engendered by our consent to inequality and injustice. But it is also true that we can never access this geography objectively, no matter how present it might be in the news, both print and televised. Our access is filtered in a variety of ways, which we must decipher, that prioritize some or other form of fragility or some or other factor of insecurity. There is never *one and only one* geography that keeps "us" *all* informed. How do we explain this variety? How are the various groupings of peoples composed by such a geography? Are they composed of citizens of the same nation? By men and women bound by the same feeling of affiliation, by shared ideals, religion, or culture, or by a common history?

This is the question. It ties the problem of responsibility, which the vulnerability and the mortality of the other should invoke *everywhere* and *for everyone*, to the question of truth. In our life with others, vulnerability and mortality plead for attention, care, and aid, as recalled and exemplified by so many of the world's nongovernmental organizations. And yet, what constantly happens (and therefore constitutes another inescapable dimension of our existence) is exactly the opposite. We have only a *variable, partial,* and *selective* perception of the fragility of others, of their suffering, and of the forms of insecurity to which they are exposed. Indeed, in some cases the last thing we want to understand or accept is how people are *more* or *differently* [*autrement*] vulnerable because of their (cultural, religious, or other) affiliation.

What we call, confusedly, the "diversity of cultures" is not foreign to this perceptual *variation* and its *discriminatory* nature. But it would be wrong to consider the delineation of such variability by some or other circle of belonging as a fact. It would be hasty and rash to think that we are predestined to be more attentive to the fragility and wounds of those with whom we "recognize" a common "identity" and to ignore the fragility and wounds of others.[2] Such a hypothesis would in fact endorse the American political scientist Samuel Huntington's hypothesis of a "clash of civilizations," which asserts that our cultural community predetermines the sentiments of friendship and hostility that we feel toward others by virtue of our belonging and by virtue of the identity that we confer on these others. Reality is obviously more complicated. It will not be constrained by essentialist determinations. We cannot neglect the political and ideological reasons and motivations that preside over the production of this variation. Political, economic, military, and industrial forces, and their backers in the media, all contribute to this variegated perception of the vulnerability of others. Because of this (and because of the fact that nothing divides or fractures the world more profoundly than the denial of responsibility that this variegated perception signifies), our differences of perception, appreciation, and recognition elicit questions about truth and falsehood rather than about nature and essence. For this reason, we must speak of "geographies of vulnerability" *in the plural*. The word "plural" refers not so much to the diversity of cultures as it does to the combination of intellectual and aesthetic operations, the rhetoric, and the framing of images that preside over their production.

Before analyzing these operations, we should recall that these geographies, because they are, more often than not, tied to war and conflict in which the boundaries they demarcate are implicated, are never simply the product of our individual imaginations. They are part of a strategy that is indispensable to the establishment and propagation of a "culture of the enemy" and that is indissociable from the exercise of sovereignty. The presentation of "victims," the display of suffering, and the narrative of ("heroic" and "barbaric") acts are all *produced* under supervision. They are published and broadcast so as to compose an "official truth," if not a "state truth," which upholds the *raison d'état* that no country at war can escape. The "truth" that puts some aggressions on display and condemns others to oblivion determines which wounds cannot possibly receive too much attention from the "public's" eyes and ears and which wounds are more appropriately ignored. The question of truth, in other words, comes up forcefully in those recurring situations in which there is a distortion between, on the one hand, the unequal globalization of vulnerability and, on the other hand, the calculations, pretensions, and partial and partisan interpretations of inequality, in the name of some or other prerogative or in defense of sovereign interests.

The globalization of the world therefore displays two faces, each in tension with the other, as aggressions and wounds vie for attention. It always produces the same sudden or calculated irruption of what I have been describing, following Camus, as "murderous consent," that is, the resigned acceptance or encouragement or promotion of the violent death of some grouping or other of individuals, however defined. If we wish to conceptualize *the world otherwise*, then we see that we cannot do so without critical, perhaps "deconstructive" analysis of the *pseudotruths* that make us believe, as members of a people or a community, that wounds and deaths are valued differently according to which side of some constructed, discursive, imaginary, visual, or televisual line of separation they occur on. There is always censorship. "Geographies of vulnerability" are the cultural and political product of what we are not allowed to show, say, explain, or simply interrogate. They are the product of efforts to influence opinion regarding both what we should and what we should not notice.

In her analysis of the trauma provoked by the events of September 11, 2001, Judith Butler reminds us of the near consensus that trauma produced, both in the media and in public opinion, regarding what was possible, decent, legitimate, or admissible to ask, and what, on the contrary, by the simple fact of asking it, was considered an intolerable justification of the attacks and an insult to the memory of their victims. Critical interrogation of America's foreign policy, Butler recalls, elicited suspicion that one was exonerating the aggression. All subsequent criticisms of America's war effort were rebuked for minimizing both the injury that was suffered and the imminence of the peril (that is, of vulnerability). Two camps, convinced that they possessed the truth regarding the state of the world, both accused one another of "murderous consent" and divided American public opinion *very unequally*. Critics of American policy were accused of "consenting," after a fashion, to the murderous attacks on New York and Washington, D.C. They tried in vain to convince the apologists of American policy not to be oblivious and detached, blind and deaf, to the suffering that that policy—even in its response to "terrorist threats"—was inflicting on the world. "The cry that 'there is no excuse for September 11' has become a means by which to stifle any serious public discussion of how US foreign policy has helped to create a world in which such acts of terror are possible."[3] In times of war (and, from this perspective, war might well be permanent), the censorship imposed by the state, relayed by the media, foisted *on* but also *through* public opinion, is complicit in the lopsided perception that we construct of the vulnerability of others. This is all the more the case when censorship is denied by those who practice it, yet denounced when it is practiced by the enemy or adversary. Inaccurate news, fabricated images, distorted words, and outright lies are attributed to others. It is they who truncate and distort the truth—so as to appear in the eyes of the world as the "victim" and to minimize and obfuscate the violence of their own actions. All conflicts are thus accompanied by wars of words and images in which the stakes are always the same: to impose a biased perception of what separates truth from falsehood regarding the aggressions that are suffered, the murders, and the violations of just war norms and international conventions. Such is the (military-political-media) law of war today, just as it was yesterday, at the beginning of the twentieth century, in August 1914.

The great Viennese polemicist Karl Kraus is unequaled in his grasp of the ways in which war frees itself from any and all relation to truth and how it mobilizes words as weapons to evoke the opposite of what they signify. He denounced that mobilization tirelessly, a century earlier than Judith Butler, as he witnessed the conscription, and even the degrading collaboration, of the great literary figures of his time in the flood of blood and fire that surged across Europe. By 1915 Kraus and his satirical journal *Die Fackel* (The torch) were swimming against the tide of public opinion— the journalists and politicians of his day were his bête noire (and they returned the courtesy). He embarked on the long task of writing a rambling drama entitled *The Last Days of Mankind* (completed only in 1918). In the course of the play's five acts, each composed of more than forty scenes—"whose scope of time by earthly measure would comprise about ten evenings"—we hear the voices that rose to support the war and that mingled together from day to day: voices of journalists first of all, but also of politicians, military officers, aristocrats, onlookers, and war profiteers.[4] Because Kraus never stopped denouncing the recourse to a corrupted language, bereft of rigor and formal standards, complacent and compromised, composed of words and phrases devoid of meaning, he wove the saber-rattling rhetoric that he overheard, the supposedly enlightened commentary, the street conversation, the table talk, the bar prattle—along with the little compromises that such language strikes with the principles of logic and the formal requirements of truth—into the fabric of his drama.[5] He treated the effects of language like an x-ray of public opinion, or like a snapshot, repeated annually, of all the sedimenting justifications of violence that war instigated, the stylistic tropes, the sophistry, and the ways of seeing and speaking that habituate a society to the kind of distribution of vulnerability that is required by a "culture of the enemy." As we read the hundreds of tableaux that make this drama (or farce) a gallery of the grotesque, we are tempted to smile and even laugh (as we should) at the humor that escapes from all these little linguistic compromises and that give such force to Kraus's writing. But we stop laughing when we realize that we are reading a meticulous "account" of the linguistic processes that accompany and perhaps foster all war. These processes, which we hear thanks to Kraus's characters, have never, mutatis mutandis, been silenced. It is not difficult to apply the words of Kraus's brief preface to wars other than the one that preoccupied him:

> The action, leading into a hundred scenes and hells, is impossible, fissured, and hero-less, just as that other action was. The humor is but the self-reproach of one who did not go mad at the thought of having witnessed and yet survived the events of this time with his mind intact. Except for him who reveals to posterity the shame of such sharing, no one has a right to this humor. The present generation, which permitted the things recorded here to happen, should place the obligation to weep before the right to laugh. The most improbable deeds reported here really happened. The most improbable conversations that are carried on here were spoken word for word. The most glaring inventions are quotations.[6]

Kraus's characters, ridiculous and/or sorrowful, compromised and/or consenting, do not resist the judgment of history for very long. I will call to mind the voices of these characters throughout this chapter to remind us how our relationship with language nurtures murderous consent.

The first thing they make apparent is the bifurcation of the question of language—a bifurcation that Kraus ceaselessly mocks and exploits as a rich reservoir of irony. The relationship with language (and, through language, with truth and falsehood) applies to everyone's discourse but is attributed by that discourse itself specifically to the enemy. We are therefore summoned to analyze not only what everyone is doing with words as they get caught up in the semantic whirlwinds of war (the stock phrases, the perfunctory judgments, the jingoism, and the formulaic recitations) but what everyone is assuming to be the enemy's distinct relationship with language when they refuse to believe what "they" (the enemy) show, describe, or narrate. "Brainwashed," "duped," "out of touch," "blinded," "fanaticized"— no qualifier is too strong to characterize the relationship to truth, however counterfeit or distorted, that prevails on the other side. Who is compelled to lie and who is free to speak, who can describe and report the events like they happened, and analyze the situation objectively? Who can denounce and condemn without bias? Such questions accompany conflict constantly. And because the response to these questions is generally partisan, they contain the premises of murderous consent.

In act 1, scene 11, Kraus evokes this prejudice in the guise of a prologue that consists of a long exchange between a "Patriot" and a "Subscriber" to the *Neue Freie Presse* (the major Viennese newspaper whose editor in chief was one of Kraus's favorite targets). Their conversation focuses on censorship, a recurrent theme in Kraus's play. The two interlocutors berate the foreign (Italian, British, French) press for having instituted censorship and simultaneously deride it for leaking reports regarding the desperate military situation of the Entente. In Germany and Austria, they explain, no journalist would allow himself to make such assertions, under penalty of severe legal sanctions. Patriotism (the mark of a grand and cohesive nation) demands that we support the war effort and that we silence the critics. It forces us to suspend unsettling questions in a way that ultimately makes it impossible to know if it is better to say the truth or to lie. Censorship, in other words, scorns equally both truth and falsehood.

Patriot: And are things any better in France? Not the least bit; didn't you see this in today's paper: "Imprisonment for Disseminating the Truth in France?" Now really! Just because someone told the truth, a lady in fact—she said Germany was prepared for war but France wasn't. So if you tell the honest truth to their face for once—

Subscriber: No. Those who are in power in France can't take that. Waging war, yes. They like that well enough. Attacking Germany, their peaceful neighbor, out of the blue—that's what they like.

Patriot: Golden words. Germany is waging a defensive war; not a living soul in Germany was prepared for war. The big industrialists were virtually stunned.

Subscriber: That goes without saying. And when that poor soul in France told such a simple truth in plain words that even a layman can understand—

Patriot: Just a minute, you've got that wrong. The woman was convicted because she—

Subscriber: Well, because she told the truth!

Patriot: Yes, but after all she did say that Germany was prepared for war—

Subscriber: But the truth is that Germany was *not* prepared for war.

Patriot: Yes, but she said Germany *was* prepared for war.

Subscriber: But that's a lie.

Patriot: But she was convicted because she spoke the truth—

Subscriber: Well, why was she convicted?

Patriot: Well, because she said Germany *was* prepared for war.

Subscriber: But how can she be convicted for that in France? For that she should be convicted in Germany.

Patriot: How's that again? Just a minute. No. Or—yes—listen, this is how I explain the matter to myself; she did tell the truth, of course, but in France—you know what they're like over there—she was convicted because she had lied.

Subscriber: Just a minute. You're all mixed up. I think it's more like this—she had lied and they convicted her because in France they can't take the truth.[7]

We see the logical contradiction in which the two interlocutors are trapped. They must simultaneously chide France for censoring the truth (which assumes that the woman was condemned for having spoken truly) while maintaining that Germany was not prepared for the war and thus was the victim of aggression (which implies that the woman lied or at least spoke falsely). When stupidity triumphs over reason, bad faith as awkward as this makes us smile. It would not be so serious if it were not for the fact that both the subtext and the stakes of the conversation, as in so many exchanges in the play, concerned the decisive question of how the aggressor was to be designated—if, in other words, the conversation did not end by justifying vengeance, reprisals, and a wide range of other punitive acts. In other words, it would not be so serious if the conversation did not culminate in the alleged need to distinguish between victims unjustly harmed by aggression, on the one hand, and, on the other, those who deserve to endure violence because they are responsible for it.

"It's Not Only in Wartime Humanitarianism That We're Ahead of Them . . ."

Being-in-the-world is partitioned by a plurality of "geographies of vulnerability" that prevent the perils, the aggressions, the victims, and the dead from being seen, perceived, or counted the same way. It remains to be determined what makes such a plurality possible. If it is true, as one begins to suspect, that it requires some discursive "operation," then what is this operation? In this chapter I touch on two operations (*naming* and *narration*) that are most certainly responsible for some of the major lines of fracture that shatter our belonging to the world—divisions which reveal that globalization [*mondialisation*] gives only the illusion of a shared world. They do so because the only significance of such partitions is the proliferation of the murderous consent that they engender. As such, they are the principal cause of the most daunting chasms that have been carved into our belonging to the world.

The first, which is common to all war, both civil and international, is *naming*, that is to say, the use of certain pejorative names (synonyms of unjustifiable violence and the violation of all rules) exclusively to characterize the enemy and to designate his actions, in spite of the fact that nothing is less obvious, less certain, than peremptory discrimination (a partitioning of crime) of this sort. Precisely because it is used "exclusively," the name is reserved for stigmatizing the acts of others in public opinion, both to ensure that no one will attempt to excuse them and to justify the response, however murderous, that such acts invite. Naming designates some as guilty, or potentially guilty, while designating others as victims or possible victims. This is why the logic of naming is always frightening: it serves to validate all forms of oppression, violence, all transgressions of human rights, and all infringements of the right to humanitarian intervention. And it sanctions torture.

In fact, everything begins with naming. What do we name "murder" and "mass murder"? What act of war do we call "criminal"? What constitutes an act of "terrorism"? What acts are there that we would never judge as such? Inversely, we hear now and then how scandalous it would be to imagine, even for an instant, that we might pose the question in similar terms regarding another party in some other conflict. What state do we call a "rogue" state? What states are we forbidden from calling rogue states?[8] Who or what will we allow ourselves to characterize as "cruel" or "barbarian"? Every time we utter—or even avoid or forbid ourselves from uttering— one of these terms, it is difficult to distinguish between what is the effect of the idealizations and sublimations that attach us to a collective identity and what is the work of a superego that prohibits *us* from distancing ourselves from a community that is accused, we imagine (always hastily), of some act that we refuse to call a crime (as if it were possible to hold that community responsible, as if it could possibly be at risk of being held collectively responsible) and, finally, what is the effect of all the resources that have been mobilized to serve the "state's truth."

A particularly significant passage from the dialogue of the Patriot and the Subscriber, again from act 1, scene 11, specifically addresses naming. The logic and the reasons behind naming adversaries and qualifying their acts emerge with great clarity to the extent that they invoke the *violation* of international conventions as justification. Or, inversely, they advance an interpretation—whose bias and bad faith Kraus makes clear—that is partial and partisan, and therefore potentially murderous, of what should be considered a violation for some but not for others. Because the official press is always the first and principal point of transmission of all such interpretations, the question raised by the dialogue, however subtly, concerns who interprets and who has the (sovereign) power to decide on an interpretation. What forces enter into opposition, and what means are used to impose an interpretation?

The dialogue concerns the treatment of prisoners of war. The Patriot begins by relating (after having read in the press) how in Tyrol, on the Brenner Pass, Austrian soldiers "had" to execute four Russian prisoners in cold blood because they refused to dig trenches and, therefore, work for the enemy (one of these was the "leader" of the rebellion). We should remember that forced labor is forbidden by the Hague Convention:

> Patriot: Probably the ringleader. He had the nerve to stand up and make a speech against Austria. Listen—
>
> Subscriber: I'm listening.
>
> Patriot: Our men—the Austrians, I mean—like the kind-hearted fellows they are, were too excited when it came to firing, and they just couldn't hit them. The captain himself had to take a hand and shoot

the bastards down with his service revolver; well, what do you say to the kind of liberties those Russians take with us?

Subscriber: With us here? Why not talk about the insolent way they treat their Austrian prisoners? In case you haven't read yet what's in today's paper. I've got it right here. Listen to this. "Russian Troops Illegally Force War Prisoners to Participate in Hostilities." From army press headquarters it is reported that, since the Russians were driven out of Galicia, hardly a day has gone by without the disclosure of some hitherto unreported infringement of international law by Russian troops, so that there is hardly a single clause in the Hague Convention that cannot be shown to have been trampled underfoot by the Russians.

Patriot: Very good!

Subscriber: Just listen to this—

Patriot: I'm listening.

Subscriber: Recent police investigations in the formerly occupied areas of Galicia have shown that during the entire occupation, by order of the Russian commanding officers, all able-bodied men and women were, if necessary, in addition to being given other types of work, conscripted specifically for the digging of trenches—

Patriot: What do you say to that!

Subscriber:—for which purpose they were marched as far as the Carpathian Mountains. The Russian authorities are, of course, not troubled by the fact that the enemy is expressly prohibited by the Hague Convention from imposing on the peaceful inhabitants of occupied areas the rendering of services that are in effect directed against their own country.

Patriot: Of course they're not troubled! The bastards![9]

The same acts (though not quite the same, since one case involves murder and the other does not) are simultaneously covered and not covered by the conventions, depending on which camp is the perpetrator and which is the interpreter. The execution of the Russian prisoners by the Austrians is seen as legitimate and fully justified because of their refusal to work for the enemy. But when the Russians impose the same work on the Austrians, it is denounced as a violation of international conventions. The conventions are applied and, even more, invoked with reference to different standards. There is no common metric of violence on one side of the front and on the other, and it is the absence of such a metric that enables both the condemnation of some and the exoneration of others. In today's language we would say that the "same" acts (or acts of similar violence, similarly murderous and similarly in violation of the international conventions that establish *jus in bello*, such as, for example, prohibiting the violation of the prisoner's human dignity, not to mention torture) characterize both *rogue states* and states that defend the values that the former allegedly flout.

The consequence of such split judgments is inevitable, and twofold: murderous consent on one side and vilification on the other, in equal measure. The more the enemy is (exclusively) discredited, the more it will seem legitimate to attenuate or exculpate the crimes of those who are counting (and can count) on our unconditional and blind support, no matter what they have said or done. Double standards are one of the principal comic forces of Karl Kraus's drama. He remains appropriately attentive to their translation into language. The (theatrical) form that they assume, that of a performative contradiction, is almost always the same. A statement, as soon as it is uttered, *performs* the opposite of what it says. It proclaims respect for human dignity, law, international conventions, for example, while justifying their violation. The very conventional, if not quite consensual, exchange between the Patriot and the Subscriber illustrates this flawlessly:

> Patriot: That was an excellent article by Professor Brockhausen, the one in which he said that in this country defenseless war prisoners have never been mocked, not even verbally.
>
> Subscriber: He was right. That appeared in the paper the same day as the Lemberg City Commandant's statement that Russian prisoners being transported through the streets had been abused and attacked with sticks by a segment of the population. He explicitly stated that such conduct was unworthy of a civilized nation.
>
> Patriot: He admitted that we *are* a civilized nation.
>
> Subscriber: Of course but there's really no point on which we don't distinguish ourselves from the enemy—who, after all, are nothing but the scum of humanity.
>
> Patriot: For example, in the civilized way we speak even when referring to our enemies, who are really the filthiest bastards on God's earth.
>
> Subscriber: And above all, unlike them, we're always humane. . . .
>
> Patriot: . . . And it's not only in wartime humanitarianism that we're ahead of them. It's also in something else much more valuable: staying power.[10]

The denial of humanity is not always so explicit. But whenever the use of some qualifier ultimately signifies that the wounds or deaths of those that it names count for nothing, when it *authorizes* some distortion not only of laws and conventions but also (sometimes in the name of these same laws and conventions, interpreted exclusively) of our responsibility as enjoined by the vulnerability and the mortality of the other (for example, the vulnerability and mortality of those injured in battle or of civilians caught in a cross fire), when it is reflected in our unconditional approval of violence or is read in the qualifiers that justify it, then it will always participate in or succeed in effecting this kind of denial. The denial of humanity is the culmination of this act which reserves names for, and applies them to, a given community, however defined (religious, cultural, national, "ethnic," etc.).

And yet Kraus's impressive gallery of characters, who in scene after scene subscribe to just such a logic, should not fool us. We should not assume that the exclusive and discriminating attribution of these pejorative qualifiers is *spontaneous*. As suggested above, as soon as it serves the interests of a sovereign state and its supporters, it generally becomes what one calls "official truth." The declaration, the diffusion, and the infliction of such namings, presented as the objective description of *the state of the world*, are acts of sovereignty. Such acts are all the more vindictive when the sovereign state declares itself to be at war—"at war with terrorism," for example, or "with rogue states" or, as was claimed in 1914 on both sides of the front lines, with "barbarism" and the "enemies of culture and civilization." Such *names* are disseminated using the considerable resources that the sovereign state can mobilize. Their power to discriminate, destroy, and even murder varies according to the power that states exercise over or extract from the media (the printed press, radio, television, etc.).

The question of naming is therefore a strategic one. Inversely, however, we should acknowledge that the names and adjectives ("cruel," "rogue," "barbarian," "terrorist") that participate in naming are not always employed unreasonably. And nothing should lessen, minimize, or relativize the violations of law, life, and the respect for human dignity that such words connote. Acts of cruelty occur throughout the world when men and women, armed groups if not states, resort to terror and maintain that it is a means of existence. But we should not forget that this recourse is also strategic and therefore informed by interest. Only rarely are the forces implicated in conflict exempt from committing the violations for which they rebuke others. What is at stake in such strategies is, in the end, always the same: the constitution of what I have been trying to understand as "vulnerability's partisan geography." This is what we must remember: what naming is *authorizing* is almost always a suspension of our responsibility. It is the eclipse, for all those who might be associated more or less closely with one or other of these names, of the attention, care, and help enjoined (that should *always*, despite everything, be enjoined *for everyone*, as argued repeatedly in this book) by their vulnerability and their mortality.

Judith Butler, reacting to the hegemonic consensus produced in American public opinion by the events of September 11, highlighted the phenomenon in these terms:

> The articulation of this hegemony takes place in part through producing a consensus on what certain terms will mean, how they can be used, and what lines of solidarity are implicitly drawn through this use. We reserve "acts of terror" for events such as the September 11 attacks on the United States, distinguishing these acts of violence from those that might be justified through foreign policy decisions or public declarations of war. . . . In the meantime, there remains ever-increasing ambiguity introduced by the very use of the term "terrorist," which is then exploited by various powers at war with independence movements of various kinds.[11]

All designations of aggression trace the frontiers of a partisan geography of broken lives, deaths, and mourning. Naming is a performative act that determines the distribution of (or discrimination between) those whom we must consider as victims (and whom it is incumbent on us to help by all means possible—even the most murderous) and those for whom no compassion, no attention to what is wounding, crippling, or bruising them, and no notice of what is destroying their lives or those of their loved ones or depriving them of shelter and subsistence are required. The counterpart of naming, as "the state's truth," wherever it emerges—and it emerges everywhere—is the refusal of responsibility. Naming lets us shut our eyes and ears and tolerate (and sometimes desire, in good conscience) destructions, aggressions, violence, and transgressions of *jus in bello*, without caring what they mean. It lets us treat such destructions as if they were of secondary importance relative to the cause that justifies such acts—a cause that henceforward is both borne and veiled by a murderous name.

This is why names (for which exclusionist justifications can always be found) participate in what I have called elsewhere the "sedimentation of the unacceptable."[12] They habituate us to marking a separation, however unjustifiable, between those who we think should be protected against violence by whatever means necessary and those for whom the violence they might experience is not considered an issue of basic principle [*ne saurait être principielle*], given the threats with which they themselves are identified. Sedimentation seeks to affect the way that we regard people whom we consent (in the best case) to see hurt—people who are other and to whom a collective identity, whether social, religious, political, ethnic, ideological, etc., is ascribed. It is how we regard them and talk about them. It is the acquired habit (which has become consensual) of entertaining a certain image of them, forged in the phantasm of their "threatening" difference, and of remaining stuck in that discourse forever. In this sense, time works in favor of violence. In time, the sediments that compose its soil accumulate and are deposited. No one escapes what becomes customary to see and think. The pillars of opinion (the media), wanting to conserve their audience, play along with this familiar theme of separation, no matter how murderous it might be, even to the point where they become its principal relay.

Isn't the Messenger Guilty, Too?

Naming is not the only discursive phenomenon that participates in the formation of a particular geography of vulnerability and the murderous consent that accompanies it. The second phenomenon—of crucial importance, the experience of which is revived by every conflict, every war—is the partial, partisan, and, for this reason, distorted narrative of events. It integrates what the historian Marc Bloch in 1921 called "false reports of the war." It was also a privileged theme for Karl Kraus in *The Last Days of Mankind*. At issue are the evocations of the past and the more remote genealogies that intrude on our perception of the facts and facilitate the propagation and reception of "false reports."[13] What is the nature of this *intrusion* that is at the heart of this phenomenon? If it is true that the "reports" play an integral role in the construction of the enemy's image by nurturing hostility, then we must understand how they arise and evolve. Bloch suggests that we begin with the observation that the unreliability of witnesses, the errors of interpretation, and the uncertainties of transmission do not suffice to account for false reports. They fail to explain what is essential, that is, the psychological, emotional, and affective conditions of their collective sedimentation and how they relate to memory: "Humanity expresses its prejudices, its hatreds, its fears, all its strongest emotions, unconsciously, in errors. Only . . . great collective misgivings are able to transform a misperception into a legend."[14]

But where do these emotions, fears, and prejudices come from? From what depths of the memory do they emerge? And if it is true that an important part (in any case, the part that concerns us) of what these reports are peddling contributes to the escalation that occurs in our narration of atrocities, barbaric acts, and cruelty, then how are we to understand our *predisposition* to believe them? We know that there is nothing more difficult and hazardous to apprehend than a "collective mood" [*état d'âme collectif*]. It would be wrong to seek refuge in the always superficial idea of some national psychology to account for such predispositions. But we can try to trace their genealogy. In this case, what I seek to bring to light is the complex genesis of the representation of a protagonist [*adversaire*] as "enemy," taking into account all the prior experiences, discourses, legends, dates, and place-names that contribute to the production of this representation. The intrusions that I discussed above enter into my account at this point. In his *Réflexions d'un historien sur les fausses nouvelles de la guerre*, Marc Bloch shows how, in 1914, the mind [*esprit*] of the combatant was haunted, on both sides of the front, by the anecdotes, tales, and legends of the Franco-Prussian War of 1870, as preserved in novels and images and as ratified by the scholarship of military experts. But these were not all. The blurred (and largely chimerical) memories of more ancient hostilities rounded out this genealogy:

> Moreover, a crowd of old literary tropes linger in the mind, as unconscious memories—all these themes that the human imagination, fundamentally quite modest, keeps turning over again and again from the dawn of time: stories of treason, poisonings, mutilations, of women gouging out the eyes of wounded warriors, as formerly recounted in song by bards and troubadours and made popular today by novels and the cinema. In this way the predisposition of the emotions and the representations of the intellect prepare the transformation [of error] into legend; this is the material of tradition that provides legend with its constitutive elements.[15]

The narratives that intrude on the perception of events (and distort their reporting), the range of actions that they address, the temporal duration over which they preside, and the way they reach back in time to call to mind facts that help orient our emotions are all, we should observe, infinitely variable. If they belong to the collective unconscious, their age-old substructure can be resurrected and exploited. Writers (poets, novelists) participate in this resurrection, as do historians and scholars of all disciplines when they use their talents to help construct a "culture of the enemy." When this happens, they all perform the same function (as required by the regeneration and management of the desired hostility): they all become an instrument of resentment, a test site where or in which the desire for vengeance can crystallize.

False news, however, is not composed exclusively of rumor. Nor is it always spontaneous. Because people are predisposed to listen to false news, it is manufactured—always and everywhere—"with the fixed goal," writes Marc Bloch, "of rousing public opinion—of bolstering a slogan—or simply of embellishing the narrative."[16] False reports relayed by the print and broadcast media work vigorously to inflame hostility. No weapon is more frighteningly effective than the gathering, editing, and formatting of the accounts of witnesses. Karl Kraus demonstrates this with biting irony in a scene (act 1, scene 14) from his play in which we observe, in an imaginary interview, the conditioning of such a witness. Three journalists (Fuechsl, Feigl, and Halberstam) try to convince the actress Elfriede Ritter, who has just returned from Russia, to testify, against her will, to the mistreatment she suffered while being detained there. They cannot stoop too low in their attempt to get the actress to acknowledge that her *experiences* correspond to their prejudices and to their calculations regarding what their readers want. They cannot stoop too low to get her to endorse their vilification of Russia. The point is not to forge a grand historical narrative (which also plays a role in the story) but to produce the required "orientation" and even fabrication, manipulation—intimidating and threatening—of a short tale, recast as a categorical and incontestable element of a broader narrative, which represents Russian society and administration as a world of cruelty:

Elfriede Ritter (*wagging her finger admonishingly*): Doctor Fuechsl, Doctor Fuechsl, that's not what I said. On the contrary, I said that I had no reason to complain—absolutely none.

Fuechsl: Aha! (*writing*) Today, the actress looks back upon her torments with a kind of ironic detachment.

Elfriede Ritter: Now really, Doctor Fuechsl, I really must say—this is outrageous— . . .

Fuechsl (*writing*): Still trembling with agitation, Fräulein Ritter tells how street mobs dragged her along by the hair, how she was harassed by the authorities at the slightest complaint, and how she was terrorized into keeping silent about it all.

Elfriede Ritter: Doctor Fuechsl, you're joking, aren't you? I can even tell you that the police were very helpful. Why, whenever they could they practically took me by the hand. I could go where I pleased and come home when I pleased. I assure you that if I had felt like a prisoner for even one moment—

Fuechsl (*writing*): The actress relates how she once tried to go out, and how the police immediately took her by the hands and dragged her home again. She literally led the life of a prisoner.

Elfriede Ritter: Now I really am angry. Gentlemen, it's not true. I protest. . . .

Fuechsl: I can only tell you that such matters are not to be fooled around with. What! A person, a first-class actress returns from Russia and has nothing to say about the sufferings she endured there? Ridiculous! Believe me, your very life as an artist is at stake.

Elfriede Ritter (*wringing her hands*): But—but, my dear doctor, I really thought—I—please—I only—wanted to tell the truth—forgive me—please—please—please, forgive me—

Feigl (*irate*): You call that the truth? I suppose, then, that we're liars?

Elfriede Ritter: I mean—I'm sorry—I really did believe it was true—but—gentlemen—if you—think—it isn't true—I mean, you're journalists—you must know better—you understand—as a woman I just don't have the right perspective—do I? Good God— you understand—there's a war on—people like me are so easily intimidated—I was so happy to get out of enemy territory in one piece—[17]

The spin and montage of eyewitness accounts, in response to the public's expectations (in the same scene, a journalist exclaims, "My dear, listen, the public, you must understand, it wants to read"), help construct a narrative whose alleged purpose is to inform the public, *truthfully, clearly, and transparently,* of the state of the world. Yet they constitute one of the discursive elements of warfare, which circulates and is exchanged like currency as Karl Kraus forcefully shows throughout his play. In the streets, in the cafés, on the front, news (whether reassuring or terrifying) is shared, broadcast, and distorted.

Today the circulation of narratives through new information technologies is not constrained by political frontiers. Sovereign states, despite efforts to the contrary, have less power to control them. Even in *The Last Days of Mankind*, Viennese rumormongers were commenting on articles that appeared in the English, French, or Italian press. Now, a century later, their successors share through the Internet images and links from around the world. And yet, the narrative that is broadcast from and to the world as a whole is not more consistent, unified, or conciliatory. No one who might wish to bring nuance to the commonly held idea of the "uniformization" or "globalization" of the news would have much difficulty showing the extent to which, even in our day, *all singular being-in-the-world* is subject to the enduring power of multiple narratives to divide our common belonging and to expose us to the ferment of hatred that they sustain, to the imaginary of the enemy that they nurture, and to the separations that they impose. Divided by such frontiers, both real and symbolic, we know that we do not have quite the same relation to the world because the events that wound us (and those of which we are the heirs) are never (and never were) related to *us* in the same way. Regarding the diversity of the world's cultures, no one can deny that the plurality and mutual incompatibility of the narratives that relate the world are among the things that separate us from each other. These narratives would not much matter (or would matter less) if they were not constitutive of what Judith Butler calls the "frame for understanding violence," that is to say, the frame through which violence is either condemned or justified. We could apply Butler's portrayal of the United States after the September 11 attacks to countless analogous narratives:

> The point I would like to underscore here is that a frame for understanding violence emerges in tandem with the experience, and that the frame works both to preclude certain kinds of questions, certain kinds of historical inquiries, and to function as a moral justification for retaliation. . . . There is as well a narrative dimension to this explanatory framework. In the United States, we begin the story by invoking a first-person narrative point of view, and telling what happened on September 11. *It is that date and the unexpected and fully terrible experience of violence that propels the narrative.*[18]

These "frames for understanding" constitute the first link in the chain of violence. As soon as violence is provided with an interpretation of the facts that justifies its application (a news item, a suspicion, a rumor), as soon as it extracts that justification from some specific atrocity or act of cruelty, real or fantasized, true or false, it must continue to hold on to that interpretation at all costs. As soon as murder is nourished by the image of the "enemy," as soon as naming and narrating join forces to validate that image, those who take it for granted cannot change it. They cannot renounce the reasons or the semblance of "legitimacy" that it provides. Murderous consent, and the geography of vulnerability that accompanies it, are caught in a downward spiral, which, as we know, is generally transmitted from generation to generation. Marc Bloch's evocation of this chain of violence is suggestive. The terms of his analysis apply to all violations of *jus in bello*, to all reprisals, all acts of revenge or denials of one's humanity, wherever they occur, or whatever excuses might accompany them: "The instant the error had caused blood to spill, it was definitively established. Men driven by blind, brutal, yet sincere anger had torched and gunned down. Now it was important that they maintain an unflinchingly steadfast faith in the existence of 'atrocities,' which alone could give their furor the appearance of fairness. We can assume that most of them would have reeled with horror if they had had to recognize the profound absurdity of the panic and terror that had pushed them to commit so many dreadful acts. But they never recognized anything like that."[19]

The intergenerational transmission of violence through commemoration is nourished both by the observation of commemorative dates and by the instrumentalization of that observation, as something desired, pursued, and secured with murderous effect by the sovereign state. When murderous consent is grounded in the "state's truth," which assumes the construction and diffusion of an "official account," the most effective recourse for the institutions that are charged with consent's sedimentation and propagation is to invite a population to share, in a way that is both traumatic and commemorative, in one or more memorial observances. Lurking in every memorial date—however legitimate and necessary its commemoration—are two acts of violence, the one that is being recalled and the one that is ultimately being authorized and justified. Because commemoration is split between an impossible grieving, on the one hand, and resentment or the desire for vengeance, on the other, participation becomes a source of conflict.

As we know, this conflictual situation can coincide with the differences that we include under the term "cultural diversity." But it must be emphasized that it is not the determination of some essence, nor is it some principled hostility between "cultural communities" allegedly destined by nature to oppose one another, that explains conflict. To find the reasons for such hostility we need to look at the efforts of ideological, political, and/or religious forces to work on "public opinion" so as to impose on the world their narrative and their interpretation of important commemorative dates—a humiliating defeat, an indisputable victory, an act of treason, or a barbaric deed. The remembrance of the dates that these forces try to cultivate is ambivalent. Remembrance pays homage—legitimately—to the victims, but it also deafens us to *rival narratives* or to any sharing in *the commemorative dates of others*. The commemoration of the acts of violence that we have endured excludes self-examination, critical interrogation, and, in general, the displacement of our perception of our own vulnerability by considering that of others.

The political, ideological, and religious exploitation of commemorative dates causes the narrative to be monopolized by an exclusive "I" that resists decentering or "disappropriation" of the narrative, thus preventing us from *thinking and living the world otherwise.* When events are recounted from the point of view of a sovereign "I," of an "I" that is assured of its place in the world, its prerogatives, its "full" and "just rights" [*plein droit*; *bon droit*], sure of its values and the universality of its values, the "world" is being said [*se dit*] in the first person. To say the world, however, means "to strike a balance" regarding our responsibility to provide attention, care, and aid, as enjoined by the vulnerability of *all* and not merely that of this self-centered "I." Several Nietzschean questions regarding truth emerge from this observation. Who determines which wounds count? Who decides, and on what authority, what is cruel and what is not? Who records history and how is it recorded so as to make possible such a decision, such a demarcation between what is barbarous and what is not, between what is "terror" and what is not? Above all, whom can we convince that this partition is just and universally valid?

We know, of course, that no force can durably commandeer the privilege of narration. *No longer* can history be recounted in the first-person singular. *No longer* can a nation, a power, even the greatest, confiscate the history of the world. On the contrary, because narration is always already decentered, we see that every time such a *will to appropriate* emerges, its sole raison d'être is catastrophically and destructively to recenter, reappropriate, or reinstitute a narrative "I" whose sovereignty is nevertheless always illusory and always fictional. Nationalism cannot be understood otherwise. The politics of memory and grieving that it deploys, its relation to the dead and the survivors, has as its principal goal to achieve a retreat back toward the elusive center. *It* wills that the dead who count in history be *its* dead, to the exclusion of all others. When nationalism is accompanied by xenophobia or some organized suspicion regarding all that is foreign or some underlying and more or less explicit form of racism, the allergy to otherness becomes the determinant element of its centripetal strategy. Unable to guarantee the nation absolute invulnerability, it turns vulnerability, whether real or fantasized, into the core of its vision of the world and its encounter with the international. We are therefore not surprised when Butler makes the decentering/recentering sequence a determinant element of the traumatism wrought by the events of September 11: "This decentering is experienced as part of the wound that we have suffered, though, so we cannot inhabit that position. This decentering is precisely what we seek to rectify through a recentering. A narrative form emerges to compensate for the enormous narcissistic wound opened up by the public display of our physical vulnerability."[20]

Because the strategy of recentering always ends up minimizing the vulnerability of others—and is therefore synonymous with "murderous consent," wherever it prevails—we cannot allow it to have the last word. On the contrary, we must invent a new kind of distancing [*écart*]—one that is simultaneously ethical and cosmopolitical, hence *ethicosmopolitical*. Butler's reflections point us in this direction. Far from treating some cultural or civilizational belonging as an immutable attribute, Butler tries to wrest the thought, the imagination, and the emotion of grieving away from the centripetal strategy, which, by contrast, seeks only to ratify or increase, blindly and unjustly, the inequitable distribution of vulnerability.

This requires, first, that history be narrated otherwise. It requires that we agree to free history from its traumatico-nation-statist context, while refusing to deny—we must never deny—the persistent and painful wounds of the past and present. This suggests a different narrative and *a different memory of the world*, one commensurate with a *being-in-the-world otherwise*, one that would expand our *living-with* to embrace our responsibility for the attention, care, and aid that is enjoined everywhere by the vulnerability and mortality of the other. The *entirely other* [*tout autre*], whatever the "cultural community" with which she identifies, has a right to expect this, barring some endorsement of the particular, partial, partisan (and therefore unjust) character of some predetermined "geography of vulnerability." The question that Judith Butler asks her fellow citizens, and the West in general, is therefore final and without appeal. She can extend the question, and redirect it, at the price of a few displacements, to other parts of the world, because its application is fundamentally universal: "Is our capacity to mourn in global dimensions foreclosed precisely by the failure to conceive of Muslim and Arab lives *as lives*?"[21]

How many lives are we talking about? But, first, what is meant by our *failure to conceive of the lives of others* (since this is the case everywhere, even if unevenly) *as lives*? Failure means falling into one of the many traps that are composed of words and images that *eclipse* our responsibility for their vulnerability. The truth of such words and images is that they condition us, more or less deliberately, not to see the death of these others as *wholly* death, that is, as the death of the world, of this world that is signified *intensely* by each life (as a reading of Grossman and Levinas suggests).[22] The truth of such words and images is that they condition us not to imagine that we could possibly weep for these others. If this *eclipse* constitutes an ineluctable dimension of our *being-in-the-world*, the lie consists in hiding the fact that this eclipse is also the truth of discourses and images of what is presented, constructed, assembled, and displayed as *The World*. The lie, in other words, resides in our ignorance of the chasm that this eclipse opens up in our representation of the world. To refute it (and my efforts up to this point have had no other purpose) is the beginning of responsibility.

The Frames of Mourning

The question of truth is therefore linked to that of the world. It concerns procedures that either favor or undermine our ability to perceive *any given* being-in-the-world as a real life. Responsibility, ethical and political, *ethicosmopolitical*, is affected by the production and reception (including the critical reception) of words and images that should make it possible (when so many other words and images prevent it) to exclude *no human life* and, therefore, to prevent the interdependence that defines our living-with from splitting the "with" that constitutes it into two kinds of relations: those that bind the living-with to lives that count and those that unbind it from others that, for some reason or other, are treated as unimportant.[23] Nothing produces this split more effectively than the extinction of a life (the disappearance of the world that it signifies) that is thought not to matter. It occurs every time it is settled, accepted, or decided that this is the way it shall be. To state it more boldly, there is no belonging to the world that does not imply a "politics of mourning." Every sovereign state has one. Nothing better summarizes what I have been calling murderous consent than the abyss that is hollowed out between this politics, however multifaceted, and the ethicosmopolitics that could set it right.

It is a politics of mourning that the state at war deploys for *its* own dead. This politics responds to several imperatives and pursues several objectives. These include uniting the nation in the collective homage that it renders to the war dead while justifying, in the eyes of their families (mothers and fathers) and public opinion, the political decision that caused their deaths. Grieving (whether by the nation or the individual) rubs up against its limits in the necessary sacrifice that is asked of people and "accepted." It is legitimate to mourn our dead, but we are prohibited from questioning and, even more, from attacking the arguments and the rhetoric, the encouragements and the injunctions, that led the dead to *give* their lives. The homicidal logic of war demands a just cause for which lives are freely and voluntarily sacrificed. The honors that are rendered to the war dead presuppose and attempt to validate, at least implicitly, this thesis. Mourning is framed, *in the first instance*, not only by the grand narrative of "patriotic consent" but rather by images selected according to the principle that any reversal by public opinion against the war must be avoided.

One of the scenes (act 2, scene 29) of *The Last Days of Mankind* evokes, again with biting irony, the political and social norms of grieving in wartime. It opposes two characters, the Optimist and the Grumbler (the voice of Karl Kraus), and takes up once again the question of truth and falsehood, but this time on the difficult terrain of feelings and emotion:

Optimist: All right, what then would be your idea of a hero's death?

Grumbler: A calamitous act of chance.

Optimist: If the fatherland thought that way, it would be in trouble.

Grumbler: The fatherland does think that way.

Optimist: What? It calls a hero's death a calamity? An act of chance?

Grumbler: Just about that. The fatherland speaks of it as a "cruel blow of fate."

Optimist: Who? Where? There is no military obituary that does not say it is a privilege for a soldier to die for the fatherland. There's never a death announcement in which even the most unassuming private individual does not proclaim plainly and proudly that his son died a hero's death. Even though under other circumstances that same man would talk about a son's death as a "cruel blow of fate." For instance, look at this in today's *Neue Freie Presse*.

Grumbler: I see it. But turn back to this page. Here the Chief of Staff, Conrad von Hötzendorf, thanks the mayor for his condolences "on the occasion of the cruel blow of fate" that fell upon him when his son was killed in the line of duty. He used the same language in the family's announcement of his son's death. . . . A Bavarian princess congratulated a relative of hers on the occasion of his son's heroic death. At such social heights *there exists a certain obligation to behave like one of the furies.*[24] The Chief of Staff not only accepts condolences, but time and again he laments the cruelty of fate. The man who is a bit closer to this kind of fate than the entire cast, that is, closer than the soldiers who may be its victims, closer than the fathers of the soldiers who may lament it, he who is author of this drama of fate, and if not that, its producer, or, let us say, its director, and if not that, at least its stage manager—it is this man who speaks of the cruel blow of fate. And he tells the truth, and all the others are compelled to lie stricken by his personal grief, he has discarded the obligation to be heroic and, as is only right, has returned to reality. The others remain imprisoned—they must lie.

Optimist: No! They are not lying. People respond to a hero's death with deeply felt sorrow. The prospect of dying on the field of honor often enraptures the sons of the common folk.

Grumbler: Unfortunately it also enraptures the mothers who have renounced their power to save the age from this disgrace.[25]

This dramatic exchange puts all the elements of thought on grieving (evoked above) in perspective. First, it illustrates the tension that exists between *two forms of cruelty*, that of loss, the "cruel blow of fate," and that of the norms that frame its interpretation and expression, norms that prohibit the free manifestation of pain, anger, and rebellion against the absurdity of death and, even more, against the words that try to justify it—norms, in other words, that prohibit rebellion against the shame of war.[26] Second, it suggests that the question of mourning is inscribed in a more general frame of a politics that consists as much in accompanying emotions, and even eliciting (while carefully monitoring) them collectively, as it does in controlling how they are displayed. Just as all wars revive the experience of these two forms of cruelty, and just as the media's coverage of loss fortifies it by gathering and diffusing the testimonies of loved ones, pain and personal grief are not allowed to obstruct pride. It is appropriate and in conformity with the social norms imposed by war to demonstrate pride, if not to "affect" it (as Kraus, through the words of his gadfly, accuses Viennese society of doing), in order to preserve the identity between death and heroic sacrifice. Here, again, it is all about consenting to killing. What is at stake in such a politics is nothing more and nothing less than the ability of a society to accept its loss and in so doing to recognize as legitimate the sovereign (political and military) decisions that are responsible for it.

But the framing of mourning by the state is not concerned only with a people's running tally of *its* deaths—the dead to which it considers itself attached by bonds of belonging to a shared community. It is not concerned only with our solidarity (which everyone is called to feel) toward the families that have been struck by "cruel fate" and with whom all are invited to identify. It is also concerned with the *exclusive* character of both these bonds and our "solidarity."[27] It is concerned with the intrinsically *selective* dimension of mourning and its politics. It is worth recalling that in every conflict, in every war, solidarity inscribes a line of demarcation, a line of fracture (a disruption in our being-in-the-world) between those whom we are required to grieve, within prescribed limits, and those *others* who have no right to grief—a line of fracture between the mothers and fathers whose pain moves us, and who enjoin our consolation, and those others whose grief is unknown or overlooked. Something else and something different is said and shown of these others, so as to serve a "culture of the enemy" in which so much discourse and imagery have been invested. It is as if all the relations that war destroyed, all that war mangled and broke in the lives of these others, thrust like us into grief, now had to be minimized, belittled, apprehended through a veil of bias, and distorted or even falsified, as if the lives to which these other men and women were bound were less valuable. Everything conspires to make sure that their dead are barred from the frame of solidarity in mourning. Recalling how Camus urged "complicity" and "solidarity" in opposition to all the forms of murderous consent to which history exposes us, we now see why such complicity and solidarity must be disrupted. This is how hatred is passed on from generation to generation, as an inheritance.[28]

This "framing" and this partition of mourning that establish and impose the distinction between the lives that qualify for grieving and those that do not are at the center of Judith Butler's reflections on war, as developed in two books written after September 11 and the interventions in Afghanistan and Iraq. The first, *Precarious Life* (mentioned above), appeared in 2004, and the second, *Frames of War*, in 2009.[29] If it is true, as I hope to demonstrate here, that all murderous consent derives from the eclipse of our responsibility for the aid, care, and attention that is enjoined by the mortality and vulnerability of the other, then the object of murderous consent is always some specific life. We do not consent to *everyone's* murder. At the heart of our consent to violence (this cannot be overstated) is its *selectivity*. The whole problem, therefore, is knowing what enables this partition, this fracturing of being-in-the-world. The questions raised by this partition are all the more difficult in that they do not elicit a simple answer. Our ability to grasp the "mechanism" whereby we resign ourselves to or indulge in or applaud the "murder" of some determinate other assumes that we can disassemble its logic (the false principles that they who "consent" put forward as justification). But this would imply that we understand both what, *in* life, makes consent possible (the death drive, cruelty) and what violence achieves *in this same life* (understood as living-with with others).[30] For this reason we must ascertain how some lives, specifically (in contrast to others), are apprehended and perceived such that, in the end, we "consent" to their mutilation or loss. We have to ascertain what discourses, montages, political and media framings allow this.

Today more than ever our apprehension and perception are inseparable from the images of war, violence, and suffering that come to *us* (the whole question, again, is to know what exactly this *us* is designating). What role do these images play in the constitution of what I called the "geographies of vulnerability"? The question is a pressing one because it kindles a multitude of simplifications. Because war and violence in general are channeled through the media, and because multiple interests, economic and political, are bound up in the framing, montage, and diffusion of these images, we are tempted to assume that they can always be manipulated in pursuit of various ends and, therefore, be made to speak in one way or another. In other words, we are tempted to believe that the reality to which they refer is always virtual. Nothing better illustrates the serpentine paths of murderous consent than the comfort we derive from shielding ourselves against these images of violence and even ridding ourselves of them by assuming that they are *all false*, going so far as to cultivate the suspicion that in their global dissemination they are participating in some or other dark conspiracy. Susan Sontag evokes this reaction forcefully and vehemently at the end of her book *Regarding the Pain of Others*. There she takes to task all those who reduce reality to its images and all those who otherwise indulge in travesty:

> [To speak of reality becoming a spectacle] assumes that everyone is a spectator. It suggests, perversely, unseriously, that there is no real suffering in the world. But it is absurd to identify the world with those zones in the well-off countries where people have the dubious privilege of being spectators, or of declining to be spectators, of other people's pain, just as it is absurd to generalize about the ability to respond to the sufferings of others on the basis of the mind-set of those consumers of news who know nothing at first hand about war and massive injustice and terror. There are hundreds of millions of television watchers who are far from inured to what they see on television. They do not have the luxury of patronizing reality.[31]

And yet it remains true that interdependence in a world of images raises critical questions. It would be simplistic to deny the need to address them. The questions are of two sorts. First, as Susan Sontag recalled as early as 1977 in her first writings on photography, we have a right to interrogate our power to transform images. We have a right to interrogate the fact that an image can both embellish and deform, both harden and attenuate, the reality it displays, accentuating some facial characteristic, some aspect of a profile, some facet of a situation and effacing others. As Sontag reminds us, this power has been acknowledged in the case of photographs of war and of atrocities. It would be naïve to assume that the forces implicated in their global diffusion do not take advantage of this power. We know that all such images are subject to a process of selection concerning, first, what can be photographed and filmed (access to sites and the authorization to record), second, the channels through which they are broadcast, and, finally, how they are archived, reproduced as iconic images, or destroyed. Even if the state's monopoly on such selection is increasingly challenged by new technologies that escape its control, such selection continues to implicate the media and political and military authorities in decision-making. Although their sovereignty and sense of responsibility may vary from one situation to the next, they will still gauge what can acceptably be shown (or not) and how reality should be framed with respect to which interests.

From my perspective, I should emphasize the fact that this decision, in and of itself, implies from the outset a geography of vulnerability—*and, even more, of mortality.* Photography from its very beginnings raised the question of what we can and should do with images of the dead. When is it decent, useful, interesting, or effective to show (or not show) cadavers? In the event of war, this means asking how displaying or hiding such images might weigh on the course of hostilities, if not directly, then by affecting public opinion's perception of the conflict and its attitude toward the adversary. Here again, there is nothing simple about the geography that emerges. Showing one's own civil and military casualties in a violent conflict is not the same thing as showing those of the adversary. And the experience of confronting the casualties of a war in which we are implicated by some sense of belonging (national, religious, community) is not the same (and efforts are expended to convince us of this) as being shown the bodies of those who have died, far way, in some epidemic or other health or meteorological catastrophe, or even in war, if sufficiently remote and forgotten. Susan Sontag reminds us of this in forceful terms that resonate with attempts here to make sense of consent:

> The more remote or exotic the place, the more likely we are to have full frontal views of the dead and dying. Thus postcolonial Africa exists in the consciousness of the general public in the rich world— besides through its sexy music—mainly as a succession of unforgettable photographs of large-eyed victims. . . . These sights carry a double message. They show a suffering that is outrageous, unjust, and should be repaired. They confirm that this is the sort of thing which happens in that place. The ubiquity of those photographs, and those horrors, cannot help but nourish belief in the inevitability of tragedy in the benighted or backward—that is, poor—parts of the world.[32]

Our interdependent relation to a world in which images of war and, more generally, of suffering and violence suffuse rumor and speculation invites critical questions of a second sort, which concern our complacent familiarity [*accoutumance*] with what these images show. This is one of the axes around which Susan Sontag orients her thinking, going back to her first works on photography. It is significant that this concern resurfaces twenty-five years later. Are we justified in saying that distance renders all emotions on our part superficial and that, as a result of being bombarded by such images, our relation to the world—at least a large part of the world—becomes banal and indifferent by force of habit? Can we make people bear the weight of even the most tenuous, least heard, and least admissible forms of murderous consent? Is there some *emotional deficit* that is creating this fracture in our being-in-the-world, this fracture in our belonging, the analysis of which constitutes the focus of this book? If we were to respond to these questions positively but monolithically, by arguing in effect that these images are not telling us anything new, we would merely be acknowledging the fact of human cruelty while turning our backs on it. Such a response would validate murderous consent by complaining that there is no hope in truth. There is accordingly nothing to do and nothing to show because it has already been said and done, even if in a way that will always invite contestation. Again, to go down this path, which I have crisscrossed many times in this book already, is to court nihilism.

Susan Sontag did not choose this path. Whatever we might think of the way that images are produced, framed, used, and even manipulated, their repertory is so vast that we cannot minimize their power to haunt us or underestimate the inevitability of such a *haunting*. Murderous consent does not vanish, nor is it suspended or disrupted. It does become problematic, however (already a major difference), when some *phantom* reclaims or holds on to its prerogatives. Being haunted by images does not mean that we accept them uncritically as absolute truth—even if we want to use them as proof of the atrocities to which they testify, generally posthumously. Nor, of course, does it mean that we can reject them out of hand. It does mean, however, that we permit them to raise problems regarding the meaning of our belonging to the world. In other words, it does mean recognizing—whatever the conditions of the production and diffusion of such images—that *their truth will always be their power to problematize this very meaning*.

> There now exists a vast repository of images that make it harder to maintain this kind of moral defectiveness. Let the atrocious images haunt us. Even if they are only tokens, and cannot possibly encompass most of the reality to which they refer, they still perform a vital function. The images say: This is what human beings are capable of doing—may volunteer to do, enthusiastically, self-righteously. Don't forget. . . .
>
> If the goal is having some space in which to live one's own life, then it is desirable that the account of specific injustices dissolve into a more general understanding that human beings everywhere do terrible things to one another. . . .

Such images cannot be more than an invitation to pay attention, to reflect, to learn, to examine the rationalizations for mass suffering offered by established powers. Who caused what the picture shows? Who is responsible? Is it excusable? Was it inevitable? Is there some state of affairs which we have accepted up to now that ought to be challenged?[33]

How should we understand the way that images of violence, which occurs *everywhere*, and of the suffering that violence causes work to *problematize* the meaning of our belonging to the world? To answer this question we must go beyond Susan Sontag's reflections and interrogate the perception that we have of the lives that, we learn (or not) in various ways, have been mutilated and destroyed. We have to ask ourselves how these lives, as such, enter (or do not enter) into the frame of the violence that we perceive in the world. The question of speech, images, and truth intersects the question of mourning, as discussed by Judith Butler in her more recent work. Nothing contributes more to murderous consent than political power's efforts to ensure that some or other life *is recognized as such* and another is not. "Recognizability" is not a given. It is constructed. It is a function, Butler says, of the "frames" that order it by discriminating among lives. Discrimination is achieved principally by distinguishing between lives that must be protected and lives that need not be, particularly if they are seen as threatening. This distinction holds not only in times of war but also in the case of policies that restrict immigration, which have a tendency to stamp an image of threat on the populations of entire continents. The result is that those who are protected are *entitled to mourning*, while those who are not protected are not so entitled, such that, in the end, the "geography of vulnerability" that I evoked earlier in this chapter culminates in a "geography of mourning." The map of the world today is the product of a profusion of murderous consents having, as their object, forgotten wars, refugee camps, famine, and pandemics. Such is the global condition of "precarity": "Such populations are 'lose-able,' or can be forfeited, precisely because they are framed as being already lost or forfeited; they are cast as threats to human life as we know it rather than as living populations in need of protection from illegitimate state violence, famine, or pandemics. Consequently, when such lives are lost they are not grievable, since, in the twisted logic that rationalizes their death, the loss of such populations is deemed necessary to protect the lives of 'the living.'"[34]

Such eclipses of our responsibility, however, do not mean that we are in fact relieved of it. Nothing conforms more closely to the logic of murderous consent than does the assumption that it is the *captive* of these frames that organize our perception of the vulnerability and mortality of others, as if we, prisoners of speech and imagery, were obliged despite ourselves to "consent" to violence. Although one of the objectives of this book is to bring murderous consent to light as an inescapable dimension of our existence (as I stressed in the Introduction), another equally important objective is to explore the many ways that we can oppose it. Among these are Camus's revolt, Levinas's goodness, and, as explored in the following chapter, Anders's shame. How do we escape the limits that the frame imposes on our responsibility? Karl Kraus's approach, in and of itself, already constitutes an answer to this question. The way he turns speech against itself to reveal, almost obsessively, its performative contradictions overturns the conventions that frame the way we designate and perceive the enemy. The same could be said of Butler's analyses. Nothing would be more opposed to the spirit and engagement of her work than to draw the conclusion that our perception is confined by its framing. Just as the frame is subject to the (political, military, national, media) context that engenders it, it can also be wrestled free (as happens now and then) from that same context. In addition to producing new frames (through alternative media), it is important that the circulation of the frames that are foisting norms [*norment*] on our perception of the world should be accompanied by their decoding, and that their distribution and reproduction should become their *démontage*. As decoding and *démontage* occur, the contents of such frames (the wounds, the destructions, the violations of rights and law) can be set free so as to restore some part of the truth. In this case, an additional response to life, in opposition to the murderous consent that inhabits it, becomes discernible: that of *a belonging-to-the-world that is in principle critical and deconstructive.*

5

The World

Nor do I know when death will come to me. Any number of times each day I tug at my hair and count the strands that pull out. Terrified of the spots that may appear suddenly, at any moment, I examine the skin of my arms and legs dozens of times, squinting with the effort. Small red mosquito bites I mark with ink; when, with time, the red bites fade, I am relieved they were bites and not spots.

Atomic bomb sickness inflicts strange, idiotic bodily harm: you remain fully conscious, yet no matter how dreadful the symptoms that appear, you are aware of neither pain nor numbness. For those suffering from it, atomic bomb sickness represents the discovery of a new hell.

Incomprehensible terror when death beckons and anger at the war (the war itself, not the defeat) intertwine like serpents and even on the most listless of days throb violently.
  —Ōta Yōko, "An Autumn So Horrible Even the Stones Cry Out"

The name Hiroshima is universally recognized. It has become the synonym of both a silence and an absence.[1] We could fill entire libraries with books on nuclear deterrence, on the various nuclear strategies (including that of the United States in 1945), on the efforts of nonnuclear states to equip themselves with nuclear arms, and, it follows, on the risks of proliferation. Far less common, however, are the books written or translated into European languages that take us back to the scene of death and destruction that was Hiroshima. Few are the testimonials, novels, novellas, or philosophical analyses that help us evaluate, politically and morally, what happened there on August 6, 1945. Rare are the works, in other words, that help us represent or imagine the nothingness that this event signifies.[2] It is as if the effectiveness of deterrence presupposed this "trigger event" to make it credible, while simultaneously the effacement of the suffering, the broken and destroyed lives (spread across several generations), even unconsciousness with regard to it were needed to make deterrence tolerable, to remove culpability, and even to render it banal. Of course, there have been "world conferences against nuclear weapons" and "peace movements" that cannot be separated from the memory of that day. And certainly everyone is at least vaguely conscious of the fact that we live in a world exposed to the threat of nuclear war, as of the fact that nuclear weapons were indeed utilized, on two occasions, at Hiroshima and Nagasaki. For Kenzaburō Ōe, who observed many such conferences and movements and gathered accounts from the victims, the politics and the recollection of that day were (and remain) far from compatible or consistent with one another. There are, however, several literary accounts coming out of Japan that help keep its memory alive. These include Masuji Ibuse's novel *Black Rain* (1966) and Ōe's own *Hiroshima Notes* (1965). The novellas of Tamiki Hara (1947 and 1949), Sankichi Tōge's *Poems of the Atomic Bomb*, and Ōta Yōko's *City of Corpses* have been published collectively in English in a volume entitled *Hiroshima: Three Witnesses*. With the exception of *Black Rain*, however, much time had to elapse before these testimonials appeared in translation. And they remain rare.[3]

Finally, one should highlight the disproportion that exists between the massive scale of the event and the relative paucity of deep reflection, other than simple dread, that it inspired.[4] Most of the great philosophers of the second half of the twentieth century judged it unnecessary, beyond some rudimentary reflection, to dwell on the *event* or to examine critically the official reasons for and justifications of it. Even less attention has been paid to the widespread and silent consent of the political class to nuclear weapons, despite the many protest movements directed against them. It was understood that making an *example* of Hiroshima and Nagasaki had proven the necessary "efficacy" of deterrence (and not, as we casually say, merely "ended the war"). Consequently, the *memory of the event* was made a prisoner of the geopolitical and strategic questions of the Cold War, just as the question of nuclear arms today is understood in the context of the potential terrorism of so-called "rogue" states. Finally, the victims of Hiroshima and Nagasaki were brushed aside as denizens of an imperial and military power that was notorious for its military's war crimes and for the fanatic indoctrination of an entire people. Everything therefore conspires to help us forget. As Kenzaburō Ōe writes in a text from October 1964, entitled "On Human Dignity": "To put the matter plainly and bluntly, people everywhere on this earth are trying to forget Hiroshima and the unspeakable tragedy perpetrated there. We naturally try to forget our personal tragedies, serious or trifling, as soon as possible. . . . It is not strange, therefore, that the whole human race is trying to put Hiroshima, the extreme point of human tragedy, completely out of mind."[5] Might we not reasonably speak of a "retrospective banalization"?

The World Once Again Seems Complete

Some voices have refused to stay silent: Nobel Prize–winning physicists, crowds of anonymous dissenters of all ages and origins, and Karl Jaspers, who alerted the world to the risks of a peace founded on fear. But no one gave vent to a more thoroughgoing anxiety than Günther Anders, who made the struggle against nuclear weapons the fight of his life. Anders wrote "The Bomb and the Roots of Our Blindness toward the Apocalypse" (Über die Bombe und die wurzeln unserer Apokalypse-Blindheit) in the early 1950s. It was reprinted in his 1956 masterpiece, *The Obsolescence of Humankind* (*Die Antiquiertheit des Menschen*). In 1958, on the occasion of the fourth congress against A-bombs and H-bombs in Tokyo, he visited Hiroshima and Nagasaki. There he recorded his impressions in *The Man on the Bridge: Journal from Hiroshima and Nagasaki* (*Der Mann auf der Brücke: Tagesbuch aus Hiroshima und Nagasaki*). Soon thereafter, he published *Burning Conscience*, his correspondence with Claude Eatherly, the pilot in charge of weather assessment who relayed to the bomber the presidential order to drop the bomb.[6] These last two books are particularly remarkable in the way they give utterance to a plurality of voices. Anders's thought in effect takes shape as a kind of fabric woven from his many encounters and the testimonies he heard. It is fed by words collected in opposition to oblivion and silence as well as by the objections, resistance, and denials that his thinking confronted. With every step he takes in his effort to understand and inform, Anders places at the core of his thought the obligation to do justice to the dead and to the survivors and an acute alertness to this new form of vulnerability and mortality that the world confronts in nuclear weapons.

Nothing is more opposed to this sense of obligation than the "banalization" of the devastation wrought by the two bombs, as if, given the historical context of their deployment, that devastation was of secondary importance; as if the civilian victims—men and women, children and seniors, first blinded then struck down in their homes, in their places of work, or on their way to school—do not count for much when the "meaning of history" (identified with the defense of security) is at stake. It is useful to begin with Anders's tense conversation with a proponent of nuclear deterrence, which took place somewhere in the skies above Hiroshima, during a flight from Tokyo to Bangkok. When this person learns that Anders is an activist who is working toward nuclear disarmament, that is, one of those people who are constantly warning their fellow human beings of the danger posed to the world *in its totality* by the proliferation of atomic weapons, he recoils and refuses to speak to someone who could defend such a position. Then he reconsiders and indulges Anders in a self-important indictment that supposedly demonstrates *a contrario* the absolute necessity of nuclear weapons.

It is not by chance that Anders reproduces his interlocutor's words as faithfully as possible. In effect, the arguments that Anders's interlocutor develops merit our attention. In a few sentences, they effectively condense all the conventional elements of the official justification, still heard today, of those who seek retrospectively to defend the destruction of Hiroshima and Nagasaki. The argument is based not so much on the (still debatable) claim that we had to bring the war to an end but rather on the claim that their detonation served as an indispensable exemplum if peace were to be maintained following the victory of one side over the other.[7] In other words, the nuclear attacks were necessary for the survival of the "freedom camp" in its struggle against totalitarianism. According to his argument, renouncing the bomb would have been "liberticidal," the height of irresponsibility. Though Anders's interlocutor does not say it explicitly, he does insinuate, *a contrario*, that Hiroshima's and Nagasaki's "exemplary" victims were the price we must be willing to pay for our freedom. The general argument leaves no doubt. Humankind's humanity [*l'humanité de l'homme*], in its essence, is imperiled by its exposure to a power, totalitarianism, "in which evil has become incarnate." "You know that I am now talking about totalitarianism. Totalitarianism may leave us our existence in a banal physical sense; it probably must do so—yes, it *must*: its diabolical pleasure consists precisely in the manipulation of dehumanized people, and for that it indeed needs us—but it cannot rest until it has been satisfied, until it successfully transforms men into totally unrefined parts of the total apparatus; not until it has transformed all men into fragments of the perilous apparatus."[8]

Anders's interlocutor stigmatizes a system that is "liberticidal," even "libertiphagial"—a system that consumes and devours freedom and cannot nourish itself otherwise. As a consequence we are confronted with a fundamental and unconditional choice that surpasses all others in its implications: either totalitarianism or freedom, as understood and defined here. It is a choice imposed by an essentialist logic, and it produces two implications. First, everything that is not totalitarianism *is* freedom. This implies that we can locate with absolute certainty an intrinsically airtight border between the two, where nothing is blurred or uncertain, and where the "world *understood as* free" reveals no gray areas. This certainty extends to *everything* concerning nuclear weapons, nuclear tests, their effects on populations and the environment, and the risks they pose. The world (this is the dogma!) is thus divided into two blocs: one gathers the forces of good and the other embodies evil. It goes without saying that the fall of the Berlin Wall did nothing to shake this logic. It simply displaced it. As soon as the end of the Cold War was decreed, announced, and celebrated, in the late 1980s, we were confronted with a new enemy of the "free world," a new threat that justified, now more than ever, the exclusive maintenance and even enhancement, in the "good camp," of a nuclear strike force. This is the source of the second implication of the choice "totalitarianism or freedom." The "free world" must forgo no intellectual or physical means to preserve its integrity. Its nuclear arsenal is fully justified by this obligation to protect itself from the demonic powers that are plotting its destruction.

But this logic exhibits a strange paradox, which Derrida could surely have qualified as "auto-immunity." If it is true that nuclear weapons are a threat even to the countries that produce them, and if it is true that they are also the product of a choice (although, as we see today, the choice to produce nuclear weapons is increasingly difficult to limit and control), and if it is true, therefore, that the choice *also* incurs risks, then we have to admit that the choice itself is not being made freely. The choice has been foisted on politics, *against* morality, by those we identify as the enemies of the "free world." Whether real or imagined, these enemies are dictating their law to us. They are forcing the world that *calls itself* free to renounce morality and accept all the forms of murderous consent that this renunciation entails. The "free world" is one whose freedom is conditioned by threat. The effects of this paradox reveal themselves immediately, most notably in the fact that every decision concerning nuclear weapons is classified, including those that directly jeopardize the future of individuals on whom these decisions are imposed. Here we find the "auto-immunity" of the logic deployed by Anders's interlocutor: in the "free world," the exercise of sovereignty is linked to the anxious preservation of one or many secret decisions that apply not only to "free" people but even, and more momentously than any other decision, to all of humanity. We confront once more the question raised earlier about famine: what is the value of liberty when its exercise is rebuffed in a domain that, by right, should not be detached from morality and assigned only to, and by, politics? The apostle of deterrence cannot evade this question, although he is not much bothered by it—in the same way that a similar contradiction fails to inconvenience the acolyte of torture in the "war against terrorism." Anders's interlocutor concedes only that we have to accept (it is the credo of security) that the totalitarian threat "prevents us from being moral": "Because we would've already—and you can't deny it—we already would've been robbed of our freedom, if not (I know that it sounds cynical, and it pains me to be so, but to overcome this pain is one of the most painful duties for us today)—I say, we already would have been deprived of our freedom if destiny had not placed the evenly matched means into our hands, the means whose apparent inertia and deterrent force are equal to the totalitarianism that threatens us."[9]

Anders's interlocutor does not stop there. He wants to give his argument the allure of an existential meditation. If we must accept the formidable consequences of atomic war, he says, it is vital that we awaken existence from its dormancy and restore to it a sense of sacrifice. Nothing is given, nothing is certain—we must be mindful of the price that we are willing to pay for a more *authentically* free existence. One cannot lay too much stress on the disastrous effects that flow from the logic of this invocation. There is no more forceful way to deploy the constitutive elements of murderous consent. It always comes down to this: over and over, we grant death the superiority of its nobility, its grandeur, its sacrificial regalia, and turn the attachment to life into weakness or cowardice. Life assumes value only in and through the trial by death. Death rises above humanity by raising humanity above itself. Only death, therefore, can restore humanity to its essence. It is undeniable that there have been moments of resistance to oppression in history where such sacrifices were necessary. But nothing is more suspect or questionable than the discourse that demands death and disguises its historical urgency by denigrating or devaluing life. The acolyte of deterrence falls into this trap. He speaks in a tone reminiscent of the grandiloquent declarations of writers and thinkers who have forever called on others than themselves to give up their lives for a greater cause. Anders's interlocutor recalls all those who, with every new war, rejoice (with unwonted pleasure) that humanity is being coerced by circumstances to detach itself from the "physical and vegetative pursuits" of life and to find meaning in more authentic values. He adopts the semantic register of availability, mobilization, and total commitment—words that themselves belong to the same totalitarian system that our sacrifice is supposed to prevent: "Maybe the greatness, or we can even say fearlessly, the *loftiness* of this test can even fill us with a certain grim pride. Life is not the highest good. . . . We summon unshakable willingness to confront a total threat with total resources and total commitment, even to sacrifice ourselves."[10] When exposed to the political or ideological assaults of this sacrificial logic, we do well to keep in mind the question that Anders asks, implicitly if not explicitly: "Sacrifice for whom? . . . Sacrifice by whom?"[11] We should retain at least two points from this set of arguments. First, at no moment does Anders's interlocutor take into consideration the specificity of the destructive power of nuclear weapons nor, consequently, the way that power affects, displaces, and disturbs our faculties of representation and imagination.

Second, the rhetoric his interlocutor mobilizes is ultimately indistinguishable from the rhetoric that accompanies all wars so as to habituate people to death and violence.

In his *Man on the Bridge*, Anders recalls that he initially kept his silence, for a moment, wondering whether it was worth replying to his interlocutor's headstrong arguments. His interlocutor's conviction seemed to draw its strength from the "ruse of reason," which treats the most commonly received ideas as the product of free reflection. His conviction also showed that acquiescence in the existence of nuclear weapons was such that much "public opinion work" [*travail de l'opinion*] was needed. As we have seen in other wars, it also implicated specific strategies as regards truth and falsehood.[12] As the plane flew over Hiroshima, Anders understood where he had to focus his attack against this ideological concentrate. He had to focus on the "banalization" of nuclear weapons. He began by observing that his interlocutor spoke of the bomb only *in the future conditional tense*, as if it had not already been used, twice, on two cities, resulting in hundreds of thousands of victims, causing irreparable physical damage, and plunging entire populations into suffering that would endure for several generations. Anders's objection summoned the memory of the dead whom we have forgotten or disavowed, the scars we have effaced, the smothered cries, the enforced silence, and, finally, again, the ears we have plugged and the eyes we have closed: "You have not mentioned what is down there, below us. Not a single time."[13]

His interlocutor was a "banalizer" [*banalisateur*]. He was surely not the only one, but he did represent the forces that actively or passively contribute to "banalization." It was necessary to recall what, from Hiroshima, was still effectively perpetuating the violence. The city had been reconstructed, and commemorative monuments had been raised, but it was all done with great concern that the memory of the bombing itself would remain as discrete and amorphous as possible. Inscriptions of memory (museums, official narratives, memorial days) were organized, prescribed, but controlled. Over the course of *Man on the Bridge*, Anders repeatedly expresses alarm at this practice. He found the violence of the effacement disorienting. He spent much time in such "places," which had been doubly drained of their memory. His conscience, his human conscience, beset by the destructions of the past and made anxious by destructions he could anticipate, was searching for something but searching in vain. Only his determination never to forget made it possible for him to discover, somewhere in the city, the tangible trace of this strange (and yet absolutely necessary) consecration of the atomic bomb's victims:

If it is possible to remember at every instant where one is, something strange happens: one realizes that this ground has become *consecrated ground* [*geweihtem Boden*]. It is hard to explain why this is so. Because why should these people, who were victims of the most extreme crime, become sacred, along with the ground where they lie? . . . Stay here and wander through the streets, and wander over the bridges! And remember where you wander, and over what, and over whom! And remember that nothing you see is real; the only real thing is that you can no longer see reality.[14]

It is in this vein that we can begin to understand the importance of Tamiki Hara's novellas and Masuji Ibuse's novel *Black Rain.* The latter explores the desire of a husband (Shigematsu) and his wife (Shigeko), both victims of Hiroshima, to prove that their niece (Yasuko) was not affected by the radiation (the "atomic sickness"). The very suspicion that she might have been would have prevented her from marrying. As proof, the uncle prepares to attach two pieces of evidence to any forthcoming proposal of marriage: the young girl's Hiroshima journal and his own. The narrative intertwines both the suffering of survivors, several years after the end of the war, and the terrifying account of the hours immediately following the nuclear attack. Shigematsu's journal recounts his efforts to cross the burning city, the view of calcified bodies on every street corner, the crazed wandering of mutilated beings who could not understand what was happening to them, the burns, the hair falling out by the handful, teeth shed like shoes, the black scars that never disappeared. From the devastated neighborhoods (which have since been rebuilt), to the train station, the bridges, the schools, the university, the battlefield, all blanketed by corpses, Masuji Ibuse *reconstitutes* the map that was destroyed. Out of nothingness, the annihilation, made unimaginable by Hiroshima's reconstruction, reemerges through the force of his writing:

> Still we came upon corpses, and yet more corpses. Driven by the heat and trapped by the smoke, they had flung themselves face down in their suffering, only to be unable to rise again and to suffocate where they lay.[15]

> We reached the rice fields. Walking along the raised paths between them in the direction of the electric car tracks, we came across a number of schoolgirls and schoolboys lying here and there in the fields, dead. They must have fled in disorder from the factory where they had been doing war work. There were adults lying about too.[16]

If Anders is critical of his interlocutor, it is because the latter *cannot* make, or *does not want* to make, the effort to imagine what happened in Hiroshima—to exercise his imagination as a form of attentiveness. If he speaks about nuclear weapons with such assurance, in a way that sounds so detached and abstract, it is because he lacks the ability to envision what happened there thirteen years earlier, on August 6, 1945. Such assurance, we could say, always ends by erasing the prefix from the word "re-construction." In time (which can be short), the substitute effaces what it replaces. It fills the space left empty by the ruins, or it deprives of continuity what it excised from time. Because life must "continue," because wounded beings must also "reconstruct" their lives, the restored cities leave little trace of this rupture, of the interruption to which we respond, in some sites (like the abandoned streets of the martyred village Oradour-sur-Glane), by saying that time has been frozen: "If you had been there, I mean, down there in Hiroshima, you would have seen that everything has been rebuilt. And with such an outrageous completeness that nothing bears witness to the destruction. The world looks complete once again. Despite the two hundred thousand deaths. Unfortunately, the city still looks complete."[17]

This is a decisive point. With this incidental aside, we arrive at the heart of what connects murderous consent to thought of the world. Everything supports the illusion of completeness: "The world," writes Anders, "looks complete once again." And yet, though it seems that way, it is not. It is an illusion to believe that the world is complete again—an illusion to cling to the effacement, the forgetting, the indifference, or the ignorance. The illusion consists in acting, living, and thinking as if the dead of Hiroshima had not opened a breach and gouged out a cavity in the completeness [*complétude*] of the world—it is as if they had not placed this same world in debt to itself. What debt? In light of the preceding chapters, one can offer a partial response: the world *owes it to itself* to be concerned by its incompleteness [*incomplétude*], because here and elsewhere there are still victims, survivors, and everywhere beings who have been made vulnerable by the multiple forms of insecurity to which they have been exposed. It is a question of the responsibility that acknowledges [*donne droit*] the vulnerability and mortality of others before all other considerations. But even this will not suffice. We must go a step further. It is also a question of whether such a responsibility can overcome limits, of all sorts, to understand itself, to experience itself singularly, and to be shared as "concern for the world"— in other words, to engage in the extension *without limits and without frontiers* of the attention, care, and assistance that the vulnerable implore. Our awareness of what is missing is in this engagement. Only our awareness of such a debt can bring about a movement, an emotion, an effort of imagination, the goal of which is not to *complete* the world but, first, to recognize its incompleteness. Multiple forces seek to wipe it from memory or to portray it as collateral or negligible, or perhaps as necessary or inevitable. But this movement receives its injunction to act and to think from the very breach or fracture for which, from its origins, it assumed responsibility. Witness to this injunction is borne by the lives of activists and associations worldwide who stand with the vulnerable. Their response is to remember the victims and to care for the survivors. It is what is owed them. We rediscover this debt in the calls for "never again" that issue from the lips of survivors in the aftermath of violence: "I (we) want to remember, I (we) must remember, so that this *never happens again*, so that *never again* will I (we) be ashamed of what humans do to other humans." "The reconstruction is disloyal to the dead. They themselves never complain. I mean, the dead. They never complain. And those who do not answer the call never notice. As missing, I mean. The scandal is not that the dead are invisible, but that the missing are absent, and their absence is invisible."[18]

Being "faithful to the dead," in the skies above Hiroshima, consists primarily in recognizing and remembering that the use of atomic weapons cannot be discussed merely in the future conditional tense, despite the geopolitical, strategic, political, and military-industrial interests that would have us act *as if* that were the case. Anders expresses this sentiment succinctly but emphatically: "It has come to the indicative," he writes, "an indisputable indicative."[19] Yet his interlocutor continues to deny this obvious fact; he refuses to consider "what happened yesterday" in the name of "what is the threat today." To pursue his objections Anders is obliged to go through his adversary's arguments point by point. Since he does not want to speak of the past, since he has no ear for memory, Anders agrees to speak to his adversary in the future tense and engages with him on his own terms of threat assessment. Anders—the radicality of his thought is on display here—endows insecurity with a more powerful capacity to provoke. This is why the first thing, the foundational [*principielle*] thing in his eyes, is to home in on the deceitful nature of the initial alternative: "Atomic *or* totalitarian threat." The assumption behind this pseudochoice is debatable because it makes *as if* a world exposed to the real risk of nuclear war does not imply a more formidable *alienation*, on a planetary level, than the privation of freedom, against which, according to this apostle of deterrence, it is supposed to protect humanity. Anders writes, not without anger or provocation, that if indeed the sword of Damocles is dangling above the heads of humanity, no matter what world they belong to, free or not, we must use our imagination and recognize that, "like prisoners in concentration camps, we can define their lives only as 'not-yet-killed.'"[20]

Anders advances his indictment by placing in perspective the difference, in nature and degree, of the danger posed by totalitarianism, on the one hand, and nuclear arms, on the other. In the case of the latter, we must imagine annihilation with no going back and no way out, total and definitive destruction. The grip of totalitarian systems on the lives of individuals is provisional (we can always hope that they collapse), but the nuclear threat is permanent. The date August 6, 1945, signifies, before all else, this *new permanence*. Camus made this same observation as early as August 8 in an editorial in *Combat*: "Even before now it was not easy to breathe in this tormented world. Now we find ourselves confronted with a new source of anguish, which has every likelihood of proving fatal. Mankind has probably been given its last chance."[21]

Freedom, as defined by Anders's interlocutor, is never definitively lost—people whose freedom has been confiscated have, we know, been able to reclaim it. As the images of the liberation of Paris or the fall of the Berlin Wall remind us, the recovery of freedom is one of the rare joys that the spectacle of history in the making can provide us. But this is not true of the specter of humanity's self-destruction. No enthusiasm, no jubilation awaits us. Once this specter has begun to haunt us, nothing can rid us of it. Fifty years later we can better assess the nature of the threat, but the international community, nevertheless, seems powerless to prevent or even slow the proliferation of nuclear arms. The two threats, totalitarian and nuclear, do not inscribe human existence in the same temporality. They do not relate to time in the same way. The nuclear threat, unlike the totalitarian threat, consigns all humans, together, to the selfsame finitude, that of their simultaneous disappearance. As in works of fiction that explore this angst or fantasy, time itself comes to an end, *for everyone* (or nearly everyone), at the same instant.

For Anders, the distinction between the "free world" and the "totalitarian world" must be understood in the context of this "for everyone." Individuals from both worlds are exposed to technological processes that are beyond their ability not only to control but even to visualize (particularly in their effects), and that overflow the boundary that this distinction (*free* or *totalitarian*) is supposed to ensure. On this point, the analysis of *The Man on the Bridge* rejoins the central thread of *The Obsolescence of Humankind*. Both dramatically signify that the protections that, we assumed, had secured humanity's existence everywhere have escaped our mastery to the point that they signify *loss*, whether we are willing to admit it or not. Anders, at this point, proffers a final objection, well suited to the intimidating prose of our apostles of deterrence: the loss is *transgenerational*. Loss is indeed, henceforward, the principal, most decisive, and most determinate thing that generations can pass on to one another. The entire logic of sacrifice encounters its limits. When we are asked to envision, courageously, the sacrifice of our lives, we should know that we are offering to sacrifice not only (or necessarily) our lives alone but those of our children and grand-children as well. The looming extinction not only effaces every recipient and beneficiary of our sacrificial offering but produces suffering of the particular sort that is forever conjured by the word "Hiroshima," as evoked by Tamiki Hara's *Summer Flowers* or Masuji Ibuse's *Black Rain*: "The whole left cheek was a blackish-purple color, and the burned skin had shriveled up on the flesh, without parting company with it, to form ridges across the cheek. The side of the left nostril was infected, and fresh pus seemed to be coming from under the dried-up crust on top. I turned the left side of my face to the mirror. Could this be my own face, I wondered. My heart pounded at the idea, and the face in the mirror grew more and more unfamiliar."[22]

"We Were Ashamed to Be Human"

How are we to understand the words of the survivors or to give grounds for [*donner droit*] their silence? In the introductory pages of *The Man on the Bridge*, Anders recounts, as if the meaningfulness of his entire journal, both moral and political, hung in the balance, the delegation's first encounter with the survivors. He describes the feeling that seized him and his companions, no matter what their convictions regarding nuclear disarmament or the reasons behind their participation in the conference might have been. Politics can get in the way of agreement and unity, and peaceful (or pacifist) intentions can stumble over the ulterior motives, calculations, interests, and jealousies of sovereign states. But there now arose, for an instant, a feeling that transcended all difference and dismissed all interests to the dust heap of indecency. Suddenly, the disparity between the participants' partisan (thus predetermined) political (sometimes philosophical) words and the impoverished utterances of the witnesses appeared in its full cruelty.

The "experience" echoes Ōe's own account of going to Hiroshima as a journalist in August 1963 to cover the ninth world conference against atomic weapons. The event, he confesses, utterly overwhelmed him and changed his life. There, in the beginning, he witnessed the political confrontations between Japan's various political parties in the executive committee and the diplomatic skirmishes between foreign delegations, notably Soviet and Chinese. It was as if the misfortune evoked by all the stone memorials that make Hiroshima look like a vast cemetery, Ōe writes, as well as the close proximity of the monument dedicated to "all the souls here [who] rest in peace for we shall not repeat the evil," had no power to silence the political passions on display in the conference. "The appeal is 'action more than argument,' but the dispute does not thereby recede quietly into the shadows at this world conference, it emerges forcefully into the light from the moment the conference opens."[23]

A logic of suspicion jeopardizes all disarmament conferences and, indeed, all international conferences, like those that tackle climate change. All the demands, propositions, and draft resolutions are assumed to mask calculated interests. Participants are faulted for confining themselves to this logic. It seems obvious that representatives of a sovereign state would consider it their priority and imperative to fight for the interests of the sovereignty that delegates them. Hence, they inevitably display a certain deafness and blindness. But blindness to what? And deafness to what? The whole question is here—and the response is related to what I am describing as "murderous consent."

Blindness and deafness, proven or feigned, are de rigueur at most important international conferences and are the cause of division. Every compromise, every partial agreement, is, simultaneously, a victory over both (it is better than acting as though there were nothing to take away from what was seen and heard) and, to the extent that prejudice makes it possible, a concession to both. They manifest the limits inherent in all political gatherings. In Hiroshima, however, they assume a supplementary dimension, which escaped neither Günther Anders nor Kenzaburō Ōe. Beyond the place and the violence the name Hiroshima symbolizes, a name that has become a synonym for exceptional suffering, there is, beyond the victims and the dead, the enduring presence of the survivors of the attacks. It is these survivors who reveal the utter cruelty of nuclear weapons. They are living on borrowed time. They are living for the time being, condemned. As the delegations argue, Ōe, who, unlike Anders, is not frustrated by the language barrier, goes out to meet them. Unlike those who "vanished in an instant, vaporized," these remained behind to "live out their cruel destinies, forever afraid to have their leukocytes counted."[24]

Meetings such as these structure *Hiroshima Notes*. Ōe recounts, for example, a meeting with the hospital director Shigeto Fumio, who relates how on August 6, 1945, "in the open space in front of the hospital, thousands of dead bodies had to be piled up each day and then cremated in its yard," and how he was obliged to "stay on duty, directing the wounded doctors and nurses engaged in caring for dying people."[25] Subsequently, by recording the extent of the bomb's effects year after year, he was able to identify the syndrome of radiation sickness over the course of several generations.

Through contact with the sick and their suffering, their brief remissions and relapses, and their fatal exhaustion (which Masuji Ibuse also describes), Fumio established the link between atomic bombardment and cancer. Health authorities, foiled in their calculations, were slow to acknowledge the link. If I were to search for a concrete illustration of the attention, care, and assistance that are enjoined everywhere by the mortality and vulnerability of the other, in resistance against the proliferation of all the various forms of murderous consent, Shigeto Fumio, the doctor from Hiroshima, might well provide it. Along with many others, he confronts us with an exemplary figure of this singular edification of a being-against-death that acknowledges and comes to grips with the incompleteness of the world:

> He draws on his experience, the hospital records, and clinical observations to determine the nature of A-bomb diseases and to fight them. Initially, he thought that A-bomb illnesses could be cured within a few years—until he found that leukemia was among the illnesses. Certainly the atomic assault was the worst disaster to befall mankind, and there is no way to know how radiation affects human bodies apart from clinical work and the discoveries made in actual clinical situations.[26]

> Dr. Shigeto took upon himself the misery of Hiroshima, and has continued to do so for twenty years. How tenacious he has been![27]

Ōe recalls—the memory never deserts him—the large cohort of faces and bodies, the litany of suffering that puts politics in debt, that puts all those who share in politics in debt. They—not merely those who are active in political life, but everyone—cannot be indifferent to that debt. If politics were not compromised by lies and half-truths, by the will to move beyond the misfortunes of the past and advance toward the future, no one would remain impervious to this debt. But Ōe tells a different story. Like a wedge driven into politics' certitudes, the gaze and words of the victims become insistent, like an ethical injunction. Ōe makes palpable the isolation of those who live in the anguished expectation that their sickness will catch up with them, who live in the distress of "old people with cancer or leukemia . . . who could do nothing but despair." In homage to the aging survivors, who greet the pacifist demonstrations that pass before their door (as if they could be the bearers of hope for those other than themselves), Ōe asks, in reverence of the Calvary of having to live on borrowed time, the one question that really matters: "who among the demonstrators, having seen your hands held out in confident expectation, could not have felt a debt toward you?"[28]

This, then, is what the accounts of the witnesses expose to thought. Politics, that of the militants and others as well, owes them. But, Ōe explains, between those who are in debt to politics and those to whom politics is indebted (the *hibakusha*, the "survivors"), there lies an abyss. The scene is tragic. The demonstrators in the park hardly notice the families of the dead who, apparently ignorant of the demonstration, have come to place flowers and burn incense before the monument. Ōe, viewing the event, explains: "they seem to be playing the part of the chorus in a Greek tragedy, adding dignity to the agony and ecstasy of the drama on the conference platform."[29] Indeed, what is happening onstage, in that moment, is the opening of an abyss of incomprehension and indifference between the aging philosopher-survivor, who is both the voice of ethics and the representative of the victims who live on borrowed time (men and women whose lives are riveted to the progression of the sickness in their bodies), and the politicized crowd, eager for watchwords and slogans, impatient, and insensitive to the moral significance of the survivors' lesson. The debt, incommensurable, remains unpaid, both by policymakers and by spectators, unconcerned (this is the tragedy) with acknowledging and accrediting [*rendre droit*] the new forms of vulnerability and mortality that the nuclear disaster engendered. And yet, this is the debt that we have indeed inherited from Hiroshima. Ōe reminds us of this already in the prologue to his *Notes*, where he evokes the neglected *hibakusha* from the island of Okinawa. There is no escaping their appeals for medication, care, and assistance: "how can the Hiroshima experience ever be brought to an end in anyone's heart?"[30]

Five years earlier, Günther Anders was similarly charged with bearing "Hiroshima within me," when he first confronted the gaze and voices of the victims of the bombing.[31] The experience I described above as an ordeal, however (how else could one describe it?), is inseparable from a concomitant experience, unanticipated and unheard of, which invalidates all identitarian discourse that assumes that an individual's affective, emotive, or intellectual reactions are always apprehended within the straightjacket of some cultural, ideological, or religious belonging or are confined within spheres of national or civilizational affiliation. It is the experience that is reported by, and that unites, the readers of a variety of texts, translated into multiple languages, such as Ōe's *Hiroshima Notes*, Masuji Ibuse's *Black Rain*, and Tamiki Hara's *Summer Flowers*. We discover that we have been "touched" or "struck" in the same way as others, men and women, coming from very different horizons. It is the experience of the "universality of the heart." It wells from a shared feeling, one that caught Anders's attention in *The Obsolescence of Humankind*, and to which he accords considerable importance in his reflections on Hiroshima. It is the experience of shame: "You will ask, what is this feeling which we all felt identically? The answer, which was mentioned in later conversations and always from different mouths: the feeling was that we were *ashamed* of each other, and *we were ashamed to be human*."[32]

Shame: this is the sentiment that attests to the "universality of the heart." It is a sentiment commensurate with Camus's rebellion and with Levinas's kindness. Like each of these injunctions, and like the "attestations of the human" that are the teaching of Paul Celan, shame is responding to murderous consent. What is its response? It is a moralist response. It brings agitation, trouble, and resistance to the order of political certitude. How must we understand it? How can we feel ashamed to be human—ashamed, to say it another way, of "humanity" or of "*our* humanity"? At a minimum, shame assumes the existence of a fissure [*fêlure*] or fracture [*cassure*], not unrelated to the breach [*faille*] in belonging to the world that I have been associating with murderous consent throughout this book. To be ashamed of humanity, of our humanity, implies that something has been weakened, if not broken, in the "confidence" that we can place—or thought we could place—in humanity or in the credit that we think—or imagined—we can, even should, accord. Something has come undone. We can anticipate already that, somewhat further on in *Man on the Bridge*, Anders will link the question of shame to that of nihilism *today* and will speak of the need to restore a "moral situation" based on, or in the horizon of, this fracture.

Anders names this breach, which bears the mark of all the positions he has taken, "desolidarization" [*désolidarisation*, translating the German *Desolidarisierung*]. This is what shame means, always: the painful, necessarily *unresolved* [*inaboutie*] tension that results from desolidarization. To be ashamed of oneself or one's acts is to attempt, precisely in situations in which it is impossible, to distance oneself from what one has been, what one has said, or what one has done (or failed to say or to do). Shame is the tension that belongs to the aporetic longing for an impossible yet necessary *separation*. I wish, one wishes, we wish, that what has been done or said had not been done or said, had not taken place, because it damages or weakens what I think, he or she thinks, we think is *owed* [*devoir*, "to owe," "to be obligated"]. Owed to whom or to what? This is what is at stake in the question of responsibility; and it takes us back to the theme of indebtedness: "This may sound strange, maybe even arrogant, or even like an outrageous desolidarization. It might be. We did not have the time to think about it. The first reaction was certainly one of denial: the refusal to recognize that those who were capable of doing this are like ourselves, the refusal to attribute them to us."[33]

As Derrida might have said, citing what he calls "hyperbolic ethics," it is this aporia that makes recalling our debt a responsibility. But what demands sustained attention at this point, what considerably complicates our analysis of shame—and particularly, "the shame of being human, humans who regard each other"—are the overlapping connections that (simultaneously) make and unmake humanity. "Desolidarization" evokes more than one understanding of solidarity, as shown by Patočka's use of the term when, twenty years later, in *Heretical Essays*, he called for a "solidarity of the shaken" that problematizes the meaning both of the word and the world.[34] The solidarity of the shaken is effectively and indissociably a movement of "solidarization" [*solidarisation*]. In reality, there are three relations implicated in shame. The first concerns the rupture of all ties with those responsible for murder. In shame one cannot desire or imagine acknowledging a common humanity with murderers, even when doing otherwise seems impossible. Levinas was often asked, "Does the executioner still have a face? A face that expresses the transcendence of the infinite?" The (aporetic) rupture provides the beginnings of a response to this question. Whenever violence has a face, even if deformed by hate and given over to a mere caricature of itself, it drives me to feel shame; it prods me toward the impossible possibility of desolidarization. We shall see below that the specificity of nuclear weapons is their ability to be triggered from a distance. If they are ever used again, they will usher in (and complete) a world in which the *face-to-face* interaction between victims and their executioners no longer exists.

And yet (and this is the paradox), at the very moment that the trial of shame arises, it brings about two extraordinary forms of solidarity that, in Anders's words, "restore" humanity there where it seemed irremediably jeopardized. Both forms give humanity a new chance, but only *on the condition* that they stipulate is imperative. Because nothing is erased and no assurance or reassurance is given, they do not signify the preservation or the conservation of a humanity that is reconciled with itself. They merely trace, as a last opportunity or last chance (as Camus would say), the uncertain and never-completed path of a restoration, of being restored *differently*. This is the only path offered by the painful memory of all forms of murderous consent:

> So that I am not misunderstood. The decisive element is not the desolidarization [*Desolidarisierung*] contained in the feeling of shame [*Schamgefühl*] but rather the community of desolidarization, that is, the new solidarity that has become reality. This is why it is unjustified to be indignant about shame (which I often experienced when I

returned home). As for me, I have never felt the meaning of "humanity" with such strength and poignancy as in the hour of desolidarization. If your neighbors—regardless whether they are African, American, German, Russian, Burmese, or Japanese—are silent for the same reason, then the humanity in us is not damaged but restored; maybe even really established.[35]

What are these two unheard-of [*inouïs*, or "uncanny"] forms of solidarity? The first brings together, in desolidarization, those who share [*partagent*,"share" and/or "divide"] in it, that is, in the present case, those who have lost the capacity to speak because they have eyes to see and ears to hear. This first form transcends all denominational, political, and ideological affiliations. It delineates the community of the "shaken," for whom the "meaning of the world," as seen through the eyes and accounts of the victims, becomes once more eminently problematic. For this reason, however, it is the second form of solidarity—which accompanies shame—that effectively holds everything together. This second form consists in the bond that gives substance to the attention, care, and assistance that each of those who share in desolidarization brings singularly to the "survivors," however inadequately. Because solidarity is never equal to their suffering—and because it survives the victims' deaths in its determination never to forget—it persists in binding together those who share the feeling that Ōe calls "Hiroshima within me."[36] It goes without saying that solidarity is not limited to those who harbor suffering in their memory. It belongs to all the witnesses and victims of this twentieth century of extremes, and all those who retrospectively will have turned their attention to them.

But the analysis of shame does not end here.[37] It returns several times in the pages of *The Man on the Bridge*. First, there is the shame of the *hibakusha* themselves. They are ashamed, not of having survived the bombing, however provisionally, but of their weakness and fragility, of the care they are ashamed to ask for, of the medication that fills those who require it with guilt. They are ashamed of their sickness. It disturbs those around them and therefore drives its victims to hide, to keep out of sight, to stay away from the hospital. It is this shame of the victim that Kenzaburō Ōe himself feels some years later and that is the most painful part of what the cycle of violence can perpetuate from one generation to the next:

> It is in Hiroshima that a great many girls stay indoors because they are ashamed of the ugly keloid scars on their faces. How can we understand the sense of shame that the A-bomb victims feel about their experiences, without also being ashamed of ourselves? What a frightening inversion of feeling!

A girl is ashamed of her face disfigured by keloids. In her mind she divides all people on earth into two groups; the sense of shame is the line separating persons with keloid scars from all others without them. The girls with keloids feel ashamed of themselves before those who have none. They feel humiliated by curious glances of all other people who have no keloid disfigurations.[38]

Then there is the shame that Anders feels when confronted with the denial of suffering, the indifference that prolongs suffering *into the present*, or when confronted by the neglect of suffering still *to come*—shame, therefore, for those who enjoy a "good situation" ["*bonne assise*"], as Levinas would say, assured of their place in the world and confident in its order and progress. They will always resist the pull of this feeling of shame and will mock or discredit it in the name of more realistic imperatives. Shame has this in common with Camus's rebellion and Grossman's and Levinas's kindness: it opposes murderous consent *against all good sense*. This is why shame cannot be reduced to a feeling that is merely endured, and why shame does not cause those who feel it to get bogged down in some kind of paralyzing passivity. Like rebellion and kindness, shame assumes responsibility:

> Today's shame: the shame of what people *have been* capable of doing to one another; the shame, thus, of what they can *still* do to one another today, thus also what *we* can do to others, and thus the shame of also being a *person*.
>
> This shame must be claimed. Those who have *done* it—the culprits, the guilty—are not acquitted of the shame they deserve, but they do not recognize that they deserve shame, so there must be a representative to stand in and assume the necessary shame for them.[39]

How might we better understand this triple temporality: shame before *what has happened*, shame before *what is*, and shame before what could still or *must still happen*? How can we understand it, in the present and in the future, as orientation? What imperative lies waiting behind the infinitive "to be oriented by shame," which this temporality seems to instigate? The preceding analyses bear ample witness to the feeling aroused by what has happened. Shame before the past is the suffering caused by a rupture in our moral relations, understood as attention to vulnerability and mortality, with which the release of the bombs over Hiroshima and Nagasaki is complicit. It marks a rupture because their victims were overwhelmingly civilians, going about their daily chores, as we are reminded by the laconic cry of a woman, lying flat on the grass, her arms raised toward the mushroom cloud: "Hey, you monster of a cloud! Go away! We're non-belligerents! D'you hear—go away!"[40]

The "shame of what people have been capable of doing to one another" is a torment that the past inscribes in the present. But Anders's most radical analyses show that shame in the present is also shame for the present, not merely of *what happened*, what opened the unbridgeable fracture (the breach in being-in-the-world and the fissure in humanity), but of *what perpetuates*, *prolongs*, and *maintains* the suspension of a moral situation. It is shame for the political, ideological, and cultural forces that oppose, in the face of and in hostility to this torment, what I thematized above as the promise of its (a moral situation's) restoration. Anders expresses his thinking at the end of a narrative that we must first listen to, the words of a survivor, as echoed in all the reports collected by Ōe in *Hiroshima Notes*, as well as in a passage of *Black Rain* that expresses the same despair of abandonment:

> When I regained consciousness, I was badly burned and my wife was also in terrible shape. We climbed through the rubble. Then my wife stumbled on something. It was a man. We didn't recognize him. And we couldn't see whether he was dead or still alive. But he recognized us. "Leave me, child," he whispered, "flee!" The voice was strange and outlandish, but I knew it was my father's voice. But when I looked at him, I said to myself, "No, it isn't him." "Away!" he screamed (no, I don't think that he screamed, but it sounded like an order). "Away, or you'll stay here!" So it is him, I thought, and I ran to get him some water. But when I tried to give him water and I saw that he refused it, I said once again, "It isn't him." And I was frightened. And I said to my wife, "Do as he says!" and pulled her with me, and so we left him, we left him lying there. On the way, we saw many others lying on the ground, who we also left there. Each time I thought to myself, "This is my father." . . . But I am not finished with what I did or didn't do there. And you wouldn't be finished with it, either.[41]

As he transcribes the narrative, Anders recounts first the pain and shame his audience feels, not so much for this man, whom no one can claim to judge, as for the "atomic situation," its pointlessness, its disorientation, that drove him to suspend, against his will, the moral obligation that consists of caring for those to whom one is connected by family ties, at any and all costs (perhaps at the cost of one's life), until one's dying breath. What is shameful is not the flight itself (we cannot possibly share the momentousness of this failure as lived by the man of the narrative) but rather the fact that "men can put other men in situations where it is no longer possible for them to act in a human way."[42] What Levinas and Grossman call "kindness"—feeding the hungry, giving drink to the thirsty, assisting the afflicted—is no longer possible.[43]

When such a situation is generalized and normalized, when we resign ourselves to the risk inflicted on humanity by a general suspension of morality, in the name of imperatives in comparison with which the word "morality" provokes a smile (we recall the large, frozen, stereotypical, and ultimately troubling smile that Levinas evokes in "On the Spirit of Geneva"),[44] and when the thought of future and inevitable suffering and destruction reveals itself to be no more convincing than the memory of suffering and destruction from the recent past, then we have inaugurated a situation—the triumph of nihilism—that would provoke a strong reaction by the likes of Camus, Freud, Levinas, and Kraus. Because the specter of the annihilation of life, beginning with that of relationships, reigns supreme in this situation, it is, writes Anders, "the situation of nihilism today."[45] Thus we understand why shame is declined in the future tense. Because it enables us to act morally, that is, "humanely," once again, it is the necessary response to this situation. "What in earlier morality could be presupposed as self-evident—that moral or unmoral actions are possible—we can no longer take for granted. This is why the first requirement is the recovery of this situation. The postulate is thus: prevent the emergence of such situations where it is no longer possible to be moral, which for this reason are beyond the competence of moral judgment."[46]

Three remarks are in order. First, what Anders calls the "suspension of morality" invites comparison with what I have been calling "murderous consent," to the extent that it consists of the eclipse of the care, assistance, and attention that the vulnerability and the mortality of others enjoin. When individuals find themselves in a situation where they no longer live within a fabric of "moral relations"—a *living-with*—it is almost always conditioned by such an eclipse. When the suspension is as extreme as that recounted by Anders's witness, when it is the abandonment of our own loved ones to which we are forced to consent (an abandonment that, in fact, applies to all others: "Each time I thought to myself, 'This is my father,'" Anders's narrative relates), then the suspension signifies *dehumanization*. It tears to shreds everything that enables us to define an existence as "human." When we can no longer offer help or respond to the cries of the vulnerable, life itself is reduced to the bare conditions of survival, not blind or foreign to the suffering of others, but *reduced* to the impossibility of providing relief, to reaching out, to putting others first. The second remark is that the "atomic situation" opens a breach in our belonging to the world in a way that bears no comparison with any other. Its specificity resides in three points, each of which requires careful analysis. First, it challenges our capacity to picture or imagine what in this situation might constitute "consent." Second, it shatters the bond between the possibility of massive destruction and the development of a culture of the enemy. Up to now we have thought that all murderous consent assumed hatred of the other and the stereotyping and defamation that go into the cultivation of that hatred. But the atomic bomb is controlled and detonated from a distance. It is amenable to rational calculation in a way that implicates neither the intoxication of combat nor warrior enthusiasm, zeal, or frenzy. The apostles of deterrence count on our rationality to convince themselves that nobody would ever risk nuclear war—as if we could not imagine some Doctor Strangelove, adrift in his apocalyptic vision of the end of time, turning the entire world into the object of his death drive. Finally, the third point that describes the specificity of the atomic situation is that it dramatically transforms the perception of the world that it has fractured. It frees it of all divisions (national, civilizational, continental) and establishes a mode of belonging in which *all are the neighbors of all*.

There remains a third and final overarching remark. In the analysis of murderous consent there is a nagging question that is difficult to escape: do all these developments and witnesses signify that we are doomed to murderous consent by our nature or essence? Is it an incontestable, inevitable, and inescapable dimension of human life as living-with? Levinas and Grossman have already, from the depth of the horror of Hitler's death camps and Stalin's gulags, discerned the way out of the downward spiral of such thinking. The small voice of Ikonnikov, obstinate and unreasonable, resisted the supposed fatality of being resigned to murder, of accepting it, or promoting it. But Anders, though very close to these authors, finds another point of resistance against this fatality: shame. It is not much and, simultaneously, it is quite a lot: shame unmakes, unknots, or recuses all "solidarity with murder."

"Close Your Eyes and Give in to Your Imagination"!

Yet this implicit, tacit, and barely conscious "solidarity with murder" has weapons at its disposal that seem invincible. Among them, the most insidious and tenacious is our lack of imagination, our limited ability to represent evil as such. It is not just a question of our grasp of the effects of Hiroshima or our anticipation of the consequences of the never-ending threat of nuclear warfare. When I evoked the tenaciousness of famine in the world and the silence it elicits in the media and in politics, I was already made mindful of the existence of some defect or deficiency or failure.

And if I have turned to literature throughout this book, it is to palliate this deficiency. As noted in the preceding chapters, it is not philosophy that is bringing commentary to literary texts but literature that is buttressing philosophy, there where needed, there where conceptual analysis calls for, and even demands, a different mode of representation. If literature has had to come to the rescue and prove, and continue to prove, how indispensable it is, particularly in this book, it is because the many and varying forms of murderous consent take aim at philosophy and leave it disarmed. If literature is privileged, it is because it works at the limits of representation. It displaces its frontiers; it evokes and makes imaginable that which exceeds our powers to represent what we are interrogating; it distresses or perturbs, like cinema, the barriers it inevitably confronts, regardless of what the source of the obstacle might be, whether education, prejudice, or ideology. To see otherwise, to see farther, to recall as well as to anticipate: these are the resources that literature affords to those who are gripped by this notion of shame, as discussed by Ōe and Anders.

Anders's appeal to the imagination is a guiding thread that connects his writing on Hiroshima to other texts of his: "Today, anyone who is limited to the perception of the visible misses reality. Because reality is full of little fantasies. Anyone who doesn't have enough imagination, or who fears imagination and prevents it from adequately representing the fantastic, remains a dreamer. The alleged perceptual world is an ivory tower, empiricism is escapism. Today, really seeing is only possible with closed eyes; today, the only 'realist' is the person with enough imagination to imagine tomorrow's fantasy."[47] When certain voices—though far too few—dared to alert political authorities (American, British, and ecclesiastical) to the extermination of the Jews of Europe, describing the gas chambers and crematoria, their stories probably seemed far-fetched to their interlocutors—far-fetched or fantastical, exaggerated, out of proportion, as so many people at that time believed. The Nazis' rational, calculated, physical elimination of millions of individuals so far outstripped the powers of the imagination that people could not accept the idea of such a crime. When the reality of the Soviet gulags could no longer be ignored, when it became apparent that Stalin had orchestrated the deportation, disappearance, or elimination of tens of millions of Soviet citizens, most Communists around the world refused to accept it. They could not conceive that such an action was possible. A crime like this could only be the invention of the enemies of revolution, a phantasm, the monstrous invention of some reactionary imagination. But denial such as this is crime's good fortune. Denial, the refusal to admit what seems inadmissible, our willingness to minimize, attenuate, and correct what seems unimaginable, is always invoked as justification of murderous consent, at least partially.

As for the articulation of an ethics and politics that oppose the proliferation of murderous consents, we need to invert the standing of the imagination. It must not be considered as primarily a faculty for inventing murderous utopias or be confined to servicing reverie without object. The imagination can no longer be viewed in this way because we need it to discern a reality [*un réel*] that is potentially, if not already, murderous. To imagine does not mean to make present to consciousness something that does not or could not exist. It means, rather, to represent what most people do not see but what nevertheless seems inescapable—to anticipate what happens, to anticipate what threatens unavoidably to happen. To imagine is not to calculate or foresee. It is rather to prohibit oneself from excluding the possibility that something that is not could never be, which is to say, the possibility of something worse: "Today, the utopian is no longer the person content or amused by imagining a nonbeing or a dream image; inversely, it is the person who imagines himself as a being, as a Still-being [*Noch-sein*], who could (or probably will) be nonbeing tomorrow, and who assumes this Still-being without the slightest justification."[48]

This inversion introduces an initial modification into our understanding of nihilism, one that considerably exacerbates and increases its importance. Being a nihilist does not necessarily mean displaying a will to destroy or even the desire to see the world destroyed—it also means, more insidiously, the refusal to imagine the possibility of a worst case. Utopia in this context consists of dreaming of the world as imperishable, of acting as if its destruction is implausible, of endowing it with robustness, security, and confidence, such that, against the backdrop of the fractures opened up by past terrors, the extension of the abyss to the world as a whole goes unnoticed. For Anders, such are the constitutive features of our contemporary utopia, in its most current nihilist dimension: to continue to see the world, despite the victims of Hiroshima and Nagasaki, as if its destruction were unthinkable. To put it otherwise, it is because nothing seems necessarily to exclude, a priori, the possibility of humanity's self-destruction that the naïve belief in the continuing existence of a world, true to itself, begins to look like "a pure *utopos*."[49] The memory of the past thus unites with the anticipation of the future. Connecting both past and future to the present, Anders notes in *Man on the Bridge* on August 6, 1959, fourteen years, to the day, after the bomb fell on Hiroshima: "Close your eyes and give in to your imagination. Because today, only the indolent rely on their eyes."[50]

The failure of the imagination would not be so terrible if it were not linked, intrinsically, to the very nature of the atomic bomb. Like all weapons of mass destruction, the characteristic feature [*le propre*] of the atomic bomb is that the person or people who deploy it (or order its deployment) can have only a distant and very abstract perception of its effects. This is why the impossibility of representing the destruction provoked by nuclear weapons goes hand in hand with an *emotional deficit*. If it is true that murderous consent is indeed the essence of nihilism, it is a nihilism that is aggravated by the disparity between the weapon, as represented by those who produce, stockpile, and test it, and the reality of its effects, that is, its infinitely murderous nature. Proof is found in the difficulty that Anders encounters (and which we continue to encounter in our day) when he tries to tackle the question of atomic weapons on this basis and make people admit that we are actually talking about mass murder and that the proliferation of these arms, which is difficult to contain, signifies the growing probability of their use, up to and including total annihilation. Anders shows no hesitation in taking on this difficulty. In the first pages of "Commandments in the Atomic Age," which he addresses, in July 1959, to Claude Eatherly, we read:

> Not only our reason has its (Kantian) limits, not only *it* is finite, but also our imagination, and even more so our feeling. At best we can repent the murder of *one* man: more our feeling does not perform; we may be able to imagine *ten*: more our imagination cannot perform; but to destroy a hundred thousand people causes no difficulties whatsoever. And that not only for technical reasons; and not only because the acting has been transformed into a mere "acting with" and into a mere releasing, whose effect remains unseeable. But rather for a moral reason; just because mass murder lies infinitely far outside the sphere of those actions which we can visualize and towards which we can take an emotional position; and whose execution could be hampered through imagination and feelings.[51]

Consent is blind not only because its anticipation of the effects of an atomic explosion is abstract and partial but also because—despite its cruelty—mass destruction no longer requires hatred. In all cases of mass murder up till now, we could assume that the murderers were aware of the deaths they caused—that is, they saw (they lived with) the beings whom they consigned to death. Their execution was wanted. In most cases, assistance, participation, and perception went together. At the very least, mass murder required an "army," "special forces," or some repressive apparatus whose death drive had to be let loose, magnified, and sustained by speeches and images. In the words of Levinas, the face of the other had to be replaced by a caricature.[52] That there was a connection between the work of the drives (which carry out this transformation) and the possibility of cruelty seemed obvious and inescapable. It is why the problem of truth is connected to the question of murderous consent.[53]

The atomic bomb, however, makes hatred incidental. This is not to say that states now do without a "culture of the enemy," assuming they still even care about trying to convince their public that it is necessary to remain prepared to use nuclear weapons. It simply means that, technically, massive destruction *without hatred* is now conceivable—or, inversely, that the possibility of mass destruction could come down to the self-destructive madness of a single person. This is why we fear the proliferation of nuclear weapons. We fear that they could fall into the wrong hands. To bring about the apocalypse the world no longer needs to be ripped apart by irreconcilable hatreds. The death drive of a single person will suffice. In the case of an atomic explosion, the victims will never see their executioners, who themselves will experience their victims' eradication in only a fragmentary and distant way, as an "impoverished" experience. And yet, again, it is not appropriate to speak in the future conditional tense. As Anders tirelessly reminds us, such abstraction and fragmentation are, already, the experience of Hiroshima:

> What we perceive remains fragmented: either it is *only* the preparation or *only* the effect. And that is particularly true for the most important situations, that is, when we decide on the being or nonbeing of others, or when we decide for ourselves to be or not to be. This mutilation of perception corresponds to the mutilation of our emotions. What I don't know can't hurt me. What we prepare without seeing the effects of our preparations or the victims, what could hit us without our first seeing the attacker's preparations—this remains unworkable for our feelings. Such is the unworkability that occurs here in Hiroshima.[54]

The victims of Hiroshima will never have seen the faces of those responsible for their suffering, nor could they have hazarded a guess as to their will to destroy. As all the narratives testify, the victims no more understood what happened to them than they were able to grasp the nature of the unknown weapon whose development was kept secret from them. Levinas writes in *Freedom and Command* that war always attacks the face of the other at an angle.[55] In the case of nuclear weapons, this angle is the product no longer of hateful characterizations that reduce the other to the "forces" and/or "weaknesses" that are attributed to it but rather of the nonperception that is engendered by distance—the distance separating the place of action (the launch) from the place of suffering (the destruction). Distance turns beings without malice into murderers who no longer need to feel or sustain any particular enmity toward their adversaries as they decide (or follow the order) to eradicate them.

The consequence is this: all the anthropological categories that we have mobilized up to this point, along with the questions that unsettle responsibility, have been upended, beginning with this one: "How do we designate the relation of the murderer (or murderers) to the victims if neither the concept of 'enemy' or 'adversary' is adequate, especially in the psychological sense of the term if not in the political sense?" Obviously, political power retains the privilege of designating the enemy (and to present it as a threat to the "people," "nation," "religion," or "civilization"). Inversely, political power no longer needs to plant and nurture a culture of hostility to render the enemy's destruction possible. For Anders, nothing is more worrisome than this decoupling of politics and psychology, which constitutes one of the most characteristic features of what he describes as the "obsolescence" of the human being, its dotage, its diminution, its disquieting expiration. Even though the association between psychology and politics is daunting, as we well know, their disassociation provides a glimpse into an even more terrifying *disaffected cruelty*, which we can only resign ourselves to calling, with great effect, "telemurder" [*télémeurtre, Fernmord*]:

> Nothing could be more naïve, more deceptive, or more thoroughly harmful to our endeavors than to believe that the two fronts that exist today are that of hatred and that of absence of hatred. Today, it is not so simple. In fact, hatred is absent from *both* fronts. The coming telemurder war [*Fernmord-Krieg*] will be the war most exempt from hatred in history.
>
> But on the basis of this determination, as reassuring as it may seem, we cannot pin our hopes to it—because it is only reassuring for the superficial. The merely negative absence of hatred [*Haßlosigkeit*] does not guarantee anything. On the contrary, this absence of hatred will be the most inhuman absence of hatred that there has ever been; and absence of hatred and absence of scruples become one and the same thing.[56]

Ultimately, the lack of imagination signifies nothing other than this: the cruelty of war's effects no longer depends on the cruelty of its agents. Murderous consent becomes—and this is what awaits us—consent by default. The turnabout constantly troubled Anders. Today we easily take its measure in manifestations (which Anders could not have foreseen) that might seem inoffensive to the extent that they are presented to us as simple, inconsequential distractions. We need only examine the array of war-themed video games—their promotion and success, the fascination they exert, and the drives they trigger—to become aware of its importance. Such games generally invite the player to destroy the greatest possible number of enemies on the video screen—that is to say, removed, at a distance—but they do not invite the player to react emotionally to the fact that killing is the main objective of the game, as important as winning. Such games engender a certain *habituation*, which is perhaps among the most insidious forms of what I have elsewhere called the "sedimentation of the unacceptable."[57] They habituate generations of children to believe that mass death is nothing more than a technical gesture, a manipulation, a click that triggers an apocalypse of fire and blood, but without obvious cruelty. The pleasure derived from such playful destruction is not without a connection to the mercantile exploitation of the death drive.

At an entirely different level, murderous consent is on display at its cruelest in Hiroshima not only because it seems to be free of cruelty but because the death drive does not even seem to be implicated. Cruelty thus resides in what assumes the deceptive appearance of a *beyond cruelty*. And when cruelty is declined in the future tense, as a simple possibility, we encounter its paradoxical nature in the fact that, under the auspices of ensuring security, it masks (this is the contemporary form of our lack of imagination) the threat that is being suspended above life in general. Cruelty advances disguised. Hence, from the beginning of his journal, Anders takes issue with the advocates of nuclear testing: "The so-called 'tests' have today become *reality*. Since they damage *real* life—the lives of today, tomorrow, and the day after tomorrow, maybe even leading to the extinction of life itself—the 'tests' are a form of *war*. Yes, the experiments signify a war against life. Here in Europe, there is an old saying: 'War is a continuation of politics by other means.' *Today, the converse is true. What today is incorrectly called 'peace' is the continuation or the preparation for war by other means.*"[58]

The most distinctive and significant characteristic of the "pursuit of war by other means," however, is its global magnitude. Such are the parameters of our age. But they do present us with an opportunity. There exists a parallel between the magnitude of the threat and the magnitude of our responsibility. If it is true that the only concept of the world that is capable of surviving history's calamities is that which measures it, both intensively and extensively, against the responsibility that is enjoined by the vulnerability and mortality of others, then, at the very least, the nuclear peril confirms the extension of this responsibility beyond all borders. It is, as some who lived at the time of the bombings of Hiroshima and Nagasaki already suspected, this aspect of our responsibility that invites us most imperatively to *think of the world otherwise.*

We Are Really Neighbors—at the Very Least as Mortals

We are led to this other thought of the world, first of all, by the global propagation of nuclear technologies. Anders underscores this in his 1982 introduction to a new edition of *Hiroshima Is Everywhere* (*Hiroshima ist überall*), which brought together his texts on the "atomic age." If the words "atomic age" sounded ominous twenty years earlier, the developments he observed over the last quarter of the twentieth century confirmed his view that humanity had indeed entered such an age. The exclusive possession of nuclear arms, he wrote, has disappeared, and we must admit that all sovereign states are potentially capable of "becoming part of the club," whatever the modalities of their participation—that is to say, regardless of their ability to pressure or blackmail others. It is difficult to imagine some historical law or even some speculative conjecture regarding future trends that would limit *in perpetuity* some or other military technology to a small number of sovereign states, despite their conviction that they alone have the right to possess it and despite their determination to preserve their advantage *for the security of the world*. At a minimum we would have to imagine that nuclear weapons, unlike other weapons, could be withdrawn from the cycle of fabrication-utilization-destruction and, moreover, could escape commercial manipulations and misappropriations, often criminal: "This is the meaning of the philosophy of history: today's atomic weapons production and technology and its tactics of total threat constitute not merely one reality amongst others. Rather, the truth is that this technology, the products that it generates, and the continuous blackmail exerted by the mere possession of atomic weapons are the medium in which history takes place."[59]

In a word, every advance in the field, every extension of the "club," already realized or merely likely, feared or confirmed, opens a new fracture in the illusion that we belong to a world whose preservation is assured. We need only note how Iran, Pakistan, and North Korea have become synonymous, in our day, with the abyss that has been carved out in this belonging. It is not merely the fact that nuclear proliferation cannot forever be opposed, however, that demands new thought of the world but the impossibility of limiting risk, in the event of a crisis, to a circumscribed region. Anders constantly returns to this point: nuclear weapons make *all of us neighbors of all*. They annul the "far away." They make men and women of every generation contemporaries not only in time but in space. The power of the threat that weighs on the world means that living-with implies sharing space as well as time. It means extending the fabric of moral and political relations, which bind us to the fate or destiny of others, to all mortals. We experience the meaning of nuclear weapons today in the way the world tests us: it is impossible to remain indifferent or foreign to what happens on earth, anywhere on earth; it is the certitude that no tension or conflict—however much limited by a circumscribed geography—can be limited to purely regional stakes.

If this is the case, it is because the sharing [*partage*] of the world, not its partition but the community [*communauté*] of its space, cannot be distinguished from murderous proximity. This, in the end, is the core of Anders's despairing perspective on the "vital space" that humanity shares in common. What is it, of the world, that we share first and foremost? What comes back to us, day after day, as events become ever more threatening? A proximity [*voisinage, Nachbarschaft*] that extends the possibility of murder to infinity: "But for us, every individual and every country are contemporaries in space and time, and each individual and each country lives in murderous proximity [*mörderischsten Nachbarschaft*]; every tomorrow lives in today's murderous proximity, every day."[60]

But proximity [*voisinage*] has another dimension that we must, simultaneously, call to mind. We recall from our reading of Levinas that the experience of the other signifies the possibility of murder and, through the transcendence of the face of the other, concomitantly, the impossibility of killing him.[61] The same holds for the atomic age and for the totality of the world. The experience is identical with "murderous proximity" [*voisinage meurtrier, mörderische Nachbarschaft*]. But, by the same token, this experience also suggests that all forms of responsibility, as they relate to murder, apply to this totality. The world is both the murder that can occur at any time and anywhere, as exemplified by terrorism—every new attack revives our anxiety—and, in our nihilistic age, the appeals for attention, and the care and assistance that respond to them, that will no longer recognize borders. In the name of such proximity, nothing that comes from the world can be foreign to anyone.

It remains that the impossibility of partitioning the world in a way that might suspend or interrupt this proximity concerns not merely individuals, collectively responsible toward one another, but first and foremost the states whose sovereignty, in principle, is put in question. The universalization of nuclear technology and its effects should result in each and every one of us being prohibited, by law, from remaining "master in his domain" [*maître chez soi*], for what one makes *of* and does *with* [*fait avec et de*] nuclear weapons (their storage, testing, and commerce) engages the lives of all. And we know that nearly all the recurring tensions related to nuclear weapons have their source in the refusal of some or other sovereign state to allow foreign oversight of their production, in application of their right, as they intend it, to defend themselves against eventual aggressors. In reality, the meaning of interference, as Anders insists with compelling far-sightedness, should be inverted. The interference is not that of international organizations that pursue their right to inspect such production but rather of the states that, because they possess nuclear weapons, effectively interfere in the lives of populations that are theoretically not subject to their control. Any given state from any given region of the world that pursues nuclear policies interferes in *the lives of everyone*. Such is the political (and no longer merely ethical) meaning of "murderous proximity":

> The principle of sovereignty has undergone a dialectical reversal. Sovereign acts have become acts of interference: the interference in the sovereignty of some or all other states. "Interference" includes "nuclear experiments" which, . . . in the formal juridical sense, seem to be subject to the competency of sovereign states. But, in truth, because it is technically impossible to contain the effects of these actions to the borders of one's own territory, they violate the sovereignty of other states. . . . If the effects radius (and the inevitable *affect* radius) on sovereign territory is modified (enlarged), the sovereignty of its neighbors also changes.[62]

Thus we begin to see the contours of a *different* thought [*une autre pensée*] of the world emerging as the rejoinder to the nihilism of our time. It interweaves three threads. The first is that we not forsake our memory of the past in the name of the future. It acknowledges that shame is *indelible* and prohibits us from adding forgetfulness to all of history's injustices. Shame reminds us constantly that yesterday's victims, like today's, cut fault lines in our belonging to the world. Acknowledging this fact in thought is to admit that the world is *incomplete*. The second thread is the ethical injunction that is conveyed by this incompleteness. We must recognize that each of the rifts [*brèches*] or fractures [*brisures*] that renew our experience of incompleteness proceeds from a circumvention, eclipse, or violation of the principle that grounds our belonging: the attention, care, and assistance that are enjoined *everywhere* by all the forms of insecurity to which the other is exposed—her vulnerability, her mortality. The third thread that we must hold on to concerns the articulation between the ethics and the politics of the world—that is to say, an *ethicosmopolitics*. How does the ethical injunction address those who are responsible for the political? It says, first, that there are attachments that cling jealously to the prerogatives of sovereignty that are, in their essence, potentially murderous. It affirms, second, that the highest responsibility of the practitioner of politics cannot simply be to focus on (or be satisfied with) the protection of those who are subject to her authority. However argued and justified, such a restriction is always redolent of nihilistic consent. If ethics is indeed capable of assigning some or other objective to politics, it can only be that of delineating, arranging, or simply making possible the singular and collective ways of a shared *being-against-death* that will suffer no exception or suspension. Only in this way can politics take the measure of the world in a modality that is no longer a pursuit of power, conquest, appropriation, or exploitation, all of which suppose the eclipse of such an order. Inversely, because this other thought of the world finds its meaning in the responsibility that is enjoined by the vulnerability and the mortality of the other (all others), it legitimates [*rendre droit à*] this ethicosmopolitics.

Conclusion

I

It finally happened. In April. The seminar in which the framework of this book was assembled had all but come to an end when the question, feared but not unexpected, arose from the back of the Salle Paul Celan of the École normale supérieure: "What about animals? You have nothing to say about animals? Shouldn't we speak of 'murderous consent' to describe our routine indifference regarding the violence that they endure, in their living conditions, the methods of slaughter, and the experiments they are forced to undergo?"[1] I answered, somewhat precipitously, that there was no doubt that they were victims of human cruelty—and that we habitually avoided acknowledging that fact and even thinking about it.[2] I added, moreover, that it was difficult to see what might warrant the claim that vulnerability and mortality, however understood, were the sole province of humanity. But nothing is simple. Because, if we admit that no particular exclusivity can be validly invoked, we would still have to consider the moral *and/or* political nature of the relations that bind (or should bind), not the human to the animal, but humans to a broad variety of animals, in the apparent absence of reciprocity. "We will have to return to this question." Several weeks later, when Jean-François Nordmann was asking how the manuscript was progressing—his interest in this topic, particularly in the issue of animal flesh as food, goes back years—the question arose again:

"Will you talk about animals?" And again, I promised I would address the question in the Conclusion.

II

In Chapter 3 I discussed Vasily Grossman's last novels, *Life and Fate* and *Everything Flows*. Shortly before his death in 1964, as the first of these two works was running into difficulties, culminating in its confiscation and destruction, Grossman composed a short story, "The Road" (1962), the significance of which is enhanced by the circumstances surrounding its composition. Like his novels, it is about war. It relates a journey across Europe, from the Apennines to the plains of Russia. It is thus a narrative about a migration, or perhaps about getting lost and wandering. In any case, it narrates the tribulations of an exhausting odyssey. It reads like an allegory of suffering. But it is not the soldier, the civilian, or the refugee who is making this journey, as were so many at that time, wandering the highways of Europe. Rather, it is a burro, named Giu, who is making the journey, a step at a time, one day after the other, under the lash of a pitiless driver. Through the feelings of this maltreated animal Grossman evokes a world of sounds, colors, odors, to which the burro reacts with pleasure or displeasure, with indifference or anger: the light playing on the sea, the smell of flowers, the heat of the sun in the morning, the blinding whiteness of the snow, the biting cold, the unremitting feel of leather on skin, and the pain inflicted by the blows he receives. The description of this singular world is devoid of any anthropomorphism: the impressions, the sensations that compose it, as far as they can be imagined and transcribed, are such that it is *not impossible* to grant them plausibility. In any case it would be facile and ultimately moot to deny that animals have such sensations. In a manner of speaking, the sensations refer only to themselves. But to those who are tempted by the Heideggerian thesis that the essential characteristic of the "animal" is that it is "world-poor," Grossman offers, singularly, from the opening pages of his short story, a gentle but hypothetical refutation:

> People would have been astonished how many things the mule noticed that day: music everywhere, the radio blaring away without a break, the stable doors left wide open, crowds of women and children by the barracks, flags fluttering above the barracks, the smell of wine coming from people who did not usually smell of wine, the trembling hands of his driver, Niccolo, when he came to Giu's stall, led him outside, and put on his breastband.[3]

The mule's large, spacious brain, used to conceiving vague images of smells, of form, and of color, was now conceiving an image of something very different, an image of a concept created by philosophers and mathematicians, an image of infinity itself—of the misty Russian plain and cold autumn rain pouring down over it without end.[4]

We should be careful not to rush to evoke parallels between this story and Grossman's novels. Giu's world is not of the same order as that of the characters of *Life and Fate*, even if both worlds are beset by the torment of war. Denying what is irreducible in them merely means not acknowledging their *singularity*. If the burro's two drivers, first one then the other, display the same brutality and the same cruelty by striking the same painful site—"the sensitive little bone in the front hoof"—it is precisely because they are incapable of such an acknowledgment. Nothing is farther from their culture and preoccupations than that admission. Even though the drivers, themselves, suffer misfortune, Giu can only *endure* their presence. That presence consists of what the drivers inflict on Giu: their smell (tobacco, wine), their voices (whistling, shouting), their attitude (threatening), their gestures (violent). Giu is the victim of their abuse. He has no power over them. Nothing of what he thinks or feels can affect them. We have to await the story's conclusion before they pay (or repay) any attention to him at all.

The circumstances in which that attention is aroused are important. The relationship that binds the burro to its tormentors is not the only "relation" that forms Giu's world. He was appointed a "team-mate" to help him pull his cart full of ammunition along the highways of Europe at the behest of the German army. His "team-mate" is an old burro, although the designation "team-mate" is more nominal than real. They are harnessed to the same yoke, but they do not seem to be bound by any of the hardships that they have to withstand. They advance side by side, drink from the same trough, receive the same blows, repeated, multiplied, to the limits of their endurance, but each remains indifferent as regards the other. They are without care for one another. Following the death of their human companions in a bombardment, a new "master," no less brutal than his predecessors, takes the reins, and a young horse replaces the old burro. Initially hostile, rebellious, evil-eyed, the horse is eventually reconciled to the harness that they share. They exchange signs of understanding, looks of complicity. A certain solidarity and affection develop between the two animals. Something unexpected, resembling "sympathy," brightens the end of the story. Then, for the first time, we hear the voices of humans:

Through their warm breath and their weary eyes, Giu the mule and the mare from Vologda spoke clearly to each other of their life and fate, and there was something charming and wonderful about these trustful, affectionate beings standing beside each other on the wartime plain, under the gray winter sky.

"The donkey, I mean the mule, seems to have turned quite Russian," one of the drivers said with a laugh.

"No, look—they're both of them weeping," said another driver. And it was true; they were both weeping.[5]

III

We can derive several observations from Grossman's story. First, when the "world of humans" is reduced to blood and fire, the massive destructions that devastate or break human lives do not spare the animals. The burros, the horse, and the drivers all suffer the bombardments, the cold, and the bouts of exhaustion, together. Yet there is no apparent need to share the hardships, and in this specific story, there is no glimmer of solidarity that might bring humans and animals together. If it is true, as I proposed in the Introduction, that we must search for a way to impress on thought the idea of a "community of the living," nothing would seem to advance this effort better than the experience of the extreme conditions that make up the fabric of our present reflections. Despite all the distinctions that we could make, it is nevertheless significant that for Grossman, these extreme conditions, which Grossman experienced personally, invite us to take into account the mortality and vulnerability that humans and animals share. The destruction of harvests, the scorched fields, the forest fires, and the devastation of the countryside make no distinctions. They affect animals and humans alike. The second observation is this: if we are willing to include animals in our thought of *living-with*, then we must divide the relations that compose it into two categories. First, there are the relations that bind animals—notably but not exclusively domestic animals—to the humans on whom they depend. Second, there are the relations that "attach" animals to all other animals, whether of the same or of different species. The relationship in the first case is unequal and the violence of potential mistreatment is *devoid of reciprocity*: the animal is *unilaterally* exposed to the irruption of such violence. In the second case, the relationship (whether feral or not) is inscribed in a different order, which we should not describe too hastily. We will retain merely this: when these relations (which include the attachment of a singular animal to *its* environment) are destroyed, the destruction occurs, not by itself and from within the relationship, but as the result of an external force (as is the case today, more than ever, of industrial farms and, for a long time, of most zoos).

IV

This is to say that if we wish to qualify the relations between humans and animals as "moral *and* political," we must not understand this characterization in the same way we encountered it in *murderous consent*. The two ways in which humans interject violence into the world of animals mark the distinction. Throughout this book the term "consent" has been applied exclusively to the relations that bind humans together reciprocally. It is essentially from *within* such relations that they can be transformed, even destroyed, and thus the belonging to the world of some or other human being can be affected. No one is assured of eluding the collapse and disintegration of the attention, care, and aid that bind us to the vulnerability and mortality of the other. In the relation *between* humans and animals, however, responsibility cannot be conceptualized in the same way. Not only is the relationship not reciprocal (the power to harm of humans and animals is not equal), but it affects the relations that compose the world of animals *both* from within *and* from without. From *within*, it affects the multiple relations that humans maintain with animals for their personal needs, and *from without*, it affects their environment, their survival, and the conditions of life that bind each animal, of every species, to every other animal, of all species. It has become unfashionable to make assertions that might be understood as definitional of humanity's "fundamental nature." But there is one such assertion that forces itself on our attention. What is unique to humanity is its ability to affect, modify, perturb, develop, and even destroy *the totality of relations* that constitute the world that is proper to each species (including our own) and therefore to each animal singularly.

V

We have discovered in these pages that murderous consent can assume both the form of a negation of human relations (moral *and* political) and the form of an unwillingness to acknowledge or even to be apprised of events and forces that destroy them. We can therefore understand how this concept might apply to the relations that bind humanity to animals in their diversity. It is clear, first, that consent of this kind is at work whenever and wherever the sphere of humanity intersects that of animality, when we deny that animals like Vasily Grossman's burro can have, or even "bear," a world.

As soon as we refuse to grant animals some or other faculty, as our metaphysical tradition is wont to do (so as to reserve these faculties for humanity exclusively)—beginning with the capacity to suffer—then there is not much out there that can prohibit or even restrain the violence that is inflicted on them.[6] Because the relations that compose their "being-in-the-world," as well as the relations that associate them with humanity, and finally the relations that tie them to an environment (a space, individuals of their species and other species) are not recognized for what they are, there is no (bad) treatment and no (murderous) experiment to which they cannot be exposed. This helps explain both battery farming and industrialized slaughter. Such "cruelty to animals" is the most ordinary thing in the world, as Élisabeth de Fontenay reminds us:

> [T]here is a refusal to see that cruelty toward beasts is the most widespread and most commonly denied thing in the world: it is a banal, quotidian, and legal form of violence, the violence of atrocities not punishable by law. For as things currently stand, it is no longer only death that constitutes the most atrocious violation for an animal, but the enclosure of its poor body and its poor life in the terrifying abstraction of the pet store and the laboratory, or in the concentration-camp-like space of factory farming. The amnesia constitutive of the reality of our ordinary practices and the daily cruelty that inheres in these practices bear a very simple name: indifference. We are not blood-thirsty and sadistic, we are indifferent, passive, blasé, detached, insouciant, hardened, vaguely a party to what is going on, full of good humanist conscience, and we are made this way by the implacable collusion of monotheistic culture, techno-science, and economic imperatives.[7]

VI

The responsibility is not of the same order. We can be deeply attached to the life of some or other singular animal, but that attachment is not *extensive* in the way it is for Camus when he invites us to conceptualize attachment under the denomination of "complicity of human beings between themselves." Certainly, we must be careful not to claim too hastily (recalling Derrida's fitting admonition in *The Animal That Therefore I Am*) that the "animal does not respond." However enigmatic its responses, the point is that they cannot be treated in the same way as the utterances that humans address to one another in order to assume our *mutual* responsibility for the attention, care, and aid that is enjoined by our respective vulnerabilities and mortality. The sense in which we speak here of a "community of the living" is therefore specific and deliberately restricted. If we wish to adopt as principle the claim that the "common characteristic" that binds this "community" together is that life, all life, supposes a fabric of relations that constitutes for each living being *its* world, in the sense that the world constitutes each being as singular, then it would not be absurd to think that the first responsibility of humanity toward animals is to preserve these relations as such, in their plurality and diversity—or at least to protect them, the animals, *in the interdependent singularity of their world*—at all events, until death. One might object that this is too little. But it might at least encourage us to take the suffering of animals into account in order to prohibit the cruelest of practices in raising and slaughtering animals and to bring us at last to a greater degree of respect for the indispensable balancing that is needed to maintain this plurality and diversity.

VII

Some will doubtless claim that all consumption of meat and fish, because it implies the death of an animal, manifests "murderous consent." Nothing prevents us from developing this hypothesis, on condition that we mark a distinction between this kind of consent and that which corrodes the "solidarity" and "complicity" of humans among themselves and thus jeopardizes their belonging to the world. The relations that are implicated in the two cases, again, are not of the same nature. They cannot be described in the same terms or placed on the same plane. However atrocious, ignoble, and insufferable the conditions in which some animals are killed, fished, or trapped, we gain nothing by putting them on the same scale or by suggesting parallels with the violence that humanity inflicts on itself. Such practices should be analyzed by and for themselves. There is no need to minimize human suffering in order to do so. Closing our eyes to "what humanity inflicts on humanity," so as better to capture and feel "what humanity does to animals," simply amounts to exchanging one form of murderous consent for another and thus to consenting yet again to murder. In other words, we should avoid thinking concomitantly about the various forms of cruelty to which these two kinds of relations pertain, with the exception of those limited situations in which heterogeneity and the irreducibility of responsibilities that it implies are kept firmly in mind as a matter of principle.

VIII

And yet, just as one might question the ineluctable character of murderous consent, weighing as it does on our existence, one might also feel the need to identify a way out (and, given my readings of Camus, Levinas, Kraus, Anders, and others, ask how one might conceptualize that way out) that, even if it does not free us completely, nevertheless provides us with ways to rein in our "nihilistic" temptation to be discouraged, demoralized, or resigned. The way out is given by revolt, by goodness, by critique, and by shame. All these, along with testimonies and narratives, are ways of *living-with* that endeavor to draw humanity together and reunite it *otherwise*, despite our divisions. Although there is no promise or program attached to this way out, one can still discern a framework that helps orient us, that enables us to withstand the unbearable (which we nevertheless must bear), that reveals and discredits all the ruses that contribute to the sedimentation of the unbearable, and that does so in the name of an ethicosmopolitics.

Derrida, in a chapter of *For What Tomorrow . . .* , calls the spectacle that "man creates for himself in his treatment of animals"—the laboratory experiments, the conditions in which animals are raised and butchered—unbearable and predicts that *in time* we will find them more and more difficult to tolerate.[8] Our relation to animals also demands orienting. It also needs an orienting framework. Fortunately, the way out I have been exploring in this book can also help advance this task. If we want to grant credit to the idea of a "community of living beings," then we will doubtless have to *rebel* against the present state of relations between humanity and other species, just as we will need to *critique* (or deconstruct) the discourses that ground or preserve the rationales for these relations. As to goodness, we should keep in mind that, for both Grossman and Levinas, it imposes itself more powerfully when it resists all calculation, all interest, and presses ahead in its unreason [*déraison*]. Nothing need prevent us from believing that it is precisely this kind of folly—a folly of goodwill—that our "community" needs in order to escape this other folly that is "murderous consent."

Appendix. Friendship: A Trial by History

Of any two friends, one will leave this world before the other. To the one left behind falls the challenging privilege of assuming the weight of a friendship interrupted by death.[1] Sometimes friendship has been suspended already, perhaps by some dispute, falling out, or misunderstanding, or a simple relocation, making the disappearance of the one definitive, already, for the other. Whatever the case, to the survivor falls the task of trying, in vain, to recapture a time that is lost, to recall to memory the words and gestures that are missed. To fulfill this work of memory, he forges an explanation, in his grief, using words that are superfluous, signs that are absent, and silence. The task requires retrieving time and reweaving the fabric of a shared story. But the story is multifaceted. It is the story of each one of the two, and of the two together. It is also, indissociably, the story of events grappled with, shared, and judged: a common History in which the bonds that tie lives together are circumscribed. For writers and thinkers of the twentieth century, it is this circumscription—in the fraternities of combat, the mutual engagements, the consent accorded to violence or refused, the acts and words of lucidity or blindness, recognized or admonished—that enabled attachments or wrecked them.

I

Such mournful anamnesis, darkened by the violence of history, forced itself on Jean-Paul Sartre on two occasions in the early 1960s. It was forced, in quick succession, by the disappearance of Albert Camus, then several months later, by that of Maurice Merleau-Ponty. From the former disappearance emerged an article published in the journal *France-Observateur* on January 7, 1960. In a short but intense panegyric Sartre recalled their falling out and acknowledged the absurdity of their rupture. He evoked the silence, the emptiness fostered by the voice that had gone missing, in an effort to understand an unjust and precarious human order, lived and interrogated in a conflictual and forever-bloodthirsty present:

> We had quarreled, he and I. A quarrel is nothing—even if you were never to see each other again: it is just another way of living *together*, without losing sight of each other in the narrow, little world allotted to us. This didn't prevent me from thinking of him, from sensing his gaze on the page of the book or the newspaper he was reading and asking myself, "What's he saying about it, what's he saying about it *right now*?"[2]

Regarding the latter, the anamnesis occupies the larger part of a special issue of *Les temps modernes* that appeared in October 1961. Because the relationship between Sartre and Merleau-Ponty was more enduring and the parallels between their lives more apparent—the École normale supérieure, the discovery of Husserl and Heidegger, the resistance movement Socialisme et liberté, the direction of *Les temps modernes*—the threads composing his tribute are more profuse. What Sartre attempts to recapture is, first (using the words of Merleau-Ponty), the way an existence, that of his friend, is "bogged down . . . from birth," predisposing him to invent, in the torment of history, *his style*.[3] The subsequent surge of events turned this torment into the mortar of their rapprochement, before becoming the crucible of an estrangement that death could not efface. The archeology of a friendship reveals multiple strata and soils that root it in multiple exchanges. For Sartre and Merleau-Ponty, the first of these was philosophy. It was never simple: "the essential words were spoken: phenomenology, existence; we discovered our real concerns."[4] But philosophical writing, which does not lend itself easily to sharing, engenders rivalries. The conversations that accompany it are merely a detached and discrete effervescence. We rarely agree on the importance of discussion or on the need to push a confrontation to the point of rupture. It is unusual to see the advances of one philosopher undermine those of the other or, inversely, to accord a share of attention and time to those advances that might satisfy their author's hopes. Sartre, in a striking declaration of complicity and, simultaneously, of inadequacy, explains this reluctance:

Left to ourselves, each of us would have persuaded himself too easily that he had understood the phenomenological idea; together, we embodied its ambiguousness for each other: this was because each of us regarded the alien—and sometimes hostile—labors the other was engaged in as an unexpected deviation from his own work. Husserl became at once the distance between us and the foundation of our friendship. . . . [Merleau-Ponty] retained a nuanced recollection of our talks. Ultimately, he merely wanted to deepen his own understanding and discussions distracted him. And then I made too many concessions to him, and too hastily.[5]

And yet, what each of these two philosophies opened up, in different ways, was a shared avenue to this other stratum in which friendship would take root: History. Not a history in which one imagines oneself to be an impartial spectator, but one that, because it engulfs self and other together, transforms both into contemporaries. Because it cannot be detached from all that makes a life a *living-with*, nothing outlines the contours of friendship more than such contemporaneity. The friendship between Sartre and Merleau-Ponty was one of resistance to the German occupation, the division of the world into two blocs, the war in Indochina and the Korean War, the rejection of capitalism (and anticommunism), and shared hopes placed in the Soviet Union prior to the revelation of the gulag. Their friendship was founded on the course of events that made them, each singularly, yet that brought them together to share their singularity and then separated them as they embarked on divergent paths (in their actions, judgments, advocacies, and "professions of faith"). It was this unfolding of history, this concrete experience of a historical movement that, having engulfed them both, would not tolerate eccentricity. It was their shared will to interrogate this common adventure, to make explicit what was implicit and unforeseeable, that led them to found *Les temps modernes*.

In his account, however, Sartre follows a different narrative thread. If history is discovered through the prism of friendship, and friendship is discovered through the prism of history, both friendship and history wrestle with the impediment of what Sartre calls, on page 1 of his anamnesis, "a quarrel that never took place."[6] Though it is true that the disagreements and the reproaches never degenerated into a clash of words that could not be retracted, like those that separated Sartre and Camus (see below), nevertheless the quarrel between Sartre and Merleau-Ponty nearly boiled over on a number of occasions, interjecting silence, bitterness, and distance into the time they spent together. Estrangement accompanied their relationship everywhere, leaving to the one who survived the disappearance of the other the burdensome task of proving to himself that the quarrel never really occurred. Sartre's account is a strange accolade, haunted, from the first to the last line, by the ghost of rupture, as if Sartre from beyond the grave was trying to tie back together the bonds that history had loosened.

Where did this disaffection come from? What was it about history that proved so distressing that the voices of the two friends fell out of harmony? It was nothing more, though nothing less (this is essential), than the hopes that the Soviet Union (and, with it, communism) had embodied in the aftermath of war. It was the question of the capacity of Stalin's homeland to bear, now and forever, the promise of universal emancipation, despite the lies, the subjugation, and the terror that were its truth. It was nothing more, in other words, than the disparate ability of each of the two friends to shut his eyes, plug his ears, justify crimes, provide them with excuses or reasons—and, ultimately, to consent to murder or to oppose it. Being engulfed by history meant, for some, following the path that led to this opposition. But for others it meant perpetuating consent and its rationalizations. Merleau-Ponty makes a choice that we can locate somewhere in the interval between three texts, spanning several years, in which he deals with the massive and systematic violence that was being exercised by the Soviet state: *Humanism and Terror*, published in 1947; "The U.S.S.R. and the Camps," which appeared in *Les temps modernes* in January 1950; and finally, five years later, *Adventures of the Dialectic*, which contains a long chapter, "Sartre and Ultra-Bolshevism," in the form of an indictment.

Books at that time were never read lightly, and the harshness of the polemics they provoked, under conditions in which the choice between "murderous consent" and its rejection was never all that obvious, bears witness to the depths to which one's being-in-the-world in its entirety could become engaged. *Humanism and Terror*, in which Merleau-Ponty refused to judge the Moscow trials, either from the perspective of democratic liberties or even in the name of morality, did not escape the rule. He asked only that we assess whether the violence, to which we might be inclined to consent, is progressive or not and to do so from the standpoint of the movement that demands it *in the name of the history* of which it is the bearer. The understanding that Merleau-Ponty sought had no goal other than to remain on the lookout for a justification that might hold up:

> [F]or the moment the question is not to know whether one accepts or rejects violence, but whether the violence with which one is allied is "progressive" and tends toward its own suspension or toward self-perpetuation; and finally, that in order to decide this question the

crime has to be set in the logic of a situation, in the dynamics of a regime and into the historical totality to which it belongs, instead of judging it by itself according to that morality mistakenly called "pure" morality.[7]

In the long article he devoted to Merleau-Ponty in *Les temps modernes*, Sartre recounts Camus's reaction to *Humanism and Terror* and the row between Camus and Merleau-Ponty that erupted in the home of Boris Vian:

> One evening, at Boris Vian's, Camus took Merleau to task accusing him of justifying the Moscow trials. It was painful: I can still see them, Camus outraged, Merleau-Ponty courteous and firm, a little pale, the one permitting himself, the other forbidding himself, the splendors of violence. Suddenly Camus turned away and left. I ran after him, accompanied by Jacques Bost, and caught up with him in the empty street. I tried as best I could to explain Merleau's thinking, which Merleau himself had not deigned to do. The only result was that we parted on bad terms.[8]

As stated in Chapter 1, *The Rebel*—with its thinly veiled allusions to Merleau-Ponty's book—appeared in 1951, four years after this encounter, and tried to elucidate the political and moral principles that Camus was trying to express on that occasion. But Merleau-Ponty had already published his editorial "The USSR and the Camps" in 1950, and his tone had already changed. This article revealed Merleau-Ponty's unmitigated disillusionment. He began by stating the need to face the facts: the massive deportations of Soviet citizens and the growing, unlimited autonomy of a repressive system. The facts were incontestable. Although the "inspiring humanity of Marxism" continued to nourish the hopes of all the oppressed peoples of the world, it was time to admit the obvious, that the October Revolution's principal and perhaps only outcome was a cruelly hierarchical society.[9] No matter what the Communists believed, the entire significance of the Soviet system had to be rethought. In 1950 Merleau-Ponty and his readers were still far from having access to all the information that would enable them, twenty years later—especially following the publication of the *Gulag Archipelago* in 1973—to gauge to their full extent the horrors of Stalinism. Nevertheless, Merleau-Ponty had already come to the inescapable conclusion that supporting the Soviet regime and its glorious accomplishments—as he had done several years earlier, along with other "fellow travelers" of the French Communist Party—meant consenting to the violence of a police state and, ultimately, to the consignment of tens of millions of Russians to servitude:

And Communists throughout the world expect that, by a sort of magical emanation, so many canals, factories, and riches shall one day produce whole men, even if in order to produce them it is necessary to reduce ten million Russians to slavery, reduce their families to despair, be it even twenty or thirty million Russians, train another part of the population in the art of policing and denunciation, and the civil servants in servility or armed egotism. This is undoubtedly how the best of the Communists are able to turn a deaf ear to ten million prisoners.[10]

But the history that engulfs us does not concentrate the violence that it produces in only one part of the world. The USSR did not have a monopoly on oppression. To argue the contrary, and thus willfully ignore the occurrence in some other country (or under some other regime) of the things that one denounced elsewhere, including the USSR, was to consent to violence in equal measure. It meant granting absolution in one place for what one rejected in another place. This was (and remains) the paradox of our being-in-the-world, which made all forms of anticommunism an object of suspicion for Merleau-Ponty (and which for others still does): "The only sound criticism is thus the one which bears on exploitation and oppression, inside and outside the USSR; and every political position which *is defined* in opposition to Russia and localizes criticism within it is an absolution given to the capitalist world."[11] Denouncing the Siberian gulag was appropriate, but using this denunciation to minimize or justify other forms of servitude and terror in the world was not. One cannot make a deal with violence. It was therefore necessary to *speak up about all violence* or *not speak at all.*

In his account of their friendship, Sartre relates the development of a certain speechlessness. As Sartre declared himself officially to be a fellow traveler of the French Communist Party in 1952, Merleau-Ponty stopped supporting the party, sought to distance himself from it, and began to censure all manifestations of complicity with oppression, deception, and servitude, whatever their source. In the beginning, Merleau-Ponty's silence expressed his refusal to enter into a compromise with violence in the name of a history that he, as his ideas evolved, could no longer justify. Later, his silence marked the breach produced by a confrontation held in check, a dialogue held suspended between incommunicable thoughts. In encounter after encounter, Sartre and Merleau-Ponty kept their judgments and criticisms to themselves so as to avoid the eruption of a public dispute. At the heart of a friendship that was growing darker with time was a disagreement that was haunted by the clamor of the world. Pondered in secret in their hearts, disagreement gave itself no other means of expression than the slow corrosion of their patience. But what applied to their experience of history also applied to what Sartre later called "the labor of rupture"— and reciprocally: "All meaningful discourse could only . . . be lies: all that remained was to withhold one's complicity, to remain silent."[12]

One incident in particular spelled the end of Merleau-Ponty's collaboration with *Les temps modernes*. As editor in chief, he attached a short introductory text to a mediocre article devoted to the "contradictions of capitalism." Merleau-Ponty's text alerted readers to the parallel "contradictions of socialism." Sartre, in disagreement with both the article and Merleau-Ponty's introductory editorial, nevertheless approved the article of his Marxist collaborator but opposed Merleau-Ponty's critical presentation. Merleau-Ponty resigned from the journal. Sartre's inelegant intervention was symptomatic of a companionship, even a loyalty, that Merleau-Ponty could no longer share. He explained his position several years later in *Adventures of the Dialectic*. Simone de Beauvoir viciously countered the book's attacks on Sartre's positions. For the first time, their disagreement became public. And yet the two friends still met—a conference in Venice, in Rome, and, for the last time, in Paris at the École normale, where they felt in their hearts the melancholy embarrassment of all who have had a falling out only to be reunited again another day, exhausted, and moved by the sole assurance of their mutual attachment:

> I can still see his face that last night I saw him—we parted in the rue Claude-Bernard—a face disappointed, suddenly impenetrable. It remains with me, a painful wound, infected by regret, remorse and a little rancor. Transformed into what it will now be, our friendship is summed up in it for ever. Not that I accord the slightest privilege to the last moment nor allot it the task of telling the final truth about a life. But everything was, in fact, gathered in that face: frozen in that silent expression are all the silences he met me with after 1950, and at times, I, for my part, still feel the eternity of his absence as a deliberate mutism.[13]

II

The quarrel with Camus, by contrast, was not characterized by silence. It was public and polemical from the outset. Its battlefield was, again, the journal *Les temps modernes*. And again, the question of communism and, with it, the violence of history cast an intractable shadow on the lives and thought of all concerned. The pretext was the publication, in 1951, of

Camus's *The Rebel*. Because it denounced revolutionary violence without reserve, because it denounced all executions perpetrated and consented [*consentis*] to in the name of history, and because it inveighed explicitly against Stalinism (and implicitly against Stalinism's fellow travelers), the book was given a highly critical review by Francis Jeanson in the May 1952 edition of *Les temps modernes*. Camus's reaction to the review was one of barely contained anger. He addressed a letter to the director of the journal, Sartre, which was subsequently answered by letters written by both Sartre and Jeanson. The tone of the letters, on all sides—dogmatic, indignant, arrogant—makes them painful to read, and the lecturing on morality and politics, and the words of abuse, words capable of shattering friendships, were unconstrained.

First, there was complete incomprehension on Jeanson's part (and on Sartre's, for that matter) regarding the point of Camus's essay, which took aim at all conceivable political fidelities and allegiances. Jeanson refused not only to follow Camus's argument but even to consider the words Camus used in his effort to dissociate himself from the cult of history and its seductions. Camus's words made clear to the militants and fellow travelers who had resigned themselves to the executions and the assassinations, and who had voiced their resignation openly because they were convinced that violence was necessary, that their murderous consent was in fact the frightful symptom of a present that was blighted by nihilism. The bitterness of the polemic had its source in Jeanson's refusal to respect Camus's text. It was not simply Camus's probing of revolution that bothered politically engaged readers like Sartre, Jeanson, and others but the implicit evocation of their own complacency in the face of violence, the insinuation of their accommodation with murder, and their unwillingness to acknowledge the sufferings of the victims that could no longer be overlooked. Jeanson therefore had nothing to say about the rebellion against political crime that guided Camus's thought—nothing, that is, except that it typified the moral posture of the good soul who suffers from the illusion that history is avoidable. Rebellion, writes Jeanson, is a "refusal of history," the refuge of a "life without history," the "escape to definitive solitude":

> How can one deny that rebellion is—and in a rather radical way— *the refusal of history*—when the former is characterized by "limits" [*mesure*], while the latter is made the very locus of "excess" [*démesure*], of cynicism, of destruction, and of limitless servitude, an indefinite series of "convulsions" and "a prodigious collective agony"?[14]

Jeanson speaks for the journal, in compliance with the objectives defined by Sartre and Merleau-Ponty. He reprimands Camus for ignoring the twofold movement within which history both captures us and imposes on us the task of understanding it. If we pursue this task ceaselessly, it is because history is making us who we are. All positions of transcendence, all desires to escape our experience, to judge it from the outside on the basis of principles that do not belong to history, are chimerical. It is not our prerogative to invent ourselves as singular beings-in-the-world capable of securing freedom from the constraints of history's burdens. And if the rebel imagines this to be the case, he or she is in fact sanctioning more violence than he or she might think. It is an old song (and its dogmatism is inextinguishable): to condemn revolution (which Jeanson readily identifies with Stalinism) is to make oneself "an accomplice, willingly or not, of that other frenzy, in a reverse sense, whose suppression constitutes the very goal and truest meaning of the revolutionary enterprise."[15] The politically engaged critic concludes with arguments that, though they fail to detract from the acuity, the accuracy, and the justice of Camus's reasoning, are nevertheless pertinent to our concerns here. We need to listen to them and interrogate them, especially when they disturb our convictions:

> To our incorrigibly bourgeois eyes, it's quite possible that capitalism offers a less "distorted" face than Stalinism; but what face does it offer to a miner, a state employee punished for going on strike, to a Madagascan tortured by the police, to a Vietnamese "cleansed" by napalm, to a Tunisian "picked up" by the Foreign Legion?[16]

But Camus did not appreciate the upbraiding, to say the least. His letter of response, from beginning to end, quivers with indignation regarding the reviewer's partisanship, bad faith, maneuvers, falsehoods, and biased misinterpretations. Camus addresses his letter to Sartre, as if he were the author of the review, or as if Jeanson, in writing it, had only been acting as his spokesman. Camus, not without disdain, refuses to cite Jeanson's name in his letter of response. He insists on two points. The first concerns the demonization of history that Jeanson claims to discern in his thought. Camus replies that it is not true that *The Rebel* advocates moral procrastination, whose only solution to the violence that pervades the world is to disregard history so as to spare oneself from compromising sympathies. It is true, inversely, that his essay, written with eyes open to the "indisputably historical suffering of millions of men," sought to denounce the promotion of this history to the status of an absolute, since that promotion leads ineluctably to the invention of reasons and excuses for crime, and even to its endorsement.[17] Camus's concern for the victims, their vulnerability and mortality, his refusal to be won over by any form of resignation, accommodation, or consent regarding history, even less its encouragement, is already a manner of being-in-the-world and of reacting to history, even if this history is not that of those militants who, engaged in a cause, claim to know history's ends and to serve them. Denouncing terror does not mean stepping outside of history or opposing its advance. Rather, it means replacing the categories that tolerate it with demands for a transversal solidarity that would tie revolt to the care for life. It means justifying the denunciation of history through the care that is enjoined by the mortality of the other, any given other:

> *The Rebel* seeks to demonstrate . . . that pure antihistoricism, at least in today's world, is as harmful as pure historicism. It is written there, for those who wish to read, that he who believes only in history marches towards terror and he who does not believe in it at all authorizes terror. It states that there exist "two kinds of inefficacy: abstention and destruction," and "two kinds of impotence, that of good and that of evil." Finally, and above all, it demonstrates that "the denial of history is equivalent to the denial of reality" in the same way, neither more nor less, that "one separates oneself from reality by wanting to consider history as a self-sufficient totality."[18]

We can readily see how this second point would be decisive for Camus. His principal complaint with Jeanson's review (and hence with Sartre— the amalgam is carefully sustained) is that it ignores the only ground on which the debate should take place, which is not that of violence in general but, rather, that of the specific crimes for which Stalinist terror is responsible. Their polemic points us back to the homologous dispute that provoked the split between Camus and Merleau-Ponty four years earlier, following the publication of *Humanism and Terror*. Camus suspects that his critics' complaints are the immediate by-product of "fellow-traveling" with the French Communist Party, whose political doctrine was adopted by *Les temps modernes* and which forbade any direct criticism of communism and denounced texts that questioned communism's revolutionary eschatology. There is no doubt that this was the beginning of the end of the friendship between Sartre and Camus. Subsequently, Camus would not tread lightly in his denunciations of Sartre, as if the offending book review had been inspired by nothing but the latter's political commitments, promises, and loyalties. Camus methodically admonishes Sartre for systematically undercutting all criticism of Marxism, for appealing to authority (Marx and Hegel) so as to characterize as reactionary all rival philosophical positions, and, finally, for treating with derision or silence any tradition of revolution that is not Marxist.

But this was not the main point. More important was Camus's suspicion that the goal pursued by Sartre's strategy was to minimize or overlook state violence in the Soviet Union, as manifested by the labor camps—or, to turn the observation around, to reject state violence as the main reason for assailing authoritarian politics, as embodied by the Soviet Union, by repeatedly presenting it as a "revolutionary experiment." Despite his own estrangement from Merleau-Ponty, Camus reprised the questions that, at or about that same time, were already darkening the relations between Merleau-Ponty and Sartre:

> He [your collaborator] passes over everything in my book that deals with the misfortunes and specifically political implications of authoritarian socialism. Confronted with a work that, in spite of its lack of realism, studies in detail the relations between twentieth-century revolution and terror, your article contains not a word on this problem, but instead hides behind modesty. . . . In any case, if one is of the opinion that authoritarian socialism is the principal revolutionary experience of our time, it seems to me difficult not to come to terms with the terror that it presupposes, particularly today—and, for example, so as to remain close to reality, with the fact of concentration camps. No criticism of my book, be it for or against, can leave this problem aside.[19]

Because everything is written in the second-person plural ("your [*votre*, as opposed to *ton*] article," "your [*votre*] collaborator," "your [*votre*] journal"), and because, in the end, the letter concludes with a radical interrogation of the troubled, complicit, but discordant relationship between existentialism and Marxism, Camus's irrepressible suspicion regarding Sartre's dogmatic allegiance, blind to the crimes that were being committed and to the suffering they caused, endows the letter with a tone that makes a declaration of their separation. A fissure had opened between the two literary figures that affected not only how they related to history and, specifically, to the Communist Party and the state but also how they related to the demands of freedom. You cannot "free man from every impediment in order to then practically imprison him in historical necessity," nor can you "take from him his reasons for struggling in order to finally throw him into some political party or other, provided that it has no rule of action other than efficacy," writes Camus, thus breaking the pact that had made this same freedom the common cause that he and Sartre, side by side, had defended together.[20]

Sartre grasps what happened. When he takes up his pen to reply to Camus, it is to assure him that he understands that Camus's letter of inculpation, characterized by virulence and determination, spells the end of their friendship:

> Our friendship was not easy, but I shall miss it. If today you break it off, doubtless that means it would inevitably have ended some day. Many things brought us together, few separated us. But those few were still too many: friendship, too, tends to become totalitarian; there has to be agreement on everything or a quarrel, and those who don't belong to any party themselves behave like members of imaginary parties.[21]

The tone is almost unbearable. The central issue is avoided. Sartre does not reply to the questions that Camus considers most important—especially the questions regarding murderous consent and nihilism. He begins by attacking the tone of Camus's accusatory letter and criticizing its literary devices. Eschewing reasoned explanation, he prefers to mount an ad hominem attack, filled with biting irony, consisting (though he will deny it) of the psychological portrait of a man whom he depicts as convinced of his superiority, arrogant, and tyrannically (even violently) virtuous. Rather than articulate his own thought, he complains disparagingly—adopting a professorial style that is almost unendurable—of Camus's political and philosophical incompetence.[22] Camus is a moralist whose lessons proclaim his hostility toward history. Camus has wandered into areas that he does not master.[23] The case has been heard and the sentence rendered. Sartre will not retreat. Even when, eight years later, he salutes Camus's memory following his tragic death and recalls the quarrel that ended their friendship, he will still reduce him to the role of moralist and keep his distance (the distance separating him from moral fact, considered foreign to politics and political practice) regarding anything that might unsettle his commitments. His very adjectives speak volumes: it is in vain that humanism is "pure," "austere," and "sensual"; it is "stubborn" and "insular"; the battle is "dubious"; the refusal, "opinionated"—above all, the "moral terrain" is considered "sure," while *"practice"* is judged "uncertain":

> In this century, and running counter to history, he was the current heir to that long line of moralists whose works perhaps constitute what is most original in French literature. His stubborn humanism, narrow and pure, austere and sensual, fought an uncertain battle against the massive, misshapen events of our times. But, conversely, through the unyielding nature of his refusals, in the heart of our age, against the Machiavellians and the golden calf of realism, he reasserted the existence of morality. He *was*, one might almost say,

that unshakeable affirmation. If one read or thought, then one ran up against the human values he held in his tightly clenched fist: he called the political act into question.[24]

And yet Sartre recalls how "absurd" and "scandalous" was Camus's accidental death. It deprived the world of a voice it needed if it was to comprehend itself and find its bearings. It deprived humanity of the glimmer of order that an evocation of (moral) principles can interject into the chaos of events. Nevertheless, Camus, like Merleau-Ponty, had already, as war raged in Algeria, opted for silence. For the former as for the latter, life ended silently, in the same way that their friendship had ended silently some time earlier. The two figures haunted the tribute that Sartre now rendered to the friends who left the world before him. Sartre had to live with their silence, like a wound that would not heal. In the end, there is no doubt that the haunting silence of friendship was for him the peremptory and spectral form that the trial of history had assumed.

Notes

Introduction

1. This argument is developed by Frédéric Gros in *States of Violence: An Essay on the End of War*, trans. Krzysztof Fijalkowski and Michael Richardson (Kolkata: Seagull Books, 2010). See also the works of Wolfgang Sofsky, notably *Violence: Terrorism, Genocide, War*, trans. Anthea Bell (London: Granta Books, 2004).

2. As we know, this hypothesis is the basis of the theory of a "shock of civilizations," as developed, in 1996, by the American political scientist Samuel Huntington in his book *The Clash of Civilizations and the Remaking of World Order* (New York: Simon and Schuster, 2011). See Marc Crépon, *L'imposture du choc des civilisations* (Nantes: Éditions Pleings Feux, 2002); Marc Crépon, *La culture de la peur*, vol. 2, *La guerre des civilisations* (Paris: Éditions Galilée, 2010).

3. See Chapters 1 and 3–5.

4. Frédéric Worms, *Le moment du soin: À quoi nous tenons-nous?* (Paris: Presses Universitaires de France, 2010). See esp. Part II (to which I shall return): "La violation," 65–111.

5. See Marc Crépon, *La culture de la peur*, vol. 1, *Démocratie, identité, sécurité* (Paris: Éditions Galilée, 2008).

6. Joan Tronto, *Moral Boundaries: A Political Argument for an Ethic of Care* (New York: Routledge, 1993); Pascale Molinier, Sandra Laugier, and Patricia Paperman, *Qu'est-ce que le care? Souci des autres, sensibilité, responsabilité* (Paris: Payot, 2009). See esp. Chapter 6 by Sandra Laugier, "Le sujet du *care*: Vulnérabilité et expression ordinaire," 159–200. See also Sandra Laugier, ed.,

Éthique, littérature, vie humaine (Paris: Presses Universitaires de France, 2006). On Judith Butler, see below, Chapter 4.

7. On precarity, see the work of Guillaume Leblanc, esp. *Vies ordinaires, vies précaires* (Paris: Éditions du Seuil, 2007). On the "ordinary," which is one of the principal analytical themes pursued by Sandra Laugier, see her "Le sujet du *care*," 165: "Care is, first of all, attention to such ordinary life. The ethics of care calls our attention to what is right in front of our eyes but do not see, whether by inattentiveness or precisely because it is too close."

8. Tronto, *Moral Boundaries*, 145.

9. Some of the activities that belong to *care* remind us of this in principle. For the doctor as for the nurse, it is inconceivable that they could "choose" their patients on the basis of their "origins," and it is not surprising that it is activities such as these that participated in the creation of the first nongovernmental organizations to embrace a cosmopolitan vocation: the Red Cross, Doctors without Borders, Doctors of the World, and Handicap International.

10. I am referring here to the long commentary that Jacques Derrida devoted to Hamlet's phrase "The time is out of joint." See Jacques Derrida, *Specters of Marx* (London: Routledge, 2006), Chapter 1, "Injunctions of Marx."

11. Worms, *Le moment du soin*, 71.

12. Each of these phrases will be discussed in the pages that follow.

13. Iris Murdoch, *Existentialists and Mystics* (New York: Penguin, 1998), 81.

14. I wish to thank Jean-François Nordmann for having drawn my attention to such questions years ago. I address these questions in the Conclusion.

1. Justice

1. See Chapter 4.

2. Albert Camus, *Caligula*, in *Caligula and Three Other Plays*, trans. Stuart Gilbert and Justin O'Brien (New York: Vintage Books, 1958), 13–14.

3. Ellipsis in the original.

4. Ibid., 15–17.

5. See, among other texts, Jacques Derrida, *The Other Heading: Reflections of Today's Europe*, trans. Pascale-Anne Brault and Michael B. Naas (Bloomington: Indiana University Press, 1992), 41: "I will even venture to say that ethics, politics, and responsibility, *if there are any*, will only ever have begun with the experience and experiment of the aporia. When the path is clear and given, when a certain knowledge opens up the way in advance, the decision is already made, it might as well be said that there is none to make: irresponsibly, and in good conscience, one simply applies or implements a program. Perhaps, and this would be the objection, one never escapes the program. In that case, one must acknowledge this and stop talking with authority about moral or political responsibility. The condition of possibility of this thing called responsibility is a certain *experience and experiment of the possibility of the impossible: the testing of the aporia* from which one may invent the only *possible invention, the impossible invention.*"

6. Camus, *Caligula*, 21.

7. See Jacques Derrida, *The Beast and the Sovereign*, trans. Geoffrey Bennington, 2 vols. (Chicago: University of Chicago Press, 2009–11). This was Derrida's last seminar at the École des hautes études en sciences sociales (EHESS), held between 2001 and 2003. See also "Psychoanalysis Searches the States of Its Soul," in *Without Alibi*, trans. Peggy Kamuf (Stanford: Stanford University Press, 2002), which calls for a new discourse on war for reasons that we will examine later on but that we can already see are related to the recurrent forms of warlike cruelty. To this we can add the seminar given between 1999 and 2001 on the death penalty, which makes this same question of cruelty one of its central themes.

8. Camus, *Caligula*, 73.

9. Camus, preface to *Caligula and Three Other Plays*, vi.

10. Albert Camus, *The Stranger*, trans. Matthew Ward (New York: Vintage, 1989), 59.

11. Camus, preface to *Caligula and Three Other Plays*, v.

12. Albert Camus, *The Just Assassins*, in *Caligula and Three Other Plays*, 248.

13. Ibid., 256.

14. On this subject, see Ahmadou Kourouma's novel *Allah Is Not Obliged*, trans. Frank Wynne (New York: Anchor Books, 2007).

15. See Chapter 4.

16. Camus, *Just Assassins*, 258–59.

17. See the Appendix.

18. On this point, see Marc Crépon, *The Thought of Death and the Memory of War*, trans. Michael Loriaux (Minneapolis: University of Minnesota Press, 2013).

19. Albert Camus, *The Rebel*, trans. Anthony Bower (New York: Vintage Books, 1956), 6.

20. See the Appendix.

21. Ibid.

22. Camus, *Rebel*, 283.

23. Ibid.

24. We have modified Bower's translation from "mutual understanding" to "mutual complicity," translating *complicité*. One can understand one's enemies. The fraternity in rebellion that Camus describes is therefore more accurately conveyed by the word "complicity."

25. Ibid., 283–84.

26. From this point of view, perhaps Camus unexpectedly agrees with certain classic definitions of nihilism, such as those that see it in the reign of technology, understood as power of domination. See, on this subject, Martin Heidegger, *Nietzsche*, trans. David Farrell Krell, 2 vols. (San Francisco: HarperCollins, 1991).

27. Camus, *Rebel*, 285.

28. See Chapter 4.

29. On this subject, see the texts that, some fifteen years later, Camus dedicates to the war in Algeria: notably, the preface to his *Algerian Chronicles*, trans. Arthur Goldhammer (Cambridge, Mass.: Belknap Press, 2013). We will return to this topic at the end of the chapter.

30. The first three letters, as we know, were published in secret (the first in *La revue libre* 2, in 1943; the second in *Cahiers de libération* 3; the third, written in April 1944, in *Libertés* 58, in January 1945). The fourth remained unreleased until the publication of all four at the end of 1945.

31. Albert Camus, *Letters to a German Friend*, in *Resistance, Rebellion, and Death*, trans. Justin O'Brien (New York: Vintage Books, 1974), 5.

32. Ibid., 8.

33. Ibid., 9.

34. It is important in this respect that, when there is an aviation or natural disaster, the first information that the media in all countries emphasize, besides the number of victims, is the number among them who are "compatriots," as if, in death and mourning—that is, in the way that this information concerns *us*—that makes all the difference.

35. Ibid., 13–14.

36. "Undeniably human" is a translation of *évidence humaine.* Justin O'Brien proposes the more literal "human evidence" in his translation of *Letters to a German Friend.*

37. Ibid., 20.

38. See Chapter 2.

39. See the reading that I propose for Freud's *Reflections on War and Death* (New York: Moffat, Yard, 1918) in Chapter 2.

40. Camus, *Letters to a German Friend*, 20–22.

41. Ibid., 22–23.

42. *Faire sens* is used more and more frequently today to signify, as in English, "make sense." It did not convey this meaning in Camus's day, however. Then, it would have played on the polysemy of *sens* as "meaning" and "direction"—hence, "confer meaning, make meaningful, *and* provide direction."

43. Camus, *Rebel*, 290.

44. Camus, *Letters to a German Friend*, 28–29.

45. See Chapter 3.

46. See Chapter 4.

47. See particularly Günther Anders, *Hiroshima ist überall* [Hiroshima is everywhere] (Munich: C. H. Beck, 1982). This volume brings together three texts: "The Man on the Bridge: Diary from Hiroshima and Nagasaki," "Burning Conscience: The Case of the Hiroshima Pilot Claude Eatherly," and "The Dead: Speech on the Three World Wars." See below, Chapter 5.

48. See Chapter 2.

49. Camus, *Rebel*, 289 (my emphasis).

50. "Beyond Nihilism" is the title of the concluding paragraph of the chapter "Thought at the Meridian" and thus of *Rebel* (302).

51. Camus, *Rebel*, 290–91.

52. My emphasis.

53. Here we get to an essential point that will be at the heart of our confrontation with Freud's and Levinas's texts. What is given first in the relationship with others: the memory of one or many murders, their possibility, or their prohibition? Where do memory, possibility, and prohibition find their roots? How are they articulated?

54. Camus, *Rebel*, 292.

55. The question of solidarity itself deserves a long study. It is certainly at the center of a novel like *The Plague*, but it also returns as a leitmotif in numerous intervening texts. It is expressed in the texts supporting the victims of repression following the intervention of Soviet troops in Hungary in 1956. For example, in the "Message to Hungarian Writers in Exile," in *Œuvres complètes*, vol. 4 (Paris: Gallimard, 2008), 589: "I only want to express solidarity that for the past year connects the fate of Hungary to all the free intellectuals of the West." Or again in the interview from October 1957 entitled "The Wager of Our Generation," in *Resistance, Rebellion, and Death*, 244–45: "My role in Algeria never has been and never will be to divide, but rather to use whatever means I have to unite. I feel a solidarity with everyone, French or Arab, who is suffering today in the misfortune of my country. But I cannot all alone rebuild what so many men persist in destroying. I have done what I could. I shall begin again when there is again a chance of helping to rebuild an Algeria freed from all hatreds and all forms of racism."

56. Camus, *Rebel*, 298.

57. Ibid., 304.

58. See specifically the first text of these chronicles (which is also one of Camus's first publications), entitled "Misery of Kabylia."

59. Camus, preface to *Algerian Chronicles*, 26: "The reprisals against the civilian population of Algeria and the use of torture against the rebels are crimes for which we all bear a share of responsibility. That we have been able to do such things is a humiliating reality that we must henceforth face. Meanwhile, we must refuse to justify these methods on any grounds whatsoever, including effectiveness. Once one begins to justify them, even indirectly, no rules or values remain. One cause is as good as another, and pointless warfare, unrestrained by the rule of law, consecrates the triumph of nihilism." Further, on the next page (27): "If, however, we wish to be useful as well as fair, we ought to condemn with equal force and in the bluntest of terms the terrorism practiced by the FLN against French civilians and, even more frequently, Arab civilians. This terrorism is a crime, which can be neither excused nor allowed to develop."

60. Ibid., 27–28.

61. This concerns one of the questions and recurring themes in the latest works by Judith Butler. See, specifically, Judith Butler, *Precarious Life: The Powers of Mourning and Violence* (New York: Verso, 2004), and *Giving an*

Account of Oneself (New York: Fordham University Press, 2005). On these texts, see below, Chapter 4.

62. Albert Camus, "Banquet Speech," accessed August 12, 2015, http://www.nobelprize.org/nobel_prizes/literature/laureates/1957/camus-speech.html.

63. Ibid.

2. Life

1. Sigmund Freud, *Reflections on War and Death*, trans. Dr. A. A. Brill and Alfred B. Kuttner (New York: Moffat, Yard, 1918), 2 (Project Gutenberg online ed.).

2. Stefan Zweig, *The World of Yesterday* (1943; repr., Lincoln: University of Nebraska Press, 1964), 230.

3. Regarding the engagement of scholars in the war, see Marc de Launay, "Professorenkriegs Literatur," in "Philosophies nationales? Controverses franco-allemandes," special issue, *Revue de métaphysique et de morale*, September 2001, 83–100.

4. Freud, *Reflections on War and Death*, 3.

5. Ibid., 4.

6. Zweig, *World of Yesterday*, 89.

7. Georges Perec and Robert Bober, *Ellis Island*, trans. Harry Matthews (New York: New Press, 1995), 11. Stefan Zweig makes the same observation on the occasion of his first voyage across the Atlantic, in search of work. See *World of Yesterday*, 189: "Also through this experience at agencies and interviews in shops and offices, I gained an insight into the divine freedom of the country. No one had asked me about my nationality, my religion, my origin, and—fantastic as it may seem to the world of today with its fingerprinting, visas, and police certificates—I had traveled without a passport."

8. Freud, *Reflections on War and Death*, 4. And Zweig evokes Europe before the war of 1914–18 in the following terms (*World of Yesterday*, 127): "The Russians, the Germans, the Spaniards, not one of them can remember how much freedom and joy the soulless, voracious bogy of the 'State' has sucked from the very marrow of their soul. All peoples feel only that a strange shadow hangs broad and heavy over their lives. But we, who once knew a world of individual freedom, know and can give testimony that Europe once, without a care, enjoyed its kaleidoscopic play of color."

9. André Gide, *Travels in the Congo*, trans. Dorothy Bussy (Hopewell, N.J.: Ecco Press, 1994), 65–66.

10. Ernst Bloch, *Natural Law and Human Dignity*, trans. Dennis J. Schmidt (Cambridge, Mass.: MIT Press, 1986), 4.

11. Freud, *Reflections on War and Death*, 5.

12. This theme attracted the attention of Karl Kraus when, during the First World War, he was composing his theatrical saga *The Last Days of Humanity*, trans. Alexander Gode and Sue Ellen Wright (New York: Frederick Ungar, 1974). While Kraus was working on this drama, Sigmund Freud was writing

Reflections on War and Death. I offer a close reading of Kraus's work in Chapter 4.

13. See Chapter 4.

14. Freud, *Reflections on War and Death*, 5.

15. I observe how much this analysis runs parallel to that of the Czech philosopher Jan Patočka, whose 1977 book *Heretical Essays in the Philosophy of History*, trans. Erazim Kohák (Chicago: Open Court, 1999), addresses the disillusionment with peace and the public and official instrumentalization of "sacrifice." See Marc Crépon, *The Thought of Death and the Memory of War*, trans. Michael Loriaux (Minneapolis: University of Minnesota Press, 2013), Chapter 4.

16. Zweig, *World of Yesterday*, 297–99.

17. See the excellent and pertinent analysis of René Major, "La soif du pouvoir," in *Au commencement: La vie, la mort* (Paris: Éditions Galilée, 1999), 141–53. See also Serge Margel, *Critique de la cruauté, ou Les fondements politiques de la jouissance* (Paris: Belin, 2010). I wish to thank Didier Franck for having reminded me of the existence of this book, which concentrates, in its evocation of the Great War, several of the themes and questions that are examined in the present book, beginning with murderous consent. See also the important works of Stéphane Audouin-Rouzeau and Annette Becker: *14–18: Understanding the Great War* (New York: Hill and Wang, 2014); and their polemical discussion in Frédéric Rousseau, *La guerre censurée: Une histoire des combattants européens de 14–18* (Paris: Éditions du Seuil, 1999).

18. Jules Romains, *Verdun*, trans. Gerard Hopkins (New York: Alfred Knopf, 1937), 151–53.

19. Freud, *Reflections on War and Death*, 6.

20. On the concept of civilization, see Marc Crépon, *La culture de la peur*, vol. 2, *La guerre des civilisations* (Paris: Éditions Galilée, 2010); and Marc Crépon, *L'imposture du choc des civilisations* (Nancy: Éditions Pleins Feux, 2002).

21. Freud, *Reflections on War and Death*, 7.

22. See Michael Haneke's very beautiful film *The White Ribbon*, which relates the cruelty of the education system (the repression of drives) as it existed on the eve of the First World War and the atrocities of that war. The entire film shows how a cruel education (the perversion of care), raised to a system, prepares the ground for mass cruelty, the experience of which will be repeated from the beginning to the end of the twentieth century.

23. This is the raison d'être of all wars of religion, which are generally characterized by their cruelty. See Élie Barnavi, *Les religions meurtrières* (Paris: Flammarion, 2006).

24. Zweig, *World of Yesterday*, xx.

25. Freud, *Reflections on War and Death*, 8.

26. See ibid.: "Death is no longer to be denied; we are compelled to believe in it. People really die and no longer one by one, but in large numbers, often ten thousand in one day."

27. Jacques Derrida, "Psychoanalysis Searches the States of Its Soul: The Impossible Beyond of a Sovereign Cruelty," in *Without Alibi*, trans. Peggy Kamuf (Stanford: Stanford University Press, 2002), xx. In many ways I attempt to follow Derrida's advice in this chapter, even if I give priority to the examination of the war of 1914–18.

28. Freud, *Reflections on War and Death*, 11.

29. Ibid., 12.

30. Ibid.

31. Ibid., 15.

32. Ibid., 13.

33. Ibid.

34. Ibid., 12.

35. The quotations in this paragraph are from ibid., 15–16.

36. Ibid., 16.

37. Albert Einstein and Sigmund Freud, *Why War?* (Redding, Calif.: CAT, 1991), 5.

38. I will focus on Freud's letter in the pages that follow. But Einstein's letter is well worth close attention. See Major, "La soif du pouvoir"; and Jacques Derrida, *États d'âme de la psychanalyse: L'impossible au-delà d'une souveraine cruauté* (Paris: Éditions Galilée, 2000).

39. Einstein and Freud, *Why War?*, 11 (my emphasis). There is little doubt that the European Union would have done well to recall such strength as it sought to accord itself a constitution. Its failure to win ratification by referendum should have been interpreted as a revelation of how much such a constitution was needed. But the lesson apparently was not learned, since all events since then seem only to have deepened the chasm that separates European law and institutions from Europe's population.

40. See Crépon, *L'imposture du choc des civilisations*; and Crépon, *La culture de la peur*, vol. 2.

41. Zweig, *World of Yesterday*, 223.

42. See Chapter 4.

43. Zweig, *World of Yesterday*, 224.

44. Derrida, *États d'âme*, 107.

45. Einstein and Freud, *Why War?*, 15. [Translators' note: The German *Triebe*, "drives," is accurately translated as *pulsions* in French but frequently, and less fortunately, as "instincts" in English. We have replaced "instincts" with "drives" in all English-language translations of Freud's works.]

46. Ibid.

47. Ibid., 16.

48. See Derrida, *États d'âme*, 10: "Nietzsche, for example, discerns [in cruelty] the cunning essence of life: cruelty has no limit and has no term that can be opposed to it and is therefore without end and without resistance. But for Freud, despite his affinities with Nietzsche, cruelty, as always, might be

without limit, but it is not without resistance; that is to say, it is without end but not without resistance" (trans. Loriaux and Levi).

49. Sigmund Freud, *Group Psychology and the Analysis of the Ego*, trans. James Strachey (New York: Bartleby, 2010).

50. Einstein and Freud, *Why War?*, 19.

51. Ibid.

52. Again, this question is taken up by Frédéric Worms in *Le moment du soin: À quoi tenons-nous?* (Paris: Presses Universitaires de France, 2010).

53. Einstein and Freud, *Why War?*, 20.

54. Ibid., 21.

3. Freedom

1. Vasily Grossman, *Everything Flows*, trans. Robert Chandler (New York: New York Review of Books, 2009), 131.

In a noticeably different version, the analysis dedicated to famine at the beginning of this chapter was first published in the January 2010 issue of the *Revue des deux mondes*, in a collection entitled "Penser la désorientation."

2. The author will exploit the polysemy of the French word *mondialisation* as globalization and, in a more phenomenological style, as "worldization."

3. See, specifically, Chapter 70 of the first section, which recounts the meeting between Yershov and his father in Siberia: "The old man talked while his son sat beside him and listened. He talked about hunger, about people from the village who'd died, about old women who had gone mad, about children whose bodies had grown lighter than a chicken or a balalaika." Vasily Grossman, *Life and Fate*, trans. Robert Chandler (New York: New York Review of Books, 1985), 315.

4. Grossman, *Everything Flows*, 129.

5. Ibid., 131.

6. Ibid., 133.

7. In the interview "The Proximity of the Other," Levinas underlines that Stalinist society "is the outcome of the quest for a liberated humanity," and he explains, "Marxism's having turned into Stalinism is the greatest offence to the cause of the human, because Marxism bore the hopes of humanity: it may be one of the greatest psychological shocks for the twentieth-century European." Emmanuel Levinas, *Alterity and Transcendence*, trans. Michael B. Smith (London: Athlone Press, 1999), 107.

8. Emmanuel Levinas, "Beyond Memory," in *In the Time of the Nations*, trans. Michael B. Smith (London: Continuum, 2007), 88–89 (my emphasis).

9. Emmanuel Levinas, preface to *Difficult Freedom*, trans. Seán Hand (Baltimore: Johns Hopkins University Press, 1990), xiv.

10. This lecture is found in the volume *God, Death, and Time*, trans. Bettina Bergo (Stanford: Stanford University Press, 2000), 167–71.

11. Grossman, *Everything Flows*, 30.

12. Emmanuel Levinas, *Of God Who Comes to Mind*, trans. Bettina Bergo (Stanford: Stanford University Press, 1998), 47–48: "Modern intelligence is that which saw, in Auschwitz, the outcome [*aboutissement*] of law and obedience—flowing from the heroic act—in the totalitarianisms, fascist and nonfascist, of the twentieth century. Modern intelligence has its reasons, even if eternal Reason had, one day, to renounce them. This intelligence draws them from very recent memories—and in what is still current actuality—in which human deficiency has lost its appearance as an exception in the submission to propaganda, to terror, and to all the technologies of condition wherein the omnipotence of men shows itself a correlative of the certainty that one may make anything of man."

13. Emmanuel Levinas, "Don Quixote: Bewitchment and Hunger" (February 13, 1976), session of the lecture series God and Onto-theo-logy, reprinted in *God, Death, and Time*, 169, 171.

14. See, e.g., E. Levinas, "The Other, Utopia, and Justice," interview in the journal *Autrement*, no. 102 (November 1988), reprinted in *Entre Nous: Thinking-of-the-Other*, trans. Michael B. Smith and Barbara Harshav (New York: Columbia University Press, 1998).

15. In effect, it is this last passage that Levinas cites in the conclusion of his Talmudic reading entitled "Beyond Memory," in *In the Time of the Nations*, 88–91.

16. Grossman, *Life and Fate*, quotations from 406–10.

17. Emmanuel Levinas, "Peace and Proximity," in *Alterity and Transcendence*, 131–32.

18. Ibid., 132.

19. Ibid., 135.

20. Ibid., 136.

21. Emmanuel Levinas, *Freedom and Command*, in *Collected Philosophical Papers*, trans. Alphonso Lingis (Dordrecht: Martinus Nijhoff, 1987), 16.

22. Ibid., 17.

23. Grossman, *Everything Flows*, 204.

24. Ibid., 69–71.

25. Ibid., 200.

26. Grossman, *Life and Fate*, 214.

27. See Chapter 4.

28. Grossman, *Life and Fate*, 216.

29. Ibid.

30. Ibid., 555.

31. Levinas, *Freedom and Command*, 19.

32. See Chapter 1.

33. On this "eclipse," see Marc Crépon, *The Thought of Death and the Memory of War*, trans. Michael Loriaux (Minneapolis: University of Minnesota Press, 2013).

34. See Chapter 4.

35. Emmanuel Levinas, "Reflections on the Philosophy of Hitlerism," trans. Seán Hand, *Critical Inquiry* 17 (Autumn 1990): 69.

36. Levinas, *Freedom and Command*, 19–20.

37. Ibid., 21.

38. Ibid.

39. Grossman, *Life and Fate*, 408–9.

40. Levinas, "Beyond Memory," 89.

41. Ibid.

42. Grossman, *Life and Fate*, 81–82.

43. Ibid., 83.

44. Ibid., 87.

45. Ibid., 138.

46. Ibid., 141.

47. Ibid.

48. Ibid., 150.

49. Emmanuel Levinas, *Totality and Infinity*, trans. Alphonso Lingis (The Hague: Martinus Nijhoff, 1961), 47.

50. Ibid., 198.

51. We will see in the next chapter, specifically when we read texts by Karl Kraus, that this is why the question of murder is connected to truth and language.

52. Grossman, *Everything Flows*, 118.

53. Emmanuel Levinas, "Ethics and Spirit," in *Difficult Freedom*, 8.

54. Ibid., 10.

55. Levinas, *Totality and Infinity*, 198.

56. Ibid., 47.

57. Grossman, *Life and Fate*, 407–8.

58. Ibid., 406.

59. Ibid., 405–6.

60. *An Essay on Exteriority*.

61. See Emmanuel Levinas, *Totality and Infinity*, 37: "The *way* of the I against the 'other' of the world consists in *sojourning*, in *identifying oneself* by existing here *at home with oneself* [*chez soi*]. In a world which is from the first other the I is nonetheless autochthonous. It is the very reversion of this alteration. It finds in the world a site [*lieu*] and a home [*maison*]."

62. Ibid., 38.

63. Ibid., 50.

64. Ibid., 47.

65. See Chapter 4,

66. Levinas, *Totality and Infinity*, 174.

67. Grossman, *Life and Fate*, 692.

68. Ibid., 691.

69. Ibid., 692.

70. Emmanuel Levinas, "On the Spirit of Geneva," in *Unforeseen History*, trans. Nidra Poller (Champaign: University of Illinois Press, 2004), 102.

71. See Chapter 5.

72. Levinas, "On the Spirit of Geneva," 103.

73. Emmanuel Levinas, "Nameless," in *Proper Names*, trans. Michael B. Smith (Stanford: Stanford University Press, 1996), 119.

74. Ibid., 120.

75. Ibid., 122.

76. Emmanuel Levinas, dedication to *Otherwise than Being; or, Beyond Essence*, trans. Alphonso Lingis (Pittsburgh: Duquesne University Press, 1998).

4. Truth

1. Judith Butler, *Precarious Life: The Powers of Mourning and Violence* (London: Verso, 2004), xii.

2. On the question of recognition in this context, see Marc Crépon, *La culture de la peur*, vol. 2, *La guerre des civilisations* (Paris: Éditions Galilée, 2010).

3. Butler, *Precarious Life*, 3.

4. Karl Kraus, *The Last Days of Mankind* (New York: Frederick Ungar, 1974), 3.

5. See Marc Crépon, "La grammaire de l'apocalypse (Karl Kraus et la critique du langage)," in *Les promesses du langage: Benjamin, Rosenzweig, Heidegger* (Paris: Vrin, 2001), 81–100.

6. Kraus, *Last Days of Mankind*, 3.

7. Ibid.,, 41–42 (act 1, scene 11).

8. For a critical analysis of the uses of the concept rogue state, see Noam Chomsky, *Rogue States: The Rule of Force in World Affairs* (Cambridge, Mass.: South End Press, 2000). This text was cited and discussed by Jacques Derrida in *Rogues*, trans. Pascale-Anne Brault and Michael Naas (Stanford: Stanford University Press, 2005), Chapter 9. Derrida's approach consists of interrogating the line of demarcation that is supposed to distinguish states that are called or declared to be "rogues" from the others by showing that, in reality, the abuse of power that characterizes the so-called rogue states is an inherent element of sovereignty: "This 'logic' [of sovereignty] would make it clear that, a priori, the states that are able or are in a state to make war on rogue states are themselves, in their most legitimate sovereignty, rogue states abusing their power. As soon as there is sovereignty, there is abuse of power and a rogue state. Abuse is the law of use; it is the law itself, the 'logic' of a sovereignty that can reign only by not sharing" (*Rogues*, 102).

9. Kraus, *Last Days of Mankind*, 32–33 (act 1, scene 11).

10. Ibid., 33–34.

11. Butler, *Precarious Life*, 4.

12. See Marc Crépon, *La culture de la peur*, vol. 1, *Démocratie, identité, sécurité* (Paris: Éditions Galilée, 2008).

13. Marc Bloch, *Réflexions d'un historien sur les fausses nouvelles de la guerre* (1921), in *L'histoire, la guerre, la résistance* (Paris: Gallimard, 2006), 293–316.

14. Ibid., 298–99 (our translation).

15. Ibid., 308 (our translation).

16. Ibid., 301 (our translation).

17. Kraus, *Last Days of Mankind*, 45–48 (act 1, scene 14).

18. Butler, *Precarious Life*, 4–5 (my emphasis).

19. Bloch, *Réflexions d'un historien*, 309 (our translation).

20. Butler, *Precarious Life*, 7.

21. Ibid., 12.

22. See Chapter 3.

23. I return in the Conclusion to the crucial question of nonhuman life.

24. My emphasis.

25. Kraus, *Last Days of Mankind*, 91–92 (act 2, scene 29).

26. See Chapter 5.

27. On solidarity, see Chapter 1.

28. On the cross-generational transmission of hatred, see Catherine Lepront's superb novel *Le beau visage de l'ennemi* (Paris: Éditions du Seuil, 2010).

29. Judith Butler, *Frames of War: When Is Life Grievable?* (London: Verso, 2009).

30. See Chapter 1 on justice and justification; Chapter 2 on life; and Chapter 3 on freedom and living-with.

31. Susan Sontag, *Regarding the Pain of Others* (New York: Picador, 2004), 110–11.

32. Ibid., 70–71.

33. Ibid., 114–17.

34. Butler, *Frames of War*, 31.

5. The World

1. To begin, we recall the press code organized and instituted by MacArthur's headquarters on September 19, 1945, that forbade propagating any information and commentary related to the atomic bombardments of Hiroshima and Nagasaki in the press, at the cinema, or on the radio, both in images and in words. Consequently, it was only when Japan regained its independence in 1952 after seven years of American occupation that the words of victims (the *hibakusha*) began to surface, and even then with great difficulty.

2. On this point, see C. Sabouret, "Le consensus du silence," in *Hiroshima 50 ans. Japon-Amerique: Mémoires du nucléaire* (Paris: Éditions Autrement, 1995), 36–48.

3. To these texts must be added those that aren't translated, such as, for example, the books by Ōta Yōko: *Shibakane No Machi* (The city: A tangle of corpses), which was originally banned from publication; and *Han-Ningen* (Half-human). For Ōta Yōko, see J. Rubin, "La bombe, 'Outil de paix,'" in *Hiroshima 50 ans. Japon-Amerique*, 89.

4. I nevertheless recall an article in *Combat* dated August 8, 1945, where Albert Camus expressed outraged that "enthusiastic commentary" could accompany the news that "any average-sized city can be totally leveled by a

bomb the size of a soccer ball." Unlike most witnesses from his era, he was alarmed, though not surprised, that "in a world that has torn itself apart with every conceivable instrument of violence . . . science has dedicated itself to organized murder." *Camus at Combat: Writing, 1944–1947*, trans. Arthur Goldhammer (Princeton: Princeton University Press, 2006), 236.

5. Kenzaburō Ōe, "On Human Dignity," in *Hiroshima Notes*, trans. David L. Swain and Toshi Yonezawa (New York: Grove Press, 1996), 107–8.

6. [Translators' note: With the exception of *Burning Conscience*, none of these texts by Anders have been fully translated and published in English. While much of his work has been translated into French and other European languages, we have undertaken the translation of the original German texts into English where necessary.]

7. For an illuminating synthesis of the debates between historians concerning the strategic reasons for the atomic attacks on Hiroshima and Nagasaki, see Steven Ekovich, "La destruction atomique d'Hiroshima et de Nagasaki: Incertitudes histories et dilemmas éthiques," *Géostratégiques*, no. 26 (2010), http://www.academiedegeopolitiquedeparis.com/la-destruction-atomique -dhiroshima-et-de-nagasaki/.

8. Günther Anders, *Der Mann auf der Brücke: Tagebuch aus Hiroshima und Nagasaki*, in *Hiroshima ist überall* (Munich: C. H. Beck, 1982), 155–56.

9. Ibid., 157.

10. Ibid.

11. Ibid.

12. See Chapter 4.

13. Anders, *Der Mann auf der Brücke*, 160.

14. Ibid., 63–66.

15. Masuji Ibuse, *Black Rain*, trans. John Bester (Tokyo: Kodansha International, 1969), 100.

16. Ibid., 110.

17. Anders, *Der Mann auf der Brücke*, 160.

18. Ibid., 161.

19. Ibid.

20. Ibid., 165. Anders even suggests: "it has transformed the globe into a single inescapable, ineluctable concentration camp."

21. Camus, *Camus at Combat*, 236.

22. Ibuse, *Black Rain*, 143.

23. Ōe, *Hiroshima Notes*, 40.

24. Ibid., 29.

25. Ibid., 45.

26. Ibid., 46.

27. Ibid., 134.

28. Ibid., 47 (translation altered to reflect the French text).

29. Ibid., 51.

30. Ibid., 25.

31. Ibid., 23.

32. Anders, *Der Mann auf der Brücke*, 9.

33. Ibid.

34. Jan Patočka, *Heretical Essays in the Philosophy of History*, trans. Erazim Kohák, ed. James Dodd, with preface by Paul Ricœur (Chicago: Open Court, 1999), 134–37.

35. Anders, *Der Mann auf der Brücke*, 9.

36. I cannot fail to mention that this "Hiroshima within me" echoes the final verse in Paul Celan's poem "Grosse, Glühende Wölbung": "The world is far away, I must carry you" (*Die Welt ist Fort, ich muss dich tragen*); and Jacques Derrida's magnificent commentary in *Béliers: Le dialogue ininterrompu; entre deux infinis, le poème* (Paris: Éditions Galilée, 2003).

37. We will remember that as early as 1956 shame constitutes one of the central concepts from Günther Anders's important book *Die Antiquiertheit des Menschen*, vol. 1, *Über die Seele im Zeitalter der zweiten industriellen Revolution* [The obsolescence of humankind, vol. 1, On the soul during the age of the Second Industrial Revolution] (Munich: Beck, 2002), which opens with a chapter entitled *Über Prometheische Scham* (On Promethean shame). [Translators' note: "On Promethean Shame" was recently published in English translation in Christopher John Müller, *Prometheanism: Technology, Digital Culture, and Human Obsolescence* (London: Rowman and Littlefield, 2016).]

38. Ōe, *Hiroshima Notes*, 105.

39. Anders, *Der Mann auf der Brücke*, 74.

40. Ibuse, *Black Rain*, 56.

41. Anders, *Der Mann auf der Brücke*, 82–83.

42. Ibid.

43. See Chapter 3.

44. See ibid.

45. Anders, *Der Mann auf der Brücke*, 80.

46. Ibid., 84.

47. Ibid., 48.

48. Ibid., 58.

49. Ibid.

50. Ibid., 66.

51. Günther Anders, *Burning Conscience* (London: Weidenfeld and Nicolson, 1961), 12.

52. See Chapter 3.

53. See Chapter 4.

54. Anders, *Der Mann auf der Brücke*, 87.

55. See Chapter 3.

56. Anders, *Der Mann auf der Brücke*, 113–14.

57. See my *La culture de la peur*, vol. 1, *Démocratie, identité, sécurité* (Paris: Éditions Galilée, 2008).

58. Anders, *Der Mann auf der Brücke*, 38.

59. Günther Anders, introduction to *Hiroshima ist überall*, xxix.

60. Anders, *Der Mann auf der Brücke*, 3.

61. See Chapter 3.

62. Anders, *Der Mann auf der Brücke*, 51.

Conclusion

1. As I mention this episode in the classroom, I wish to thank the students and friends who participated in this seminar. Their close attention and questions were an invaluable source of energy as I made my way through the texts, as well as the thoughts that they elicited, seeking out phrases and syntagmas on which our attention might linger. I wish to thank some of these participants in particular: Miriam Jerade, Léa Veinstein, Élise Lamy-Rested, Benjamin Oliviennes, Francine and Steven Ecovitch, Jacky Cohen, Carmen Lupescu, Céline Barral, Mathieu Pams, and Thomas Lebon.

2. See the riveting testimony of Jean-Luc Daub, *Ces bêtes qu'on abat: Journal d'un enquêteur dans les abattoirs français*, with a preface by Élisabeth de Fontenay (Paris: L'Harmattan, 2009).

3. Vasily Grossman, "The Road," in *The Road: Stories, Journalism, and Essays*, trans. Robert Chandler and Elizabeth Chandler, with Olga Mukovnikova (New York: New York Review of Books, 2010), 223.

4. Ibid., 228.

5. Ibid., 234.

6. See the remarkable studies by Élisabeth de Fontenay, notably *Le silence des bêtes: La philosophie à l'épreuve de l'animalité*, Histoire de la pensée (Paris: Fayard, 1998). The suffering of animals is a topic that preoccupied Jacques Derrida, notably in *The Animal That Therefore I Am*, trans. David Wills (New York: Fordham University Press, 2008). In it he meditates on the question asked by Jeremy Bentham, "Can they suffer?": "Bentham said something like this: the question is not to know whether the animal can think, reason, or speak, etc., something we still pretend to be asking ourselves (from Aristotle to Descartes, especially, to Heidegger, Levinas, and Lacan, and this question determines so many others concerning *power* or *capability* [*pouvoirs*] and attributes [*avoirs*]: being able, having the power or capability to give, to die, to bury one's dead, to dress, to work, to invent a technique, etc., a power that consists in having such and such a faculty, thus such and such a capability, as an essential attribute). . . . The *first* and *decisive* question would rather be to know whether animals can suffer" (27). See also Jacques Derrida and Élisabeth Roudinesco, *For What Tomorrow . . . : A Dialogue*, trans. Jeff Fort (Stanford: Stanford University Press, 2004), 70: "Because, yes, we know this, and no one would dare to doubt it. Animals suffer; they manifest their suffering. . . . We know what animal suffering is, we feel it ourselves. Moreover, with industrial slaughter, these animals are suffering in much larger numbers than before."

7. Élisabeth de Fontenay, *Without Offending Humans*, trans. Will Bishop (Minneapolis: University of Minnesota Press, 2012), 127–28.

8. Derrida and Roudinesco, *For What Tomorrow . . .* , 71. I am thinking here of, among other examples, the unbearable but increasingly common images of heaps of animal cadavers piled up following mass slaughters, ordered as a precaution against the uncontrollable spread of disease.

Appendix. Friendship: A Trial by History

1. An initial version of this appendix, though substantially different, appeared in Jean-Charles Darmon and Françoise Wacquet, eds., *L'amitié et les sciences de Descartes à Lévi-Strauss* (Paris: Hermann, 2010).

2. Jean-Paul Sartre, *Portraits*, trans. Chris Turner (London: Seagull, 2009), 173–74.

3. Ibid., 270.

4. Ibid., 272. These "essential words" suffice to confirm, if confirmation were needed, Frédéric Worms's thesis that what he calls the "philosophical moment of the Second World War" was placed under the sign of existence. See Frédéric Worms, *La philosophie en France au XXᵉ siècle: Moments*, Folio essais (Paris: Gallimard, 2009), 193–94.

5. Sartre, *Portraits*, 272–73.

6. Ibid., 267.

7. Maurice Merleau-Ponty, *Humanism and Terror*, trans. John O'Neill (New Brunswick, N.J.: Transaction, 2000), 1–2.

8. Sartre, *Portraits*, 305.

9. See Maurice Merleau-Ponty, "The USSR and the Camps," in *Signs*, trans. Richard C. McCleary (Evanston, Ill.: Northwestern University Press, 1964), 263–73, esp. 264–65.

10. Ibid., 267–68 (translation slightly modified).

11. Ibid., 269.

12. Sartre, *Portraits*, 339.

13. Ibid., 410–11.

14. Francis Jeanson, "Albert Camus, or The Soul in Revolt," in *Sartre and Camus: A Historic Confrontation*, ed. and trans. David A. Sprintzen and Adrian van den Hoven (New York: Humanity Books, 2004), 97. The original is found in *Les temps modernes*, May 1952.

15. Ibid., 101.

16. Ibid.

17. Albert Camus, "A Letter to the Editor of *Les temps modernes*," in Sprintzen and van den Hoven, *Sartre and Camus*, 121. The original letter is found in *Les temps modernes*, July–August 1952.

18. Camus, "Letter to the Editor of *Les temps modernes*," 115.

19. Ibid., 121.

20. Ibid., 123–24.

21. Sartre, *Portraits*, 123.

22. See, e.g., ibid., 138: "What if your book merely revealed your philosophical incompetence? What if it were put together from second-hand information,

hastily cobbled together? . . . And what if your reasoning were not so very correct? If your ideas were vague and banal?" See also ibid., 148–49: "Well, I shall at least share with Hegel the distinction of not having been read by you. But what a bad habit you have of not going back to sources! . . . I hardly dare advise you to refer here to *Being and Nothingness*, to read it would seem to you pointlessly arduous: you detest difficulties of thought and are quick to decree that there is nothing to understand, so as to avoid in advance the criticism that you have not understood."

23. See ibid., 156: "In short, you remain within our great classical tradition which, since Descartes and with the exception of Pascal, is entirely hostile to history."

24. Ibid., 174–75.

Index

truth, 8, 9, 35, 36, 39, 45, 83, 107–8, 109–39, 146, 165, 168, 184, 187

Ukraine, 76, 79
United States, 52, 54, 112–13, 122, 127, 140

Vian, Boris, 185

war crimes, 2, 23, 45
Whitman, Walt, 46
Worms, Frédéric, 7, 11

Yōko, Ōta, 140, 141

Zweig, Stefan, 46–48, 50–55, 57, 61–62, 68–69

Marc Crépon is Chair of Philosophy at the École Normale Supérieure, Paris. He is the author of *The Thought of Death and the Memory of War* and *The Vocation of Writing: Literature and Philosophy in the Test of Violence.*

James Martel is Chair of Political Science at San Francisco State University. His most recent book is *The Misinterpellated Subject.*

Michael Loriaux is Professor of Political Science at Northwestern University. He is the author of *European Union and the Deconstruction of the Rhineland Frontier.*

Jacob Levi is a doctoral candidate in Comparative Thought and Literature at the Johns Hopkins University.

Perspectives in Continental Philosophy
John D. Caputo, series editor

Recent titles:

Jeremy Biles and Kent L. Brintnall, eds., *Georges Bataille and the Study of Religion*.
Tarek R. Dika and W. Chris Hackett, *Quiet Powers of the Possible: Interviews in Contemporary French Phenomenology*. Foreword by Richard Kearney.
Richard Kearney and Brian Treanor, eds., *Carnal Hermeneutics*.

A complete list of titles is available at www.fordhampress.com.

www.ingramcontent.com/pod-product-compliance
Lightning Source LLC
Chambersburg PA
CBHW032132020426
42334CB00016B/1137